Learning to Live Again…
A Day at a Time

By Chris and Amy Hotaling
with Mark Leeds

Published by Talsan
7614 W. Bluefield Avenue
Glendale, Arizona 85308-8222

ISBN 978-1-884298-78-8

Manufactured in the United States of America
February 2012

10 9 8 7 6 5 4 3 2 1

Printed in the United States
Publishers ExpressPress
200 West 5th Street
Ladysmith, Wisconsin 54848

Cover Design by: Bruce A. Clack
Photography: Images by Kay & Co.

Table of Contents

Acknowledgements

Saying "Thank you" barely scratches the surface in expressing my deep appreciation to all those who have helped me in those early years of my recovery, and those who continue today to unselfishly do their part in helping me continue to re-define my life. It is impossible to acknowledge every person individually and express my gratitude. That being said, I would like to mention those who have been particularly supportive in my recovery journey.

To all the staff at the K C C-3 Inpatient Head Trauma Unit at Mount Sinai Hospital; NYU-Rusk Outpatient Rehabilitation Center; SUNY School of Optometry-Head Trauma Vision Rehabilitation Unit; Rehabilitation Hospital of Southern New Mexico; and HealthSouth Valley of the Sun, thank you for your dedication to brain injury rehabilitation.

To my former students who provided notes and words of encouragement when they found out about my injury; The NJ Brain Injury support group members who provided emotional support to both Amy and me; Friends and family members who have made every effort to understand and accommodate my needs, I thank you from the deepest part of my soul.

I would especially like to thank Dr. Robert Pincus, my long time New York City E.N.T. doctor who referred me to an audiologist. Had it not been for your attentiveness, persistence, and genuine concern about my sensitivity to noise following my brain injury, I may never have learned about my cochlear nerve damage or how Sensaphonics ear filters would enable me to overcome the challenges of engaging in social situations. I consistently speak about the benefits of Sensaphonics ear filters at conferences and other speaking engagements. Without fail, attendees ask for additional information about Sensaphonics which I readily have available.

Ali Schonfeld, my in-patient occupational therapist at Mount Sinai, for helping me to regain some basic daily living skills and self dignity.

Mark Herceg, my out-patient cognitive psychologist at NYU-Rusk, for challenging my brain and pushing its capacity each and every session. Thank you for helping me become aware of the importance of maintaining a balance between pushing myself and taking those necessary breaks in order to allow my brain to heal. Your numerous "just chill" reminders echo in my memory still today.

Dvorah Simon, my psychotherapist, for being my emotional beacon of light. You helped restore hope, happiness, and a sense of humor, which continues to carry me through each day. You opened my heart and mind to embrace and accept my new life.

Adrienne Dicembri, who replaced my original NYU-Rusk occupational therapist. Your youthful energy and sense of humor energized my spirit each time we met. As a fellow Utica College Alum, I knew I was in good hands while under your care.

Barbara Johnson-Engbert, my NYU-Rusk physical therapist. You were always available to address not only my physical therapy needs, but ready to advocate on my behalf so that I could receive the full benefit of all my therapy programs. You were my "Go To" person, my "Angel" at Rusk, and I will be forever grateful for your kind words and actions.

Dr. Edwin Richter, my NYU-Risk physiatrist, for overseeing all my medical needs. Your soft spoken positive demeanor, kindness, and encouraging words provided the hope I needed to continue working towards recovery.

Dr. Neera Kapoor, my SUNY head trauma vision optometrist who was instrumental in my vision rehabilitation. Your genuine sensitivity, compassion, and understanding of my vision and cognitive challenges, as well as acknowledging my accomplishments over these years, warms my heart and soul. Your efforts have given me a part of my life back, and I am deeply grateful.

Stephanie Kuensting, my speech/language and cognitive therapist in New Mexico. Your own personal insight and unique understanding of brain injury is a gift that I thank you for sharing with me. You are an inspiration and a true testament that all things are possible.

To my family:
Generally, I wish to thank both my and Amy's brothers and sisters, our nieces and nephews, cousins and great Aunts who have been supportive throughout our journey.
A special thank you to my Mom and Dad for all that you have done and continue to do in our life. I can only imagine how painful it must be to see any of your children experience traumatic events and to deal with feelings of helplessness that must have been overwhelming at times. Thank you for making the many trips down to New Jersey and New York City from Utica. I am grateful and humbled by your unselfish souls.

My brother Bill, thank you particularly for showing up at Mount Sinai Hospital on that cold and windy December evening when I was not expecting any visitors. I was at my lowest of low emotionally. The time we spent together on that cold blustery evening was an awakening for me and sparked a new sense of hopefulness that fueled my efforts for recovery. Thank you Bill and Leah for your openness and willingness to create an environment in your home that makes it possible for me to enjoy family time with you and my adorable nephews, Will and Drew.

Thank you to my sister Laurie for all your many uplifting motivational cards, and coming down to New York City to be a part of my first "Day Pass" experience from the hospital. Your contagious laughter and caring heart continues to feed my spirit.

I would like to thank my brother Paul, for using whatever resources you needed to use to assist in my admission process to Mount Sinai's acute care rehab unit. Your keen awareness and ability to articulate the severity of my condition and advocate on my behalf, was instrumental in helping me begin my rehab journey.

Jennifer Lyndaker-Duell, my niece. You gave up your winter break - an opportunity to make some money for college, to come to New Jersey and help your Aunt Amy and Uncle Chris at a time in our lives when we needed it most. I literally depended on you for every step I took as we made our way back and forth from New Jersey to Rusk Rehabilitation Center in Manhattan. Your kind heart and unselfishness will be forever remembered and appreciated.

To my Friends:
As much as the role of family was critical to my recovery process, the encouragement and support from close friends cannot be overlooked. To those friends whose unseen actions quietly supported me, yet have gone unmentioned, please know how sincerely grateful Amy and I are for your "behind the scene" support.

My dear friend Mark Leeds, saying thank you is simply not enough. It is through your ability as a writer, compassion as a counselor, and your genuine friendship that our goal of having the opportunity to help others who face life changing traumatic events has become a reality. I would also like to thank you for sharing our days together in Manhattan when I would come into the city for doctor appointments. You helped make my days in the city much more safe and enjoyable.

I would also like to thank Ron Scott, especially for your visits to the hospital with my favorite Harlem sweet potato pie, which brightened my day and encouraged my appetite. Your friendship is a blessing.

How can I possibly find the words to express my thanks to my long time dear friends, Jeff Carpenter, Larry and Stacey Wilbur, Dave Roberts, and Neil Clapperton. Thank you for your continued presence and your unconditional acceptance. Your many phone calls and visits helped me normalize my life, and stay connected to a world that was moving so quickly around me.

Sandi, thank you for taking a personal interest in this project and for your sincere input in preparing our book for publication. Your contributions have not only helped produce a wonderful book to encourage others but has simultaneously created a lasting friendship. Thank you for gently insisting that the message in this book needs to be told.

And to my wife, Amy, the person who is first on my mind when I wake each morning and last in my thoughts when I fall asleep each night. Despite all the odds, you have stayed by my side and never gave up on us. You are my rock, my most reliable advocate, my most treasured resource. You were my voice when I could not speak, my motivation when I felt despair, and my light when I saw only darkness. Your love comforts my heart... your comfort strengthens my spirit...and your strength nourishes my soul.

Foreword

Learning to Live Again...A Day at a Time, is the narrative of a very special man, Chris Hotaling, who on an ordinary day has an extraordinary accident that forever alters the direction of his life. A door swings open in a crowded corridor and in a split second a healthy active confident man is transformed. After regaining consciousness, he is unable to fill out an accident report, or even remember what occurred. Within days, all his major faculties are compromised: he no longer walks, talks or even feeds himself.

A week later, Chris is diagnosed with a Traumatic Brain Injury (TBI). Based on hospital and rehab journals, his notes and reflections, *Learning to Live Again...A Day at a Time* recounts his remarkable journey back from helplessness and dependency.

During the first days and weeks following his injury, when the agonizing pain just wouldn't stop, his wife Amy transcribed his thoughts, feelings and observations from Chris's halting dictation. By the time Chris settled into the Head Trauma Unit of Mt. Sinai Hospital and began to write his journal unaided, his urge to record his testimony became a full-scale obsession. It was an obsession with a positive purpose. Charting the progress of his therapy and treatment, kept him focused and motivated. It also provided a vehicle to vent his frustrations and cope with setbacks. It helped him retain his sanity. Through his journal, he regained a sense of self, defining and redefining his identity. In his own book of life, he tirelessly recorded his private epiphanies and illuminations, his self-discoveries. In his own words, he learned "to live in the moment." Although his words were inspiring, they were not written to inspire anyone other than himself.

When I met Chris in 1990, I was working as a writer for a New York City Board of Education counseling program, developing and directing a student writing program and producing an in-house publication. Chris was a new counseling hire for a Brooklyn High School in a blue-collar, mostly Italian American neighborhood. In our urban ethnically diverse program Chris stood out. He was the image of the "all-American boy," a sturdy six-footer with fair skin, blonde hair and steady blue eyes. He smiled and laughed easily.

When I entered his office for the first time there was a student in a chair across from his desk being counseled. As I got to know him over the next nine years, whatever the high school, whatever the neighborhood, there would always be a student in that chair or a roomful of students enthusiastically participating in a group or exuberantly planning some project or activity. He felt a real sense of responsibility for his "kids." He was always available for his students. Like many effective counselors, Chris made demands. He truly believed in his students' ability to transcend circumstances and environment and succeed. Without being overbearing, he provided structure and discipline.

After a couple of counseling emergencies, a trip to the vice principal's office to change a student's schedule and a one-on-one with a teacher who was failing a student with "issues," Chris and I talked. He came across as modest and calm. He was highly committed but without that nervous New York sense of urgency. Chris came from the Utica area of upstate New York and conveyed the straightforward simplicity of rural America. He was open and trusting but hardly naive. He had cut his counseling teeth with hard-core drug addicts. He knew the score, but that did not undercut his caring and empathy.

As the students left for the day and the conversation wandered away from work Chris confided his dream. He had come to New York with his wife, Amy, to study acting and pursue a career on Broadway. He spoke with a sense of determination and conviction. I could not help being drawn into his dream.

Gradually, over time, as Chris and I worked together on projects and publications he talked less and less about his acting and eventually it just seemed to fade into the background. Chris was completely consumed with "helping kids, saving kids." Every moment on the job, he was counseling, individual or group, in conference with a parent, teacher or administrator, training students to be peer counselors and meeting with teachers having problems with students. With real relish he planned trips and activities, often on his own time, to reward his hard-driving kids. He loved his job.

Chris in his prime was a man of inexhaustible energy. He managed to keep his counseling program running on all cylinders, while completing a graduate degree, announcing acts for a national talent competition which toured around the country and doing lighting for a well-known portrait photographer. All the while, he provided his wife Amy with the moral support she needed to pursue an MBA. He couldn't have been prouder. Eventually the administration of a high school where he worked hired him away from my Board of Education program. As he settled into his new guidance position, a former supervisor laid the groundwork to appoint him as her assistant principal.

Chris was a doer; he reveled in "multitasking." Chris was not a man for half-measures; he had to be fully committed to whatever he did. For Chris helping others was a vocation. His mother and father had instilled in him their own ideals of good works and the golden rule.

During the week of October 22nd, 1999 I heard about Chris's accident from a mutual friend who told me that he fell during a fire drill and would be out of work for a couple of days. "No big deal" was his concise conclusion. Unfortunately, nothing that my friend said proved to be correct. Later, I learned from a counselor at Chris's high school that he had been knocked unconscious in the course of an actual fire and was brought to a New York City hospital in an ambulance. That weekend I called his home and I was only able to speak to an answering machine. I called other people he knew and no one seemed to know exactly what was happening. Finally, I got his wife Amy on the home phone. She sounded shaken but did not say anything more than, "Chris couldn't come to the phone." And "I have to keep the line open." I had no idea that Chris was sprawled on his bed in the same room suffering the agonies of the damned. As he said in his own journal, "If this is hell, the devil's pitchfork is sticking in my brain."

I did not actually speak to Chris or learn that he had a severe brain injury until he became a patient in a brain injury unit in Mt. Sinai. It was a dreary Thursday evening with the rain coming down in buckets. Amy met me in the waiting room, alerting me to Chris's situation and the drastic change in his appearance. She took me by the arm to a physical therapy area, which resembled a small gym with parallel bars, mats and other equipment scattered around. Chris was slowly moving himself along in a wheel chair performing a heel and toe exercise with his feet, gamely mouthing "heel and toe." He called it his "mantra." Chris was as pale as a ghost and pathetically thin. His voice was reedy and not at all clear. Still he looked determined. Despite his circumstances, he was the same overwhelmingly optimistic Chris. I was shocked, close to tears. This time, it was difficult for me to embrace his optimism. His wife Amy barely spoke.

I saw Chris again the following spring at the Rusk Institute of the N.Y.U. Medical Center, where he was receiving outpatient therapy. He was sitting on a bench with a folding cane between his knees. He looked better, but still pale and thin. The sun was shining outside as we crossed the street to a concrete pocket park. Chris walked awkwardly balancing himself on his cane. He was intent on "getting back to normal." I was conventionally encouraging. He was grateful for my visit. I avoided talking about his injury and its consequences and so did he. I could not always follow what he was saying. As I left and looked back and waved he looked very sad and lonely with his face tilted toward the sun.

In March of 2001 I finally saw him again at Rusk, but this time it was I who was receiving the outpatient therapy for the results of a stroke. It was now Chris's turn to be shocked by my appearance. I was chalk white and gaunt. My face was frozen into a stare. Chris still needed a cane to navigate and we helped one another over the icy pavement to a nearby diner. It was the first of many convivial lunches that we spent together mostly laughing at our own expense. It took Chris a long time to tell me about his journal of rehab and recovery and his desire to turn it into a book. It took me even longer to suggest we join together to make his book a reality.

For more than a year, Chris laboriously dictated his hand-written journals into his computer using speech recognition software. It was a difficult painstaking process, hampered by poor short-term memory, limited motor skills, and a low threshold for mental or physical activity. Often his efforts left him exhausted and in severe pain, he was not to be deterred.

On a very cold winter's day I began to cut, revise and shape his mountain of work into a book. The journal was compelling. As I poured over the details of Chris's ordeals and triumphs I was not only impressed with his courage, but with his wife Amy's unswerving support, loyalty and love. Chris suggests that she add her own thoughts and viewpoint to the narrative and I readily agreed. Amy is an essential element in Chris's miracle. Whatever our contributions, this is Chris's book, an unsparing totally personal document of one man's ability to transcend adversity who "Learns to Live Again... A Day at a Time."

Mark Leeds

My first love, you stay in my heart
And forever in my soul
I know this is real.
And the love that we share
Will always be there
A love that will last all our lives.

It's a miracle of love
That you're still by my side.
The wonder of it all
True love can't be denied.

A Miracle of Love

Artist: Amy Hotaling

Album: *A Miracle of Love,* by Amy Hotaling

Music and Lyrics by: George Small & Sarah Larson

*Available on iTunes and at CDBABY at
http://www.cdbaby.com/amyhotaling*

Learning to Live Again...
A Day at a Time

The sections in the book that are in *Italics* are the thoughts and feelings of Amy.

Chapter One

My New Life Begins

Just an Ordinary Day

What happened on just an ordinary day changes my life forever.

As I begin to follow Mario through the steel fire door to head toward the stairway going down to the street, everything comes to a sudden stop. My world goes black. In the distance I hear my name being called. It starts as a whisper and gets progressively louder and louder. As if abruptly wakened from a deep sound sleep, I am thrust back into an atmosphere of hysteria. As I open my eyes, Mario is leaning over me shouting out my name. Flat out on the floor, I am submerged in the noise of the alarm and the students rushing out of the building. It's all a blank. I don't know what's happened.

Friday-October 22, 1999

I am walking to the corner to catch the commuter bus from New Jersey to mid-town Manhattan with my wife Amy. It seems like just another fall day. I tell her good-bye at Port Authority; we exchange smiles and I see the same warmth in her face as when we were college sweethearts in upstate New York. Amy turns to walk down 42nd street towards her office and I begin my daily trek towards my school where I work as a guidance counselor. I pass by shop owners sweeping up in front of their store entrances, restaurant staff arranging sidewalk café tables, produce company workers loading their delivery trucks, and children playing in urban parks that dot the city landscape. I make a quick stop at my favorite breakfast cart parked by my school and grab a bagel and hot tea.

I enter the building, check my messages in the school office with breakfast in hand, and join my colleague Mario in his office one floor above mine. We are the counseling arm for one of the scholastic institutes in a high school with a student body of approximately 3,500.

My school's population is an inner city blend of students, with some focused on succeeding and preparing for college and others projecting the typical urban "hardcore" low achieving image; restless, troubled kids who seem to have given up on themselves. Those that act out, do it all too often. Minimizing failure rates can be daunting at times. Somehow, I don't mind the challenge.

This year, I am responsible for the freshman and juniors; Mario is responsible for the sophomores and seniors. When I am not in guidance department meetings, institute meetings or any other unexpected meetings that come up during the course of the day, I am busy working with freshmen on a variety of guidance issues, focusing on their adjustment to high school life.

As we swallow down breakfast, Mario and I start to talk about individual students and administrative issues before the inevitable deluge of student problems and bureaucratic emergencies begin. Even though our students see that we are in a meeting they filter in and out asking us a variety of questions.

A Fire Emergency

Around 9:15 a.m. we hear the fire alarm go off. This is all too common in our building. False alarms are frequent. You never quite know whether a student pulls the alarm or if it is a real emergency. So, following standard procedure, we sit and wait to see if the alarm is re-set before heading out of the building to our outside checkpoints. The alarm continues and suddenly Thomas, one of our students, bursts in and in a panic shouts "It's a real fire, I can smell the smoke!"

Mario and I immediately tell him to stay calm and exit the building. We head down one flight of stairs to my office and I quickly grab my coat. It is a chilly fall day and I don't know how long we will be outside. Leaving my office, we see students and teachers evacuating through the double steel doors that lead to the exit staircase. There is a sense of panic. The thick smoke is bellowing at the other end of the hallway making its way towards our exit. I follow behind Mario joining the procession of students heading through the doorway that leads to the staircase to exit the building.

My world suddenly goes black. In the distance I hear my name being called. It sounds like a whisper and progressively gets louder and louder. "Chris, Chris, wake up we have to get out of here!" My eyes open slowly and I see Mario leaning over me shaking me calling my name. Flat on the floor I slowly regain my senses and hear a fire alarm in the distance. Abruptly I awake from my deep sound sleep and thrust back into a world of hysteria and chaos. "Come on Chris we have to get out of here!" I'm dazed and confused. It's all a blank. I ask Mario, "What the heck just happened?" Mario tells me that Thomas struck me in the head with the door and I was unconscious for about five minutes. As he helps me to my feet I don't feel sure footed. I am having trouble walking straight and steady so Mario puts his arm around my waist and we begin our descent down three long flights to the street. I grasp the steel railing bringing one hand over the other to further guide me on my journey to the outside.

Hit on the Head

I'm in a fog. Mario props me up against a parked car to keep me from falling over. Dazed and stunned, my heart starts pounding and I feel nauseous. Trying to understand why I feel this way, I say to myself, "Of course you're going to feel rotten; you were just hit on the head by a steel door."

Mario frequently comes over to check on me. He seems very anxious but tries to disguise it with sharp one-liners. I can't help but laugh. Meanwhile, Thomas approaches me with concern and relief on his face and says how happy he is to see me alive. "I thought I killed you Mr. Chris!" He cannot stop apologizing. I reassure him that everything will be alright.

The fire alarm finally stops ringing. The building is deemed safe and students and teachers make their way back to their classrooms. Mario helps me back into the building and tells me that we have to report the accident. I don't think it is necessary, but he insists on it. The assistant principals' office is buzzing with activity. Mario tells Donna, the acting assistant principal, what has happened. She comes right over to me, but I don't understand what she actually says. My nausea has increased and my head is pounding. Dean Perkins comes over and gives me an accident report to complete. I pick up the pen in my fingers and begin to write down what happened. Hmm, this is strange, I have the pen in my hand ready to write but my hand is frozen. I cannot write at all. There is a disconnect between my brain and my hand. Something has gone very badly wrong! I keep on trying to write, but I am unable to do it, no matter how hard I try. Mario and Dean Perkins try to help me. They look scared. I am scared.

They help me to Donna's inner office, which is quiet and subdued. Following school procedure the school police officer, a friendly no-nonsense guy, requests a Statement for his police-report. I try to tell him what I could remember, but he has to rely on what the others say. I am too shaken up and don't have a clue what happened. I mainly depend upon Mario's account.

Eventually, EMS shows up and strongly recommends a trip to the emergency room. I understand their rationale, but I am reluctant to be taken out on a gurney. It could get back to Thomas and the other students, maybe causing further trauma. After some exchanges between myself, EMS, Mario, Donna and others, I am put on the gurney and driven to the emergency room. Mario rides in the ambulance with me. At some point he calls Amy to meet us at the hospital.

The doctor, perhaps Indian or Pakistani, in the course of his examination asks me some basic questions with a broad foreign accent, "What happened? Who is the President of the United States? How many fingers am I holding up?" He's brisk and to the point. I think I get all the answers right. He examines my neck as I lay on the gurney. He tells me that I am going to have a good size headache and orders two Tylenol for me. He instructs me to have my wife wake me up periodically to make certain I am okay. There are no X-rays or MRI's; no CAT scans, no tests at all. Evidently, there were higher priorities. And that was it. Guiding myself with my hand along side the wall to help me balance, I slowly make my way down a long corridor to the waiting room to meet Mario. I hear Amy's voice. Thank God she is here. I see them both look at me in surprise. Amy rushes to help support me and gives me a big hug. They both help me walk out of the hospital and while Amy is holding on to me Mario hails a cab. As Amy helps me into the cab I say to Mario, "I'll see you tomorrow." He responds, "At least wait till Monday Chris!" "Oh yeah... I forgot that today was Friday." Never could I imagine that I would never return.

No Tears

"No tears," I tell myself. You have to stay in control and get to the hospital in a hurry. I anxiously leave a scribbled note on my supervisor's desk and head for the elevator. Once on the street I try desperately to hail a cab. Frustrated that no cabs are available I decide to sprint to the hospital.

My mind floods with fear and concern of what I will find once I reach Chris. Only a couple of hours ago we were saying our good-bye's at Port Authority. I was walking up 42nd street to my office. My mind was deep in thought about a morning meeting with corporate executives regarding a new merger. I was heading to the merger meeting at around 10:30 a.m. when the phone rings. I pick it up and it is Chris. I say to myself; why is he calling me; he knows I have a busy schedule this morning. We talked last night about how crazy my day is going to be and how I am looking forward to a relaxing weekend. Then I hear, "Aim?" Immediately I know something is wrong. He slowly says something about not wanting to go to the hospital and "don't worry, I'm okay". He isn't making any sense. I tell him "Chris, go to the hospital, there must be a reason they want you to go." He says "okay, I love you," and then someone else comes on the phone. My head is starting to spin as if I had just exited a twirl ride at the carnival. I sit down in my chair as I hear a distant voice telling me EMS is taking Chris to the hospital and a police officer will call me as soon as possible with details. I get off the phone and slowly sit in my chair feeling numb.

Like most women, I always think of the worst-case scenario when the man you love is late or does not call when they are supposed to. What if he is in a car accident? What if he is mugged on his way to the train? What if he is hurt, lying somewhere? I mean really hurt. How can I survive without him?

"Amy, come on, you're late for the meeting, everyone is waiting for you," my supervisor exclaims. I jump back to the present. I am in shock and I tell my boss what just occurred. Stunned, she tells me to stay by the phone and heads to the meeting.

Approximately thirty-five minutes later, which feels like a lifetime, a police officer calls me. I learn that Chris is on his way to the hospital and I take down the directions.

I am about three avenues away from the hospital. Stay in control... stay in control, I tell myself. I arrive at the hospital and see Mario, Chris's co-worker, and ask what happened. As he is explaining, I see Chris slowly moving towards us using the *wall for support. I am so relieved and puzzled at the same time. From what Mario tells me had happened, I am surprised to see Chris walking. We all sit down and Mario completes his story and tells me to take Chris home. He helps us get a cab and after Chris is safely inside he tells Mario he will see him tomorrow. I say to Chris, "Tomorrow is Saturday." Mario urges Chris to take it easy over the weekend, Chris agrees, "See you on Monday."*

No matter what scenario rushes through my mind on our cab ride to Port Authority, nothing prepares me for the realities that unfold in the days, weeks, months, and even years ahead. My predictable life and normal routine has come to an abrupt end.

Chapter Two

In a Nut Shell

Some Things about Me

I've worked with the hard-to reach most of my life. From my early days in parochial school as a volunteer youth group leader, I knew that it was my calling to serve others. I often times reflect on that time in my life as an awakening. My youth group coordinator was one of those influences to serve others. In his own warm and caring way he inspired young people to become empowered to lead. It was he who invited me to become a youth group leader after participating in retreats and community service. It was a time of self-realization and personal growth. There are so many incredible people I met during those years that have helped shape who I am today.

My first professional position was working as a Chemical Dependency Counselor for Oneida County in the City of Utica, New York, where I was born and raised. This position was another awakening for me. It was a difficult transition at first. Neither my life experience nor my academic education prepared me to work with chemically dependant clients and in some cases the mentally ill addict. Treating clients ranging from the very young to the geriatric, from public schools, the military and prison populations, was an incredible learning experience. It afforded me a wealth of knowledge that more than prepared me for my first position with the New York City Board of Education—The SPARK Program in the fall of 1990.

Amy and I came to New York to spread our wings and partake of all the opportunities that only the Big Apple offered. I needed to re-charge mentally and emotionally after working in the chemical dependency area. I came down ahead of Amy and immersed myself in the world of acting. I really loved performing and the whole creative process. After a brief period taking classes and participating in workshops in an acting studio in the theatre district, I was asked if I would take charge of running a camera for a soap opera workshop. Eventually I found myself behind the scenes handling a technical equipment booth for a variety of workshops. The teachers seemed eager to have me "run tech" for them. I met a wealth of talented actors and teachers at the studio. Some of them are now on Broadway and in film.

I enjoyed my sojourn in the acting world, but it just wasn't paying the rent. I was trying to figure out how to keep my head above water in the big city when the opportunity to work for the New York Board of Education's SPARK Program came along. This was a drug abuse intervention and prevention program based in the New York City high schools. Given my experience in chemical dependency counseling and background working in a school district upstate, I was hired on the spot. I liked the freedom this counseling position offered and the opportunity to again serve. As an added incentive, I was able to continue working at the acting studio evenings and summers.

Equipped as I felt for this undertaking, I was to learn so much more from the students themselves. Working with high-risk students is a challenge that I can't compare to anything else I experienced. Many of the young people I encountered dealt every day with a realty that no one should have to endure; like the twelve year old who hid her pregnancy from her parents until she was about to give birth. Often, I confronted both disengaged and involved parents about a youngster's need to be immediately placed into an inpatient drug treatment program. Regularly, I made the hard decision to place a student into a hospital for observation, after he or she confided a suicide plan. Later I needed to steel myself against their sense of betrayal. More often than I ever thought possible I filed reports with Child Protective

Services in response to a student disclosing how their parent had sexually and physically abused them. This was my commitment to service. Each day I went to work I devoted myself to helping youngsters survive and thrive under the most difficult circumstances.

I was fortunate enough to take on two other positions with SPARK during my tenure there. As a Spark Prevention Specialist, I went into the classroom to deliver prevention presentations focusing on HIV/AIDS, teen violence, smoking, and drug and alcohol abuse. Mainly the students listened respectfully, but there were always a few students who challenged everything I said. I never minded being put on the spot. I always tried to be realistic and honest in my responses. More times than not, by the end of a week of long presentations, those who challenged me the most, joined my prevention program to promote substance abuse prevention and healthy lifestyles.

The final position I held with SPARK was as a peer group specialist. This was the best job I ever had. Every student in my program went through a full year of intensive training to master the human relations skills necessary to work with students at risk. They frequently referred students to me for additional support and counseling. I started a program from absolutely nothing and by the time I left to take a guidance counselor position at my School there were over 50 active peer helpers on board. They were a very tight knit group, a kind of family, who often helped one another and proved to be each other's primary support system. I was amazed by my students' sensitivity to other students in their hour of need. They were all an inspiration to me. I was blessed to have played a part in their growth and development.

The administrators at the Board of Education recognized both my skills and commitment by making me a member of the New York City Crisis Response Team; I was always "on-call" to go to a school that has experienced some type of trauma such as a shooting, a fire, or the untimely death of a beloved teacher or student.

The changeover to being a guidance counselor called for some major adjustments. I found out my true priorities the hard way on my first open-school night as a guidance counselor. A line of my parents and students a city block long stalled because I was providing counseling instead of guidance. Meanwhile my colleague Mario's line moved with the precision of a Swiss watch. I quickly learned to shift gears from a counseling process approach to a more concrete guidance technique, essentially providing information, advice, encouragement or discipline.

Up until I took this position, my entire professional career focused on a broad range of issues with clients I counseled. As a guidance counselor, with a caseload of between 250 and 300 students, it was not humanly possible to counsel them all.

I did not know it at the time but my whole way of life was about to be behind me. I would have to meet new greater challenges and make new radical adjustments, which I couldn't even imagine. Actually, the past and future meant little to me after my bang on the head. I lived only in the painful present.

Chapter Three

What's Happening to Me?

Hell is an Understatement

Tonight the pain that the doctor assured me could be relieved with two Tylenols continues and continues. The next day the headaches are more intense. It is impossible to read or write or do the most basic tasks. No doubt, I know I am in real trouble. I am not the kind of person to question medical professionals, but clearly something more should have been done before releasing me. I decide to keep a log to follow the progress of my condition. It may provide important information essential for future diagnosis and treatment. At any rate, I have to feel as if I am doing something to help myself. I've always prided myself on being a "can do" proactive person. By getting out my thoughts and feelings I find that they don't run around inside my head as much. Journal writing is something I often encouraged my students and clients to do, and I feel at least this once I should take some of my own advice. By documenting my experience I believe that I will also be able to look back and gauge improvement. My wife Amy must make the initial entries into my journal from my rambling dictation.

Daily Journaling

After Chris's accident I tape record Chris telling the story of how he got injured. I need to know how this terrible injury happened while it is still fresh in his mind. The next day I begin to take dictation for Chris's journal.

I feel it is important for Chris to keep a journal of the daily events in his new situation; maybe in some way it will help the doctors to make him well. It is very difficult to understand

13

him at times because of his speech impediments and he becomes easily frustrated when I cannot understand him. I gently encourage him to continue.

A Variety of Headaches

Day 3: I wake up Sunday with a variety of head pain all happening at the same time. Hell is an understatement. They are tremendous headaches, spectacular headaches, like nothing I have ever experienced before. The headaches are non-stop, no letup. The pain makes it difficult even to see. I cannot read for more than three to five minutes at a time. When I try to read or write my head and eye sockets explode with pain. The vicious pounding is hardly relieved by the Tylenol and Motrin. The pain is so relentless; I can barely stand it.

A Pitchfork in the Brain

At least three different types of pain invade my skull. One feels like a chisel constantly striking the right side of my skull, trying to make it through to the left side of my brain. I feel as if the Titanic is encased in my head. This wavy vertigo-like feeling intensifies when I turn my head from side to side. It slowly stretches and suddenly snaps back like a thick rubber band. The pain in my eye sockets feels like a screwdriver being forced into the upper part of my eyes toward my brain. I am queasy, nauseous.

My speech is slow and labored. I slur my words. I have trouble communicating with my wife in full sentences. I forget what I am trying to say midway through a sentence. I cannot complete my thoughts.

I am off balance when I stand and walk. My guidance system does not work. I try to walk straight, but my body veers to left or right, like a car out of alignment. I am stunned. What's happening? I'm afraid, petrified. I need to be certain I will get better... not some day, not tomorrow, but soon in the next moment. It's now Sunday and I will not be going to Mass today, but I will be doing a lot of praying. I awake with the same agony. In the afternoon, my face goes numb. A tingling starts around my temples and goes down to my chin. I have no idea what's happening. All I know is that it's strange and horrifying, in its own way worse than the excruciating pain. I try to stay together. Is it the beginning of a stroke? Will paralysis set in? Are there still worse tortures in store for me? Meanwhile, the excruciating medley of torment in my head remains constant. No letup throughout the day.

The Emergency Room

Already my new world is nothing but prolonged and constant suffering. If it's hell, the devil's pitchfork is sticking in my brain. Amy and I are very concerned that the pain in my head and the numb feeling traveling down the right side of my head to my chin does not let up. It is only getting worse. Not knowing what may happen if we don't seek immediate medical attention, Amy calls for a taxi for the long agonizing trip to the emergency room at the Jersey City Medical Center.

The staff finds a bed for me right away and I am hooked up to a saline drip. I am also given some kind of shot to subdue the head pain. The severe pain does not take a break. The emergency room is loud, raucous, glaring with fluorescent lights. My headaches only get worse. I close my eyes and try to relax. It is not a restful environment.

On the other side of the curtain, a woman is screaming, shrieking. She's wild, vehement and hysterical. The nurse comes over to Amy and me and apologizes. She apologizes for treating an out-of-control drug addict instead of me. I really feel the addict's agony and desperation. I wish, I truly wish, I could let my pain out with a tremendous scream. I tell the nurse that I understand and it is okay.

The doctor performs a brief neurological exam. Methodically but sympathetically, he puts me through the paces. First he asks me to touch my finger to my nose and then to his finger. It is extremely difficult for me to do, particularly with my left hand. Next, I have to close my eyes and try to stand without falling, which is next to impossible. Then while standing with my legs together he asks me to look up at the ceiling while maintaining my balance. I cannot do this even for a second. I also am unable to walk a straight line. For the finale, he tests my reflexes, which are completely unreceptive. He cannot help shaking his head. He is impressed by my ability to know today's correct date. He orders a CAT scan which comes back negative. He informs me that there are neurological disturbances that have occurred from the trauma to the brain. The emergency room doctor would have arranged an appointment with a neurologist for a full exam, but Amy and I prefer to get a referral from our family doctor.

Hearing the emergency room doctor say that there are neurological disturbances and that it appears that I sustained a brain injury adds to my nervousness and concern about a possible prognosis, but I am not really thinking about my future, since my current condition is deteriorating so rapidly. I am totally in the present.

I'm Not Joe!

Chris only gets worse and on Sunday without a car, we take the ten-mile trip by taxi to the Jersey City Medical Center. I am uncertain about the care Chris will get at this ER, probably based on his experience with the New York City hospital. How equipped are they... how knowledgeable will the ER doctor be about concussions? Why is Chris's face going numb? His condition seems to me to be much more serious than a concussion.

I am frightened yet hopeful as Chris is being admitted into the emergency room. Perhaps some tests will be ordered that could give us some answers. I am frightened and yet want to know so desperately what is happening. I just hope, whatever the problem is, the doctors can fix it.

I listen to the emergency room doctor go over his findings and hear two very disturbing words "brain injury!" My mind goes numb. I wonder what this means and how do we fix it? He instructs me to wake Chris up every four hours. I have to make sure he can recall his name and he knows where he is. When we go to bed I set the alarm for four hours. I wake in the middle of the night and ask Chris the crucial questions. After the second or third time, I think of a way to truly test if he knows who he is. As I softly wake him I say "Joe, Joe time to wake up!" Chris in astonishment replies, "Joe, who is Joe? Amy I'm Chris." I laugh and say, "Okay, I just wanted to make sure you knew who you were." He looks very perplexed and goes back to sleep. A few months later I reminded him of this story and today we still laugh about it.

Monday Morning

Day 4: It is Monday, no work today, not in my state. Please God, let me get through this day. There are many moments when I think I will never make it. It's baffling. The change is so sudden and so devastating. I pray with the conviction of a child. Amy calls our internist, and I get an appointment for the same day, that's a miracle in itself. With the thumping headaches, difficulty walking, the sensitivity of my eyes and hearing, getting there by public transportation is a huge effort.

Challenge of the Hill

We do not have a car so our journey into the City to see the doctor begins with a walk down three flights of stairs, a walk down a steep driveway, a three block walk to the bus stop in which the first block is up a very steep hill, climbing steps to board a bus, and maneuvering between people walking very fast in the Port Authority Bus Terminal.

Walking up that steep hill I have to literally lift Chris's legs and move them forward. I encourage him, "Come on Chris you have to keep going." Silently I pray for him then I hug him when we reach the top of the hill and take a break. Why didn't I call a car service? It's partly the money and partly that I don't quite know what I am in for... I am really so thankful when Chris's brother Bill offers to loan us his jeep. This helps with the grocery shopping, doing the laundry and most importantly getting Chris to his doctor appointments. I do not have to deal again with the challenge of the hill.

Is the Doctor Kidding?

The doctor diagnoses my symptoms as post-concussive syndrome, a handy label and schedules an appointment to see him in one month. Is he kidding? He indicates that a little rest may relieve my symptoms. And what do I do in the meanwhile? He writes a note indicating that the time of my return to work could not be determined. Amy and I insist that he refer us to a neurologist as the emergency room doctor suggested. He arranges for me to see a neurologist the following day. Slowly and very carefully, we make our way home.

It's odd not to be going to work, but work, the job, is the last thing on my mind. In addition to the steady relentless pain and distress to my head, brain and eyes, my ears began to ring loudly. It feels like a knife is piercing my ears.

Day 5: Today we are supposed to see the neurologist. I am anxious to find out what the hell is wrong with me. My walk is unsteady. I have to lean on Amy to keep from falling. It requires a conscious effort just to stand.

Unfortunately, it turns out that the neurologist has an emergency and has to cancel our appointment. I guess I'm not an emergency.

We see our family doctor, who schedules an MRI for later in the week, which the neurologist would no doubt have requested. On the way home from the doctor, I discover that my ears are super sensitive to loud high-pitched sounds or any loud noise. In fact, a sound literally has the power to knock me off my feet. The screeching brakes and sirens of the city are an agony. Another day is passing and the ceaseless pain and breakdown of my brain and body continue. Not a moment of peace.

A Downward Spiral

Day 8: Friday, the end of another work week, when I do not do much of anything. Today we go into the city for my MRI. My walking is worse. My legs shake as if I have cerebral palsy. Over the past week I have gone from needing moderate assistance to walk and holding on to someone's arm or hand, to depending on two people to aid me. My guidance system has totally broken down. My speech keeps getting worse. Sometimes the words just won't come out right or not at all. I am in a downward spiral and it seems there is nothing I can do to help myself. What the hell is going on? When we return from the MRI, I am totally worn out as though I had run ten marathons.

Day 12: Nothing has changed. I continue to take the over-the-counter medication, but the agonizing pain does not diminish. I constantly feel all different kinds of head pain and have difficulty walking and talking. All the doctors can say is, "it will take time." They can't tell me what will take time. Everything is vague except the pain. I have to admit I am frustrated and discouraged. There is no relief and no improvement. My condition remains the same. No doctor appointments. I stay at home and rest. I am starting to feel like an invalid. All I have the strength to do is lay on my living room recliner and sleep the day away, occasionally waking up to take an over the counter pain killer in a futile attempt to battle the unyielding pains swarming around my skull.

My World Upside Down

Day 13: Thankfully, my parents drive down from Utica today to help Amy care for me. They also want to be around for my visit to the neurologist. The whole world is upside down! I should be and have been the one to take care of them. I hate to see my mom and dad make the long four-hour trip to Jersey. Everything is out of whack. I feel useless.

Although my mom is a tiny woman, maybe five foot three on her tiptoes, weighing 100 pounds and deals with a number of medical conditions of her own, she immediately takes charge both caring for me and taking on the housekeeping. She is a very strong Italian American lady and she has never let anything interfere with her role as daughter, wife, and mother. My dad is of Irish and German or Dutch stock, (depending on who you ask), with clear blues eyes. He is a golden rule kind of person; a loving, humble and very forgiving man. Today those eyes are very solemn.

My mom and dad are two people who exemplify what it means to be a parent. They are always there for their children at a moment's notice whether to celebrate their accomplishments or care for them in times of need. They are the most selfless people I know. Of course, they are not perfect, but who is?

It's All Right Son

I am relieved to know Chris's mom and dad are going to stay the week. Dad can help Chris walk. Chris's dad is a very strong man and like Chris's mother, a very giving person. I am so excited to have the help. Although I have told them some general things about Chris's injury, the stark fear on their faces shows that they are in no way prepared for the reality.

20

That night I show dad how I put Chris into bed. After helping Chris to the side of the bed, he slowly sits on the bed while I support his back. I then lift his legs slowly up as Chris swivels around placing his feet on the bed. While holding Chris's back and head and softly speaking to him, I slowly lower him down to his pillow. If I go too fast he screams out in fear. The next night dad helps him, cradling him in his arms, softly encouraging him and slowly lowering him down. Dad is very strong and has a very calming voice. I use Dad's cradling method often after mom and dad leave to go home. Chris seems to feel more secure with this method.

In the morning, I help mom with breakfast and dad is dressing Chris. I forget to explain to dad how exactly to dress him. Chris's mom and I hear a blood-curdling scream from the bedroom. I run to see what is up. Dad looks frightened and baffled. Chris is simply holding his head. I see Chris's T-shirt thrown on the floor and know immediately what happened. Dad keeps saying, "all I was trying to do was to help him put on his t-shirt." I try to reassure them and explain to dad why Chris screamed out. "When Chris can't see, he gets more and more dizzy, loosing his sense of balance and gets really scared. He feels like he is falling, falling from a high place. It is important to always let him see what is going on, and not cover his eyes." I show dad how I put Chris's shirt over his head, as if I were dressing a young child. Dad walks away with tears in his eyes. How painful it must be for dad to see his normally robust son in such terrible shape.

I sit down with mom and dad and explain how I maneuver and handle Chris ... what I find works and what doesn't.

The next morning dad tries to dress Chris again. Chris calls out for me to put on his shirt. I come in and tell Chris that I am helping mom in the kitchen, but dad now knows how to put on his shirt. Chris reluctantly agrees and dad has no problem. I stay around the door to watch in case dad needs help. Dad smiles, as he tries to encourage Chris. Chris thanks his father. His dad responds in a breaking voice, "It's all right son."

Mom and dad are a great help and enable me to return to work. Dad now helps Chris get in and out of bed like a pro.

When I get home from work I ask them if they have picked up any helpful hints for me since that they have been caring for Chris during the day. It is clear that we are all learning together.

Another Disappointment

Day 14: My mom and dad drive me into the City for the highly anticipated neurologist appointment. My poor parents, I can't believe I am putting them through this. They support me between them. I desperately grasp each of their arms. They get me into the car very slowly guiding, coaching, and encouraging me each step of the way. Each step I take feels like my last. We are all tired and frazzled as they finally help me into the doctor's office where we meet Amy. My attempts to perform the simplest movements for the neurological exam makes it crystal clear to me how much my medical condition has deteriorated since my visit to the emergency room in Jersey City. The neurologist crisply confirms that I have a brain injury. He refers me to Mount Sinai Hospital Head Trauma Unit for a complete evaluation and to an ear nose and throat specialist for hearing tests. He schedules a spinal MRI and a follow-up visit. At last, things will start moving.

That night the neurologist phones us. Amy gives me the bad news. The Mount Sinai specialist is going on vacation and will not return until mid November. Another delay! I keep getting passed around and passed up. The doctor assures us he will keep trying to get a definite appointment upon his colleague's return.

I continue to deteriorate. I have trouble following a simple train of thought when I speak. I forget what I am saying in the middle of a sentence. I can't cope with this. How can I forget what I am saying while I am speaking? One of the things I was always proud of was my ability to think quickly on my feet and speak clearly and with purpose. Now I have difficulty expressing a word distinctly, not to mention a sentence.

Day 16: Mom and dad leave, assuring Amy and me they will be back soon. They are really suffering with me. I can't help worrying about them.

Day 18: I have an appointment with an attorney to discuss the accident. First Doctors and now Lawyers. I feel as if I have lost my will power, I have to rely so much on others. I am very weak during the meeting. It takes all my energy to try to concentrate enough to relate what happened. The attorney calls a car service to take us home. This attorney is amiable enough, but who knows? He comes on the recommendation of one of my doctors. I hope he's okay.

Doctors' Visits

Day 20: I have many doctor appointments in the city on the tenth. I begin my day at the ear nose and throat Doctor for a hearing test, followed by the allergist for my regular examination and shot, and then off to the MRI facility for a C-spine and lumbar test. The MRI is an ordeal. The MRI of C-Spine and Lumbar is a 45-minute diagnostic test, examining my neck and spine for any abnormalities. I am put on a cold padded board, which slides into the MRI tunnel. It is kind of eerie in itself. The MRI makes an incredible loud knocking noise, similar to a jackhammer breaking through concrete. Given my sensitivity to noise, it feels like a jackhammer is cracking my skull open. Not only do I have a worse headache when I am done, but I am very fatigued and have to take a long rest in the waiting room before leaving.

The energy, kinetic movement and excitement of the City that I once reveled in is now overwhelming; the noise, the activity, the people and the subway exhausts me.

My brother Bill is one of the people I depend upon today and he is really coming through for me. After Bill's college graduation with a degree in architecture, he decided to follow his dream and moved to New York City to study dance. Over the years he has done quite well for himself.

Bill and I end up taking cabs from one appointment to another. At the MRI appointment, we meet Amy and my brother Paul, a student at New York Law School. Paul is low-key and extremely bright. As my little brother, he has counted on me for support and direction. We all take a cab to Paul's apartment in Queens where Amy and I stay overnight. I have a neurologist appointment in the city the following morning. The trip back to New Jersey would be too much for me, and Amy can use the extra rest.

A Change in Routine

Since Chris has several appointments in the city allotted for a single day, his brother Paul suggests that Chris and I stay over night at his apartment in Queens. I am glad not to have to struggle with getting Chris home late at night knowing how tired and anxious he would be from this change in his new daily routine. I know it will really throw him off. Chris agrees that he would be too tired to travel back to New Jersey after a full day of appointments. Exhausted from his full schedule of appointments, Chris's goes straight to bed. I go to work the next morning, set to meet them at another appointment in the afternoon. Even at Paul's I make sure his breakfast is ready for him along with any medication he needs to take. I try to recreate his familiar routine as much as possible. Later that day, I am very glad to see both Bill and Paul at the appointment. Chris seems well rested.

A Question of Suicide

Day 21: In the morning I am so weak I have to be practically carried. My brothers take me to the follow-up neurologist appointment. As usual, Amy meets us there. The doctor says that my speech is clearly getting worse, more strained and halting. He asks me how I am doing emotionally. In a breaking voice I tell him, "I feel down, sad, and frustrated." I have to improve. I need to get better. I need to return to work and get back to living. The neurologist pauses, looks serious and asks me outright, "Have you thought about taking your own life?" I am not that desperate, yet. No doubt, I feel very fragile. "No." I tell him, "that's not who I am.

On my trips back-and-forth to the doctors, I learn that I have become a completely different person. I am very jumpy, my nerves on edge. I startle easily. Each time a car passes or even edges into the road I have the sensation of an imminent crash.

Free Fall

Day 22: I sleep the entire following day. No relief. The pain is always with me. Something very strange and scary happens in the middle of the night. As I feel myself lapse into a deep sleep I have a horrifying sensation that I am falling fast with nothing to catch me. It is as if I am falling off a cliff, a free fall or a dead drop. This nightmare feeling is terrifying. The sensation is made worse when I turn my head even slightly in an attempt to get comfortable. The sensation becomes so frightening, so bizarre and chilling I lose control and begin to yell and scream furiously until Amy calms me down.

The torment continues. My head is pounding so badly I want to rip it off from my shoulders. My ears are stabbed with knives, ringing like a fire alarm.

Passing Out

Day 23: At one point, in the early afternoon, making my way from the bathroom I just give out and stop after only a few steps. I sit on the piano bench just outside the bathroom door. I am so far gone I must sit. I feel lightheaded and call for Amy's help. I must lose consciousness. As if from a distance, I hear my wife continually calling out my name and talking to me. When I open my eyes I see Amy pushing my computer chair into the room. She helps me into the chair. She pushes the chair, now carrying me, into the living room and helps me into my recliner. The feeling of helplessness is overwhelming. I want to get better. I must get better, but no matter how much I'm trying, it's just not working.

Blacking Out

It becomes more and more evident each day of Chris's inability to handle the long walk in our railroad style apartment from living room to bathroom, which is maybe about 15 feet. One day he is very weak as he comes out of the bathroom, and he calls out to me. At the moment I walk out of our home office, I see him sliding down the wall to sit on the piano bench. I grab him and understand immediately what is happening. He is blacking out. I call out to him eliciting a slight response. His weight is unbearably heavy on my small body and we both collapse to the floor. We sit there for what seems an eternity. I continue to call out to him, gently calling his name. He opens his eyes as if awakening from a deep sleep. I smile, telling him I need his help to move him to the living room. It seems as though he understands me as I explain to him that I am going to get the office chair with wheels. I place the chair close to him. I need his help to get him up and into the chair. He sheepishly nods and on the count of three he nudges himself up while I swing him around and place him in the chair. It isn't pretty, but it does the trick. I at least have him mobile so I can move him to the living room.

As I begin to wheel him toward the living room he cries out in pain. I ask him what is wrong. The movement is too much for him. I take it easy and go very slowly. It is the only way to get him back into the living room. His eyes close and he starts to slip off the chair. I call his name and he awakens again. I take the belt off his bathrobe and tie it around his chest to the back of the chair. Again I start to move slowly towards the living room. It seems to take an hour before we get to the destination. I untie the belt and move in front of him. I remember how dad lifted Chris and I use the same technique. Talking softly to Chris throughout the maneuver, I finally have him sitting comfortably on the couch. Then I collapse next to him. He sleeps... I cry... then I put a call in to the doctor.

I try to do everything in my power to make Chris's life easier. I notice certain things bother Chris. Noise increases his headaches tremendously. I keep the TV and radio turned off, and speak quietly and slowly so he can absorb what I say. Sometimes his speech is so muddled that I can hardly understand a word. I have some paper by his side so he can scribble a word or two. This is no solution since his fine motor skills have deteriorated to the point where it is very difficult for him to hold a pen. I give him a big magic marker to use and he is able to write one or two words like a kindergartener, writing for the first time.

In our long railroad style apartment it is really hard for Chris to get around. Helping Chris walk to the bathroom I count his steps so I have an idea when he needs to take a break. When I am at work and there is no one at home to aid him in his long journey to the bathroom, he has to have some support when he takes his breaks. Finally I hit upon a solution. I put a dining room chair in the middle of the long walkway, which he can use for support or sitting before continuing on to the bathroom. This works great, but as his walking deteriorates, I have to add more chairs for more breaks until I finally push the dining room table against the wall and have all six chairs conveniently spaced and lined up for Chris. Now it seems as though he takes two steps, stops and rests, takes two more steps and again rests, until he makes it to the bathroom.

Waiting

Day 25: Another week begins. Maybe things are looking up. For a short interval, the headaches are tolerable. My face remains numb. Amy picks up my mom at Penn Station. Amy tries to contact the Mount Sinai doctor, who we presume to be back from vacation to make a definite appointment. No luck. My symptoms are basically the same. The head pain continues. I rest and sleep most of the day. I have trouble at night again with that "falling off the cliff" feeling. Amy props me up with pillows, attempting to make me comfortable. She gives me Tylenol, but it has absolutely no effect.

When I am not sleeping, I am in pain. I just can't shake it. My legs are weak and very shaky. In the evening Amy and mom note that I drag my left leg when I try to walk. At one point I stop, my leg refuses to move forward. This is very frightening. Amy moves my leg for me, trying to get me going again. I am desperate; I must get into Mount Sinai now, this very moment.

Slipping Away

I feel so lost that I can't even figure out how to get Chris to take one step forward. Every day I can see he is walking with more difficulty. His left foot drags behind, then he must constantly stop to take a rest. He cannot walk straight and his crooked walk leads him into corners. I watch Chris's health deteriorate day by day. I feel so frustrated because I cannot get help for him. I feel as though he is slipping away slowly. It is like Chris and I are in a ferocious wind storm and I am holding on to his hand for dear life, but I am slowly losing my grip until we are joined only by our fingertips.

I try to finalize an appointment with a neurologist and get Chris into a hospital, but I get excuses instead of appointments. "It takes time," they tell me. No one is giving me any clear answers. I guess this is why Chris has always said doctors "practice medicine." Nothing is showing up on the CAT scans or MRI's, yet his health is deteriorating. I need answers!

Nightmares

At night, it's worse. That same "falling off a cliff" feeling comes again. I cannot help screaming and screaming and screaming and screaming. Amy wakes up and tries to calm me.

Day 27: The headaches are still pounding and the numbness in my face is constant. I have another fainting spell. I black out in front of mom. She has been here only two days. It is more frightening for her than me. She sits me in the nearest chair and waits until I can get up again. I can't get up straight away. Mom starts calling my name. I hear her calling me as if from far away, but it is impossible to respond. I am sliding down in the chair. She is calling my name more loudly and frantically. Finally, after endless repetitions, I respond and gradually refocus. She helps me into my trusty computer chair and rolls me into the living room. My whole body trembles. My control over my body seems gone; another indignity.

My Prison

I feel as if I'm locked up in a prison for a crime I haven't committed. I feel totally powerless. I fight against self-pity. I have to keep my hopes up, despite a body and brain that constantly break down. Still I cannot get an appointment with a doctor who has the authority to admit me to Mount Sinai. I try but I cannot apply my standard approach as a counselor. I cannot take one day at a time.

I try to walk, but the shaking makes it impossible. All day my head feels like it is squeezed in a vise. My eye sockets feel like screws are being twisted into them. The wavy feeling in my head is the ocean in a hurricane.

Day 30: Dad arrives to help mom and Amy. He wants to be with us for the Mount Sinai appointment which will be in two days.

A Bad Dream

I have a dream. I am at work. I enter a windowless school. I recognize my school. I casually go into a classroom to give a presentation. Suddenly a security guard appears and tells me I have to leave. He escorts me out of the classroom to the security desk at the entrance to the school. Now I notice that I am wearing pajamas, a robe, and slippers. Donna, the assistant principal of guidance, meets me at the security desk and speaks to me in a sympathetic voice. She tells me I need to stay home and get better. She acts concerned, but she is also embarrassed. Donna asks me to leave and I lose it and begin to sob on her shoulder. The dream is a nightmare and very disturbing and I am jolted out of a sound sleep.

Evaluations

Day 32: Finally I am going to Mount Sinai for an evaluation. My brother Paul and my parents are accompanying Amy and me. First thing in the morning I take the Tylenol for the head pain. Today for a change, the pain seems tolerable, but that is only momentary. We arrive at Sinai in a fairly optimistic frame of mind. I am desperately in need of help. Hopefully, Sinai will provide it.

As the afternoon in the Sinai examining room progresses, the headaches increase, the whole range of physical agonies return with a vengeance. The head pain, lightheadedness, difficulty walking, numbness, stuttering, loss of train of thought, trouble balancing and navigating, are displayed in full force; I believe the urgency of my case is dramatically revealed to the Mount Sinai neurologist. To my surprise, the impact of my symptoms on the doctor appears to be minimal. In a detached business-like way she prescribes a medication regimen, adding that she will consult with her colleagues on the suitability of an outpatient rehab program.

Paul, who is in the examining room with Amy and me looks straight at the doctor and asks with an expression of disbelief and amazement, "Could you tell me how you go about determining if someone is appropriate for outpatient or inpatient Rehabilitation?" I could see he is at his wits end. She proceeds to say that people who cannot walk on their own, who have speech and cognitive problems, and who can't take care of their own basic living needs, are the type of people they consider for inpatient therapy. Paul and Amy both look baffled. Paul asserts himself again and says to the doctor, "Haven't you noticed it takes two of us to hold on to Chris when he tries to walk, or that he can barely put two words together? Don't you see how he struggles with the cognitive testing? How is it he isn't appropriate for inpatient therapy? Amy certainly isn't capable of getting him to an outpatient program on her own, traveling into Manhattan from New Jersey each day." The doctor appears surprised by Paul's very direct questioning. After a brief pause, she agrees that inpatient may be more helpful, but that she will have to speak to the department head about a possible admission. We all thank her and leave with our spirits renewed.

By the time we return home, I am completely wiped out and ready for bed, but I cannot sleep. The pain won't let me.

Day 33: The next day, Amy and I pay a visit to the Board of Education for another doctor's evaluation to determine whether I am "work-ready." Of course, the determination is that I am not.

This is followed by another visit to Mount Sinai and further evaluations. All the activity wears me out. I can barely take a step on my own. My headaches are banging away. I cannot handle the traffic, the honking of the horns, the sirens, the fast moving people and cars. I feel like I am in a gelatinous cloud moving at a slower pace than everyone around me. That evening when I go to bed I once again have difficulty falling asleep. The falling feeling and head pain make it impossible.

No Holiday from Pain

Day 35: Today is Thanksgiving. It is hard to be thankful. I wake up around 5:30 a.m. with intense head pain and a backache. No holiday from pain. Usually, Amy and I head to Utica and visit my family for Thanksgiving. Clearly, I cannot make that long trip. Thankfully, my mom and dad stay with us so we can have a family holiday, if not a very joyous one. Paul also joins us but he is not at all in a Thanksgiving mood. It is Thanksgiving Day, but what can I possibly be thankful for? My brain has gone into shutdown mode, only the essential functions are working. I guess I should feel thankful for being alive, but somehow I don't feel very alive. As I slouch in the recliner while my family does everything they can to change my mood and lift my spirits, I find my emotions getting the better of me. I'm looking at my family sitting all around me in my living room. I start thinking about how we should all be in Utica with my great aunts, little sister and other family members who are always part of any holiday celebration. Instead, my parents, Paul, and Amy, are here watching over me with heavy hearts. It practically feels like a wake. I know I am not responsible for what has happened, but I feel responsible for the sorrow my family is trying to deal with. I just want to make it go away.

I begin crying uncontrollably. I can't catch my breath. The tears are flowing and I am apologizing to all of them for what I've put them through. I just can't stop myself from crying.

This causes a chain reaction with everyone tearing up. I am feeling even worse. I blurt out in a stutter, "I'm the one who takes care of everyone else, not the one who ever needs to be taken care of. This is so wrong, so unfair." They all try to reassure me. My dad jumps in saying, "You've been there for all of us all the time, now it's our turn to be here for you." Their words helped dry up the tears and calm me down. I guess I need permission to depend on them, and that's okay.

I have difficulty getting to sleep and get up at 4:30 a.m. with the now familiar sense of a terrifying free fall and the stupendous head pain. I shout out in my sleep, waking Amy. She reassures me that I am still in bed and safe. She adjusts my pillows and gives me the new medication from the Mount Sinai doctor, which helps take the edge off.

Day 36: My parents leave today to return home. My mom, in particular, has trouble fighting off the tears. I try to reassure her that everything will work out fine. As much as she would like to believe me I am not certain she does. They plan to return next week when I am supposed to be admitted to the Mount Sinai head trauma unit. I am in a fog the whole day. My head and eye sockets in particular are pierced with pain. But I am not giving in and I am a long way from giving up.

Day 37: After breakfast my head is aching and only increases as the morning progresses. My face continues to feel numb. Nothing helps. It only gets worse. By the evening I notice my symptoms get worse as I struggle to read my journal. My eye sockets begin to throb even more; creating a worse headache than before I started reading. My eyes tear throughout the day.

Day 41: A new month begins, December, but the old litany of pain continues. I take down the notes in my journal as the day unfolds. The note taking intensifies the headaches. It seems when I am overtaxed and over stimulated, whether trying to walk and talk at the same time; riding in traffic where things can happen fast; being ambushed by loud noises or sudden movements, my symptoms become much worse. I have hair-trigger reactions that throw me totally off balance.

I can't believe I'm having such trouble speaking. This was one of my strengths before the accident. Everything now is such a struggle for me. The more I try to express myself clearly, the more difficult it becomes. I believe my skills will come back in time, but right now I'm so frustrated and embarrassed by my failed attempt to speak without a constant stutter. I can't stand listening to myself.

I'm not, however, ready to give up or give in. I hurt now, but I refuse to be helpless and dependent. I will struggle and do whatever it takes to get back my life. I think about Mount Sinai and its rehabilitation unit as the biblical Mount Sinai ... It signifies hope.

Chapter Four

Rehab Begins

Climbing the Mountain

Day 43: Friday December 3rd is a very special day. A bed opens up at Mount Sinai's acute care head trauma unit. Amy is in the other room doing some last minute packing. Bill and Paul are standing by in the kitchen ready to do whatever Amy asks to help her get things ready for my hospital stay. I hadn't even heard them come in. No respite. I experience a loud ringing in my ears. My head is pounding. I take a deep breath. Soon there will be some real relief. That I am now going to participate in my own recovery is a thought I try to hold on to. Amy drives to the hospital. My brothers are on each side of me. I see Amy smile in the rear view mirror. I know she feels in her bones that this is a good beginning.

My brothers Paul and Bill hold on to each side of me as I get out of the car. With my legs shaking uncontrollably and unable to support the weight of my body, they practically carry me into the hospital. The hospital seems so loud and busy. It puts me on edge. The noise makes it that much harder for me to comfortably move through the hospital. I have so much trouble just putting one leg before another. I can't wait till we get to the unit so I can flop down and relax. This person struggling to take a few steps cannot be me.

They carefully escort me up to the unit where a nurse quickly helps me into a wheelchair and guides us to my room. I find it humiliating. Once I get into my room my brothers help me on to the bed and get settled in. They stand against the back wall facing me. I will never forget the looks on their face as the nurses start asking their initial questions. They seem to be in shock. Their eyes are so big. They certainly are not their usual talkative selves. I tell them not to worry and try to reassure them.

My First Day

Day 44: I'm exhausted. I see a couple of doctors who do some tests. This is my first day. I am glad I have a private room. Nothing beats a private room, particularly when every single movement startles me so much and every little noise rings so loudly between my ears. I can't bear the slightest noise of other people. Any other person is an intrusion. I can't wait for the nurse to leave. Yet I am deeply lonely. I try to imagine what Amy is doing now, but I lose track of time. I am out of time.

Milton

I am alone and added to my physical pain is a sense of emptiness. I miss Amy so much. I choke up. My eyes are tearing. I will not let myself cry. Am I crying already? I feel abandoned. The door opens. A tall man ambles in. He walks straight up to me and looks into my face. He smiles very broadly and despite myself I can't help smiling back. "Everything's gonna be alright," he says with a Jamaican lilt. I recognize the Bob Marley lyric. The head pain lets up a little as in my imagination I dive into the transparent West Indian sea and bask in the pure sunshine. He laughs and I respond in kind. It is soothing laughter. More than words are exchanged. His name is Milton. He may be an orderly, but he's the best medicine since that blow to my head. We both sing the praises of Jamaica and other Caribbean Islands, places I truly treasure and for a moment I forget to be afraid.

I wake up during the night twice. The head pain has not subsided. I am too fragile to get to the bathroom. The nurse gives me medication to help with the pain. It helps me sleep.

The nursing staff wakes me at 7 a.m. for breakfast. The first thing I see is the date, December 4, 1999, neatly printed on a dry eraser board. I guess the intention is to help me to keep track of time. I don't realize how helpful it is until the nurse asks me what the date is and I don't have a clue. I have to rely on the board. How long has it been since I was really conscious of the date or the time?

The headaches and usual pains persist. I meet the occupational therapist. James introduces himself immediately after breakfast. He proceeds to do a once over, questions and answers and an orientation. Next I meet Alvin, the physical therapist. He brings me to the gym for some basics. No time to waste. He puts plastic braces on my legs and attempts to help me stand with the support of a walker. I can barely hold myself up and quickly collapse back into the wheelchair. Alvin and James are upbeat, friendly, and very professional. I am a little disappointed to find out that these therapists are only here on weekends. They tell me that I will be assigned to other therapists on Monday. I am very tired after these first sessions, but am glad to start working on getting back to myself.

Never on Sunday

Day 45: Unfortunately there is no therapy on Sunday. Instead a nurse brings me in a wheelchair to a jazz concert in the hospital recreation room. She is very nice and well-meaning, but the volume of the piano punishes my ear drums. As much as I enjoy music, this is torture. It feels as if I am in a cave with no opening, and a fifty piece orchestra is playing at full tilt five feet from my chair. I stay as long as I can, about fifteen minutes. I then ask a nurse to take me back to my room. My head is hammering. When I return to my room I rest until dinner. I never paid much attention to noise, now I really appreciate quiet. The head pain lasts the entire evening. The nurse gives me Percocet tablets, something I was familiar with as a drug counselor. It's heavy duty stuff, but lord knows I need it. After about a half an hour, she gives me another one, which helps relieve my headaches until about 10:30 that night. It feels very strange being here. It's unbelievable, but I'm grateful to be in the hospital.

I have a very bad case of the hiccups that night. It just won't stop. Just one more thing I can add to my litany of woes. At least the head pain is tolerable.

The Therapy Team

Day 46: I wake up with head pain, but Milton is there with a gentle "good morning Chris, it's time to start the day." It turns out that he is the first person I see each day and he will also give me my morning shower. At 8 a.m., shortly after my shower, my doctor and the treatment team come into my room to assess me. They busy themselves like mechanics over an engine, mixing clinical observations with small talk. It is decided for my own protection I will be strapped into a wheel chair. I will for the time being get in and out of bed only with the assistance of a staff member. At 9:30 a.m. I have a special MRI.

I am surprised to find myself moved to a semi-private room. The guy in the bed across from mine, my new roommate Claude, is able to welcome me with a friendly smile, despite his evident pain. He seems warm and kind. Claude has what the nurses call a halo around his entire head. I can't imagine how uncomfortable it must be having your entire head in a steel ribbed cage. Claude occasionally does try to speak to me, but I have trouble deciphering what he says. I'm not sure if this is because of his injury or my own deficiencies. I find myself nodding and smiling back at him while trying to get a handle on what he is saying. I do understand two words, "oh boy," which he repeats in an exasperated way throughout the day. He must really be in a lot of pain, the poor guy. He has fits of coughing, which leave me very rattled.

After lunch I am sent for a hearing test. I think, if anything, my hearing is overly acute. When I return to my room I see my speech therapist, Colleen. She does an evaluation. She is extremely empathetic, very compassionate, patient, and very encouraging. For some reason, she seems to understand me emotionally. I trust her. She will work with me for a half hour each morning. She reminds me of Amy, a little self-effacing at first, but a real take-charge personality.

Next, I am wheeled into the physical therapy room to meet Dave, my PT (physical therapy) guy. He has a good sense of humor and we hit it off right away. I also meet Ali, my occupational therapist. There is something about her that is down-to-earth and real. I like them both. I'm eager to get started. Today they work together as a team. They test my coordination. Dave asks me to walk as he gets in front of me and supports me between the parallel bars. Ali follows behind with a wheelchair. I eventually manage to stand up and Dave encourages me to walk toward him. I just stand there. I am trying so hard to do what he asks me, but I can't. He continues to urge me on and reaches for one of my legs, bringing it forward as I tightly hold on to the parallel bars with each hand. In my mind I know what I am supposed to do, but my legs are in a world of their own, out of sync with my brain. It is like the message from my brain to move my legs is being rerouted. Why do I have to struggle to do something that always came naturally to me? This is upsetting. Dave places a mirror at the end of the parallel bars and I see myself for the first time. I look grotesque. Hunched over, my legs going in all directions, holding on to the parallel bars for dear life! My eyes begin to tear. I cry out, "Why is this happening … this is not me?" Dave again reassures me. "It's okay Chris, don't worry." For whatever reason, his voice inspires me. I believe in him and I believe in myself. I will walk, as I have in the past.

Chris' First Days in Rehab

I take time off from work to be with Chris the first couple of days after his admission to Mount Sinai. I want to be fully involved in his evaluations and be available to answer any questions that Chris cannot answer for himself. His therapist Dave puts his wheel chair at the beginning of parallel bars and helps Chris lift himself out of the wheelchair using the bars at waist level to support him. Ali, the occupational therapist, is behind Chris with the wheelchair so Dave can quickly help Chris sit down to rest if necessary. Dave directs Chris to walk towards him while holding on to the parallel bars. Chris struggles to lift his leg but it does not budge. Dave asks Chris what is wrong. Chris tells him that he is trying to make his legs move but they just won't. Dave bends down and lifts one of Chris's legs to take a step then moves the other leg. When Dave helps Chris sit down in the wheel chair to take a break, Dave asks him if he knows he is leaning forward and not standing up straight. Chris says no. Dave slides a full length mirror to the other end of the parallel bars so Chris can see how he is standing. Dave helps Chris stand up and again helps move his legs forward. Chris is becoming aware, perhaps for the first time, of his true condition. He collapses, crying hysterically as Dave helps him sit in the wheel chair and Ali assists in comforting Chris. I have all I can do not to run to him and cradle him in my arms to protect him. Dave and Ali are the experts and must know how to deal with this type of situation. I hold my tears back and struggle not to bolt out of the room. Soon Dave and Ali have Chris under control and with the mirror put away, he begins taking the steps to relearn to walk.

Tonight Chris tells me that if I can't handle it, he understands and will give me a divorce. When he actually says the "D" word; I do not believe what I am hearing. "Divorce, absolutely not. You think after all these years I am going to walk out on you. That's not how it works; you're stuck with me so get use to it." He gives me a little smile and asks, "Are you sure?" I am emphatic. "There will be no more discussion about this." I reassure him that I am here to stay and we will get through this together. I go home that night and cry like I never cried before. I cry because of the thoughts I have. I doubt myself and my ability to handle Chris's injury. If I can't deal with this, do I reconsider Chris's request for a divorce? Do I even want to deal with this? I cry because I am guilty of the same thoughts Chris has. Divorce!

A Day of Therapy

Day 47: The next day I wake up with a headache, a wavy feeling with pressure at my temples. My headache lasts throughout the afternoon. I work with Dave on standing straight and balancing with my eyes open and then closed. I do better with my eyes open. Dave leads me in a series of exercises pointing, flexing, and making circles with my feet by moving my ankles. I practice walking seated in my wheelchair, concentrating on moving my feet from my heels to my toes. The strap around my waist keeps me from falling out of the chair. I don't like the confining feeling of the strap, but it is a good thing. I view it as a tool for recovery.

In occupational therapy Ali tests my visual acuity. I see black spots when I shift my eyes around. Later I meet with my cognitive therapist, Jackie, for about twenty minutes of tests. That's my limit. My head pain increases as I struggle to concentrate and try to pay attention.

My Heel and Toe Mantra

After dinner, while strapped in my wheelchair, I perform my walking exercises around the rehab floor. Repeating over and over again "Heel ... toe ... heel... toe... heel... toe." My mantra. It helps keep my focus on the individual movements. Amy is my admiring audience. At times, my left foot inconsiderately forgets what to do, despite my repetitions "Heel ... toe." I have to lift my left leg and show it what I want it to do. It's very frustrating watching my left leg drag up underneath the wheelchair and bring me to a dead stop while trying to complete the movement. Over time, I know it will all come together. I know I will be walking again. I refuse to be defeated.

Before Amy goes home she writes in my journal as I dictate the day's events. She believes it will be a good tool in the future for me to look back on to see how I have improved and acknowledge what I have accomplished.

After Amy leaves I also practice the speech exercises I am learning from Colleen. "Easy Onset" and "Light Contact" are techniques to help formulate and release my words without stuttering. I take a good size breath and speak each word softly and slowly without pushing the sounds out, particularly the consonants, to prevent me from getting stuck on a syllable. When I speak in this way I have a sing-song kind of cadence where I elongate the syllables to help get words out without stuttering. Over time, I hope I will be able to shorten the length of time between each syllable and thereby tighten up each word, making my speech sound more fluid.

A New Routine

A new routine begins. Now I hop on a train, immediately after work and return to the hospital each evening to be with Chris. I only have a few hours to see how he is doing and catch up on his day with a large part of that time devoted to taking down Chris's thoughts and comments, which he struggles to dictate for his journal. He speaks very slowly in the monotone his new speech therapist teaches him to use to speak more distinctly, and I write exactly what he is saying. Chris is really making an effort.

I take out clothes and toiletries for his morning shower. Chris is not comfortable about people going through his personal things and it makes it easier when his aide gets Chris showered and dressed in the morning. I fill out his food order for the next day, which Chris finds difficult to understand. I leave

Chris at 10 p.m. each evening, arriving home around 12 mid night. My eyes are closing from fatigue, yet I take his clothes that need washing down to the basement and use our landlady's washer. I have to let the clothes hang dry overnight and pack them in the morning to bring back to the hospital.

I cry myself to sleep, and wake up at 6 a.m. to begin the same daily grind all over again. Like a robot, I follow this routine day in and day out. The only evening I do not go to the hospital to see Chris is on Thursday. But I have no real time off. I go home to do additional laundry, sort through the mail, clean the apartment, and try to get to bed early. On Saturday and Sunday's I travel into the city to see Chris in the hospital around 10 a.m. and stay until visiting hours are over at 10 p.m. I don't know how I continue this hectic schedule: managing my department, running to the hospital to take care of Chris, paying the bills and keeping up the apartment, while always trying to keep a smile on my face. Something is driving me to keep going, almost as if it is not me.

The Hospital is Haunted

Another night. The blinding headaches and the peculiar agonies of my brain keep me from sleeping. It doesn't help that the nurse's aides are cutting up, shouting between rooms, laughing, cackling, chomping on food, and dragging furniture across the linoleum floor. I feel like the furniture is dragging inside my skull. Every sound reverberates. On top of that, Claude is having a coughing attack. The wind blows wildly, whistling through the corridors and slamming into the windows and doors. The whole place is haunted. It's torture and it doesn't stop. Claude is a terrific guy and his wife and little daughter are really dedicated. Like Amy, they are always here making sure he gets the best treatment. Still I want a room change and wish it weren't out of the question. I ask for earplugs but none are available. I will ask Amy to bring in a set of earplugs. While the pain continues, the light of day revives me.

Day 48: Today for OT (occupational therapy), Ali joins me for breakfast to observe and offer some pointers. I can get the food on the fork pretty well, but getting it into my mouth is a whole other story. The closer I get it to my mouth, the more my hand shakes and wanders around as if it has forgotten where it is going. Ali promises to get me weighted silverware to help reduce the shaking. She is always looking for an angle to improve my quality of life.

Going Beyond Myself

Physical therapy is a real welcome today. Dave encourages me, challenges me, and forces me to go beyond myself. I work more on my balance with a gel pad underneath my feet. I still have a lot of difficulty with this exercise today, but it feels better, more natural. I like being challenged. I don't want to be coddled. I have to fight to be whole again. My vestibular system, the source of the balance and vertigo problems I am having, has been affected by the head trauma. Dave works on my balance by having me step onto and off of different sizes and densities of foam squares. He also has me stand on them for as long as I can until I begin to get off balance. He does the same with gel pads, which are about a 1/8 inch square piece of thick "jello like" squares that squish under my feet slightly from side to side as I try to maintain my equilibrium. It appears to be a pretty easy task until I try it.

I'm disappointed; Colleen is not here today. I see her student assistant, Isabel, for speech therapy. She does her best in an exercise which calls upon me to enunciate a series of sentences and give their meaning. I have a lot of trouble; my voice wobbles like my legs. Now I feel the wash of waves in my head, totally fatigued, I can't continue. Amy finishes my journal entry for Wednesday, December 8th.

I see Dave again in the afternoon. While sitting down on a big ball for balance I move my foot on a platform. The exercise triggers the deep wavy feeling. Pressure builds up in my ears and pain shoots up to the top of my head. It feels like my pulse is hammering inside my eye sockets and brain. It is so loud, so heavy and so strong, it totally wears me out. Dave suggests I lie down until the feeling subsides. After a little rest I go up and down steps using both hands for support. Alternating between right and left hands makes it much more difficult going up the stairs, especially when holding on to a rail with my left hand. I will have to work on this.

Day 49: Another day and I can hardly wait for physical therapy. Re-learning to walk at 38 is a real challenge. I show some progress in my walking today, although I'm still shaky. My visual limitations are still being explored, as well as my balance. I'm not sure of the extent of my disabilities. The people here want to send me to a neurologist who specializes in vestibular problems. They also recommend a full cognitive assessment to determine whether there are lesions in my brain. Another very full day and I am very, very tired. My friend Mark stops by to visit. He is from my old job at the SPARK counseling program. I am practicing the heel and toe exercise as Amy brings him into the therapy area. I can't help showing off a little. Mark is quieter than usual, but it feels good to see a friendly face from the past. He promises he will come again soon. It is a wonderful surprise to see him.

Tonight I have another episode of that feeling that I am suddenly falling. It's scary when it happens. It feels as though I'm being pushed off a cliff backwards with my eyes shut. I don't know when I'm going to land, and I'm falling fast, like a rock.

Day 50: I wake up at 6 a.m. with a bad pain in my right eye that travels throughout the whole upper part of my head. I finally get some medication at around 7:30 a.m.

Mornings with Milton

It is always a pleasure to be greeted by my guardian angel Milton, who always gives me a morale boost along with a shower. Boy, do I depend upon him! It is a particular pleasure to have him back after he's off a couple of days. Even at 6:15 a.m., he's very positive and full of life. He's humming and laughing as he wheels me in a specially designed wheel chair with a cut-out seat. Milton drops me off in the bathroom for a refreshing spray and splash. I can take a shower with some privacy while safely strapped into the wheel chair.

Using a Walker

In physical therapy today I take some steps using a walker. Dave is assisting, guiding, and directing me. It is very hard for me to look anywhere other than straight ahead, fixing my gaze on a large wall clock at the end of the hall. In this way, I keep my balance. However, as soon as I lose my focus I lose my balance and fall into my walker. That's the way the crossed wires of my brain work. Dave is always there to catch me. I also lose my balance if someone is walking toward me. Dave uses flash cards to improve my ability to scan from side to side and thereby maintain my balance. He walks beside me holding a flash card straight out to my left side, shifting the angles, forcing me to turn my head. He switches the flash card to the right side when walking back in the opposite direction toward the physical therapy room. Maybe this exercise brings me closer to walking. I have to learn to do things I once did automatically without getting distracted.

Block Design

Cognitive testing also has its challenges. I create patterns using plastic red and white blocks. It's amazing how hard this is for me. A second grader could do it better. I am very frustrated.

It's upsetting to think that I administered the same types of tests to others during my counseling career. Now I find myself in the opposite chair being evaluated. I never thought I would be in this position. I am trying to focus on the results and the overall assessment, which should ultimately help me to improve.

A Gold Star

In occupational therapy Ali is impressed by how much my speech has improved since she last saw me. We do an apartment rental role-play in which certain conditions need to be determined including rental price, location, and accessibility to transportation. According to Ali I excel in this exercise. It's like getting a gold star in the first grade.

Day 51: I wake up the next morning with terrific pain in my right shoulder and neck, which penetrates from my face to the right side of my head. My headache gets worse and my stomach becomes upset which lasts throughout the morning.

Walking with a Cane

My Saturday morning physical therapist tightly holds on to my security waist belt as I attempt to walk with a cane. Although I am unsuccessful with this task, it gives me hope that I will return to normal. I broach the subject with her. I look for affirmation. She tells me about why it's not correct for her to say I will get back to normal. I understand her caution, yet at the same time I expect I will get "back to normal." I refuse to accept anything less. This is what drives me; the goal of reclaiming my life. I want someone on staff, a professional to back me up. Why should I accept anything less?

Visiting Day

Saturday, December 11th, 1999. Today is a day filled with anticipation. It's not a holiday or a holy day, but it is a very special day because family and friends are visiting today. Amy and my brother Bill are already here, when Ron, my buddy and fellow counselor from the SPARK Program at my school, walks through the door. He has a sheepish smile. He is carrying the best sweet potato pie in the country, straight from Harlem. He always brought me one for Thanksgiving. Ron's kind of low key, a terrific guy with a real wry sense of humor. He fit right into my program from the start and we always worked well together. Right behind him comes Sarah, a wonderful person and SPARK counselor with a very big heart. I worked with her on many program-wide projects practically from the time I joined SPARK. I am also happy to see Mario my guidance co-worker from school and Frank, the coordinator of our scholastic institute. They can't wait for my return. It feels like a party. It raises my morale to see them all, but at the same time I am worried it will drain my strength.

Mario and Frank are still with me when Mom and Dad arrive. After giving my parents hugs and kisses, I introduce them. I consciously, carefully, use the speech strategies that Colleen taught me. I adopt a continuous speech pattern. It is like singing in a monotone, very flat, but I am able to get out my words without stuttering … every one of them.

My dad responds by replying to me in the same exaggerated way. At first I don't know how to react or what to say to him. I ask myself, why he is speaking so strangely. He sounds like a 45 record being played at 33 rpm speed. I'm glad he is trying so hard to speak slowly, but well-meaning dad speaks so slowly, he makes me feel self-conscious. Maybe I sound even worse than I imagine? I am also wondering what Mario and Frank must be thinking. So, I say to my dad, "You don't need to speak that way, I can understand you if you speak a little faster than that. You don't have to speak as slowly as I do." I try to keep up with all the activity, although I am getting weary. So many people are in one room, so many sounds to distract and voices to follow, so much confusion. It is hard to concentrate. My head is aching and my eye sockets are sore. Nonetheless, I am glad to have the company.

The Snowflake

Later that afternoon my roommate Claude's 10 year-old daughter, Pamela, makes me a beautiful paper snowflake. "Look Christopher," she says, "I made something for you and my daddy." She is the cutest little thing. She brightens my day each time I see her. I tell her how beautiful the snowflake is and how much it means to me. I have my brother Bill tape it up by the television so I can see it each day. I also tell her about my hometown. "Back in Utica, where I grew up, the snowfalls are so heavy that the snow piles up higher than the top of a little girl's head." Pamela is amazed. She loves the idea.

Amy and my mom return to the room while Pamela is talking with me. As they approach my bed, she turns to them and says with an astonished voice, "Christopher tells me the snow at your house is taller than me." Mom and Amy support what I say with warm smiles. For me, the little girl is pure sunshine and fresh air that I desperately need. What is life without a sense of wonder?

Day 52: It is Sunday. Another day for visits. I need to see people, but it has a down side. Everything is such an effort. This morning my neck, back, and head, still hurt. For the last two days this pain dominates my life. When I turn my head from left to right, the pain gets sharper. My ears ring as loud as a church bell. I do not allow the pain to interfere with my PT exercises, no matter how bad I feel. Moving from left to right increases that wavy feeling in my head. Dave has told me this would happen, but I would slowly improve as I get used to this feeling. He hasn't steered me wrong yet, so I accept what he says and keep at it. Recovery is all about endurance.

Take a Break

Today, Andrew, my new Sunday therapist, cautions me about my exercise regimen. He doesn't want me to overdo it and get fatigued. He recommends that I take regular breaks, but I'm impatient. I just want to do everything I can and the quicker the better.

I practice in my wheelchair walking from heel to toe while doing my visual exercises. I also practice my speech exercises, "Easy Onset" and "Light Contact," in the day room. Later on, I experience a sharp numbing feeling from my head down to my jaw. I don't know what's happening. Maybe it's the medication, or maybe I'm just straining. The wavy feeling is very powerful, so as Andrew suggests, I take a break.

Imitating Normality

I see my family again today. My long time friend Larry also stops by. Amy and I met Larry and his wife Stacey back in our college days. Our mutual interest in the arts brought us together at Utica College. Our friendship flowered as the four of us participated in college choral performances and competitions, as well as community theater productions. Some time after graduating from Utica College, Larry and Stacey moved down to New Jersey to raise a family. Amy and I kept in touch and when we decided to move to the Big Apple in 1990, we took the opportunity to renew our relationship.

Rosemarie, my former assistant principal, also pays a visit. It is hard to speak with so many people around for long stretches of time. I am overwhelmed by all the stimulation. The wavy feeling returns and my eyes ache. I am physically present, but my mind drifts away. I experience so much pain I cannot focus. The conversation is totally outside of me. I am not up for this. There is a disconnect between what is actually going on around me and feeling that I am not present. This "out of body" experience is frustrating and depressing. I wish I were in another place and time. Socializing is more of a burden than a pleasure. I hang back and limit what I say. I try to imitate normality, but that is hard to do when you are suffering so much. My parents try not to be glum, but their cheerfulness is not very convincing.

I have a restful night but as dawn breaks my head, neck, and back, hurt as much as the night before.

Radical Treatment

Day 53: Dave applies moist heat packs to my right temporal area, the base of my skull and neck, which helps to alleviate the pain in my neck and shoulder that has been killing me throughout the weekend. I am still feeling the wave inside my head. One of the doctors is talking about injecting my temporal area with something that might deal with my headaches. Sounds kind of radical; I'm not sure about this treatment. I think I'm going to have to pass on this one. It sounds risky. According to Dave, the doctor seems to think that it might be that my sympathetic nervous system is getting triggered by the pain eliciting a flight or fight response that may cause a surge to my vestibular system, which interferes with my balance.

I practice making turns with my walker as Dave holds on to my support belt. It feels great, although it's a little challenging to make turns on my own. My brain wants me to turn, but my body isn't quite ready to execute it. When people pass or distractions occur in the hallway, I lose my balance and begin to shake. Dave helps me calm down and refocus my attention to help me regain my equilibrium. I have a real sense of accomplishment, overall a very good day.

The Humiliation

That night I can't keep my eyes open and doze over my dinner. Amy is understanding and kisses me on my cheek as I conk out. I sleep soundly until about three in the morning. I wake up with a strong urge to urinate. Kneeling in bed to relieve myself is extremely difficult. I have a hard time balancing myself and clearly seeing what I am doing. In addition, my head is pounding so badly- like it could explode. I also have that wavy feeling. I am a complete mess and end up missing the plastic urinal. Everything is drenched. I am so upset and embarrassed! I must call for help.

I ring for the nurse who comes in quickly. As I am trying to explain what happened, nothing comes out but an indecipherable stutter. As I hear my garbled words, I stop trying to speak and slow down so the nurse can understand what the problem is. As upset as I am, I am encouraged to see that when I stop and slow down I speak fairly clearly. That's progress.

I experience firsthand what Colleen has been emphasizing. It's clear what happens if I'm not relaxed and focused when I speak. Eventually, I hope this approach will become second nature again. I'm confident it will! At least I am aware of it now. Awareness is a most powerful tool and it will help me improve day by day.

I have an eye exam today. I hate seeing spots; they distract me. The doctor says everything is physically fine. He believes the problem is in the brain. The spots I see when I look at a wall are not from the eye itself, but are caused by the signal that is transmitted to the brain. I don't ask any questions at this time. I am too damn tired.

Day 54: I tell Dave about the humiliating experience I had last night that started with the pounding head pain. He suggests that I sleep at a 30 degree angle with only one pillow underneath my head. The muscle ache in my neck and down my back is improving with Dave's heat treatments. I speak to Dave about reducing the pain medication. He tells me to discuss it with my doctor. The physical therapists always, or most always, defer to the doctors. I know the medication is helpful, but I just don't want to take it unless it is absolutely necessary. I hate the idea of being dependent on drugs, even under these circumstances.

Making Progress

I am pleased with my progress. At least today it feels as if I am making progress. I am able to increase the speed of my speech utilizing some other new speech techniques.

I walk with a cane again today. While I require a lot of assistance, the feeling of walking with a cane is still wonderful. Granted I'm not totally walking on my own yet, but I know that I am heading in the right direction. I think the drills of walking from heel to toe in my wheelchair have been paying off. The Mount Sinai program is very intensive, almost all the therapy sessions are an hour and sometimes they go over. After dinner and between sessions I am continuously doing the exercises I learn in therapy. I will not rest until I am whole again.

Yet, if someone or something startles me, I just lose it. My body starts to shake as if I am scared out of my wits. It knocks me off my balance and puts my brain into a tailspin. For the moment, my confidence is shattered. Inside of me I know this will not last. It cannot last!

Like a Child on Christmas Morning

Day 55: Wednesday, December 15th, Dave and Ali combine their sessions so we can spend time preparing for my first outing since being admitted to the hospital. I feel like a child on Christmas morning; there is an overriding sense of anticipation. I hope all the preparation and practice walking in the physical therapy gym, through the hallways of the hospital wing, and then venturing out into the main hospitals passageways during the height of a busy day, pay off. I really don't have any doubts.

It is a wonderful early pre-Christmas surprise. My cheeks feel weird, not quite sore but something like that, as I experience the cold air for the first time in a long while. I could not figure out why, until Dave and Ali alerted me to the huge smile on my face. I am so thrilled to be outside; I can't get that wide grin off my face.

The familiar streets have become an unfamiliar experience. The world is moving so fast around me; people hustling and bustling back and forth like a swift human tide, while the frigid crisp air fills my nostrils and lungs. I am an upstate person with both feet on the ground, but this is surreal. I know I am there in the moment, but it feels like I am in a dream world moving at a much slower pace than everyone else around me. I don't mind it at all since I am out of the hospital prison, in the place that I could only view longingly through my hospital window. I have some moments when I have trouble balancing and my legs do tremble at times, but Dave and Ali applaud the result of their therapy. I thank them over and over again. At last…outside in the refreshing New York air.

Chapter Five

The Power of Family and Friends

Living in the Moment

Day 56: It's Thursday, December 16th, a date of no particular consequence. No one great was born on this day nor is any great event recalled. No holidays are celebrated on this day. I go through the usual therapy without anything special happening. I see the same faces in the corridors on my floor and in the day room. It is a typical institutional day. The special significance of December 16th comes a little later.

A Lonely Night

That evening, strapped into my wheelchair looking out the window, I watch daylight gradually become evening. Daylight disappears so early this time of the year, it brings me down. It's just so depressing. To add insult to injury, my dinner, one of the highpoints of my institutional day, is really terrible. I am famished and since I haven't eaten much dinner I open my bedside drawer in search of goodies. By the time I determine there is not a stray cookie, candy or stick of gum at hand the sun is down. I am also down emotionally, and my physical appearance reflects my mood. My head is numb and my ears are ringing; my eye sockets are pounding. I feel so out of it. And to top it all off, I don't have any visitors tonight. Amy is taking a very necessary break. She is totally worn out; it's a trek to come visit me after work and travel late at night back to Jersey. She needs the rest. I try to resign myself to a very long lonely dark night.

As I stare out the window I beg God to either make me better or let me just die. I don't want to live like this. It's not fair to Amy or to me. I refuse to remain like this. If that is the way it is going to be I can't let Amy and me continue like this. It's really not fair to her. She deserves more. She can be so much happier with someone whole. Not reduced to taking care of an invalid.

I speak to God: "How can you allow this to happen? What did I do to deserve this?"

Special Delivery from the Divine

I am just about to break down and cry when suddenly, from behind me, I hear my name being called. In the window in front of me, and in the reflection, I see my brother Billy standing there … a special delivery from the divine. I feel an immediate sense of relief. I had no idea he would appear tonight. Billy smiles mischievously like he did as a kid. I thank God for sending me an angel this evening. Bill doesn't have a clue what it means to see him enter my room at that moment. Since he is aware I can leave the hospital, he invites me to dinner at one of the places around the hospital. Even though I am beyond miserable, close to bottom, I know this is the best prescription for me.

Once outside, Billy spots a vendor and buys me a knit cap and a scarf. I wasn't prepared for winter when I entered the hospital. Still, as frigid as it is, I am happy to be out of the hospital. I feel liberated and don't give a damn about the cold. We go to an old-fashioned Greek diner with swiveling counter stools and big booths and everything but the kitchen sink on the menu. What a treat. I order a cheeseburger and a coke with a slice of lemon. I eat and drink with real gusto. The cheeseburger is absolutely delicious. A burger has never tasted so good. I order some fries and consume them with plenty of ketchup. I am thrilled to return to a little piece of normality, back with the living. Of course, after the meal, I have to go to the bathroom, something I can no longer take for granted. This proves to be a bit of an effort, since Bill has to help me down a tricky narrow stairway. We take our time, moving slowly. Once we are there, he stands outside the door to make sure no one disturbs me.

Christmas Lights on Park Avenue

I don't want to go right back to Mount Sinai. I walk with Billy holding me like a fragile package, moving about a block or so to Park Avenue. There, in front of me, stand a small forest of majestic evergreens covered with white Christmas lights. It is so moving, practically a spiritual experience. My eyes tear up as I admire their beauty.

I have walked along Park Avenue on different cross streets at different times. I don't recall ever noticing just how beautiful the trees look in their Christmas finery. How many other experiences have I let pass me by without appreciating them, so involved in the hustle-bustle, the hurry up and wait of daily life, unwilling to look in any direction other than straight ahead. I suddenly feel a warm sense of inner peace. It is a defining moment for me. It fuels my soul and gives me strength. I believe that this is another sign, a gift for me. As the twinkling lights on those evergreens brightened my dark soul I ask God to continue to watch over me and to continue to give me the strength to overcome.

I think about this experience as I prepare for bed. Maybe one of the positive things about this accident was to force me to take the time for observing and reflecting on those little things that bring doses of happiness, peace, and pleasure. Maybe the purpose - and I do believe life has a purpose - of my accident is to create an awareness of the world, which exists around and inside of me. In the future, I must take the time to absorb all the slices of life that come my way. Counselors like me encourage clients "to take one day at a time." Now I believe that it's equally important for me to take one moment at a time. Maybe I never adequately took advantage of what life offers, but now I realize the importance of those basic simple things: the ability to walk about freely, think clearly, and speak smoothly, when you have something to say and someone you love to say it to.

This evening raises my flagging spirits. I feel as though my eyes are open and my heart yearns to begin the healing process. I will forever be thankful to Billy for lifting me out of the darkness.

Going Shopping

Day 57: Ali and Dave have another surprise for me today. Amy comes to the hospital in the afternoon, and the three of them bring me to a nearby grocery store. Ali asks me to choose three items. I chose aluminum foil, sponges, and freezer bags. Ali has me write them down. She asks me to put the list away. Can I remember the three items? Ali prods me to try. I can remember one of the items, but only remember the second after a number of hints. The third is entirely forgotten. This is a good lesson for me. I must be sure to write everything down. It is kind of nerve racking in the store since it is quite busy; there is a lot of movement in the aisles. I maneuver on my cane with a little help from Dave and Ali. My head hurts scanning from row to row and from aisle to aisle trying to find the items.

Eventually I find them all, but I have trouble paying for the items. When I reach the register I have to roughly figure out the tax and pay for the items. I also have difficulty locating the exact amount of money for the purchase from Ali's change purse. I feel very anxious and nervous, as though I am holding up the line for the cashier. It takes time, but I finally locate the right amount of coins and bills. This is an important step in bringing my life back to normal. I make a real effort to relax. It's great to be outside again and I look forward to my next adventure.

Shopping

As part of therapy, Dave and Ali take Chris shopping at a nearby grocery store. I take the day off and tag along to be with Chris and get a look at how his therapy is progressing. Ali explains the purpose of this exercise and what it involves for Chris. He has to cross the street, maneuver between pedestrians, enter the store, locate and purchase some items. She identifies the three items he has to buy and the amount of money he has to use.

Chris looking determined, with cane in hand, walks out of the hospital with us around him. He seems very confident. The first thing that shocks me is seeing him cross the street without noticing the traffic lights. Ali grabs him and reminds him about the lights. I worry, how is he going to handle being on his own in the city when he can't even cross the street?

Once in the store, Ali again reminds him of the three items and his budget. Appearing even more determined, Chris starts searching for the first item. Next, he has to compare prices to save money. What is interesting to me is that he picks up the brand of sponges we usually buy. Ali corrects him and suggests buying the cheapest ones because of his budget. Chris is very confused, having to choose between what we always buy and a lesser quality brand, but goes on to the second item. Half way down the isle with sponge in hand he turns to Ali and asks what the second item is. His memory fails him. On the train ride back to work I realize that Chris will never be the same. Maybe this is as good as it will get, and I better get used to it and pay close attention to how his therapists help Chris cope with his loss of memory.

First Date

Amy comes back to see me after work. I am struck by her beauty. I'm taking my girl out - at least in spirit. She wheels me to the hospital cafeteria. This is our "first date" since the accident. It's surprising how different the food tastes. It actually has some flavor in the cafeteria as compared to when it is served in my room. Maybe it is just the change of scene that makes the food taste so good. Maybe it is the company. Amy and I have a wonderful fun time on our dinner date. We could have been eating filet mignon at the 21 Club. We toast one another with New York water and then Amy returns me to the Acute Care wing.

Despite the warmth and intimacy of a shared meal, I am beat and ready for bed. Amy has to go all the way back to Jersey before it gets too late. I hate to see her go. But I know she has a long trip by public transportation home. I can't wait for tomorrow to see her again. I don't know what I would ever do without her.

Hospital Dinner Date

After work I hop on the train to join Chris for dinner. With Chris in his wheelchair we make our way through the long corridors to the cafeteria for a dinner date. I make sure he has his earplugs and hunt for a "quiet table for two."

We don't talk much while we are eating. It's a little awkward and almost feels like a first date. We are both shy and don't know what to talk about. We talk more when we get back to Chris's hospital room. We both enjoy this night out; although I am afraid he may be over stimulated.

Day Pass

I have trouble sleeping tonight. I'm all wound up by the prospect of my family's Saturday visit.

Day 58: In the morning, I put on my headset to listen to a relaxing CD and do the Progressive Muscle Relaxation exercises (PMR) that my therapists encourage me to do to help me reduce my level of head pain and get my batteries charged. I focus on trying to do some deep breathing exercises. I take deep breaths very slowly and occasionally hold my breath and exhale very slowly. While exhaling I say the words "relax." I go through this process several times, concentrating only on a breath at a time until I feel my heart rate slow down. This is just the first step. The second step is to visualize a tranquil scene that transports me to a more peaceful place. I imagine lying down taking some rays on a very long fine powdered beach. It is very secluded. I discovered this paradise when I visited our family friend, Gabe, in Barbados. I visualize the blue sky, the warmth of the sun, the fresh cool breeze, the sound of seagulls passing over me, and the sandy beach beneath me. I smell the fresh ocean air.

Today and Sunday I'll be on a day pass. This means I can go out during the day with escorts, as long as I'm back by evening. I'm going out with Amy, my friend Jeff and his wife-to-be Laura. Also my brother Billy wouldn't miss going out with me again. And it is a real treat to have the company of my sister Laurie, who still lives in Utica. She is my one and only little sister with a heart the size of the island of Manhattan. We look so similar that we could pass for twins, even though I am eleven years her senior. Since I am unable to carry any medication with me, the nurses give me as much as they can to hold me over. Between the medication and the adrenaline rush of being out with friends and family, it carries me through most of the day. When the pain starts to get the better of me I do the deep breathing and visualization exercises. This helps me manage the pain a bit more effectively without additional medication.

We start our Saturday excursion at the Jackson Hole restaurant. All I can say is the burger is even better than the one I had the other night with Billy. The restaurant is very noisy and crowded. It makes it difficult for me to really think clearly, focus, and concentrate. Despite my overall sense of confusion and inadequacy, I am so excited to be out that I don't let it bother me.

After lunch we all walk along Central Park by the Guggenheim Museum. The sun shines brightly. Everyone else complains about the cold, but I am bundled up warm and toasty. I am just so happy to the point of exhilaration to be with my family and friends and away from the confinement of the hospital, that both body and soul are warm. I don't feel the chill at all. And since I am surrounded by a good size group of people it is easy to navigate with my cane. Any time we encounter someone the whole gang forms a protective circle shielding me from the oncoming pedestrian traffic. I feel like the president with his cordon of secret service. They ask me what I would like to do, and I choose the Christmas tree at Rockefeller Center as our next destination.

The streets are very busy, but I am secure with my bodyguards leading the way. Seeing the huge tree with its multicolored lights lifts my spirits. It finally feels like Christmas. I say a prayer and ask God to continue to give me strength to see this through. I am more joyous than solemn, exhilarated.

Day Pass

The weather is bitter cold but Chris's brother Bill, his sister Laurie, and our friends and I have a day pass to take Chris out of the hospital. He is ecstatic like a little kid, grinning from ear to ear, and I guess he is freezing but he does not complain. I am worried because I'm not even sure he realizes that it is so terribly cold. He is so happy to get out and smell fresh air. After eating lunch we walk in Central Park. Chris does not want to sit down. He only wants to walk, walk, and walk until we make him take a breather on a bench. I wonder if he realizes that he may be overdoing it.

An Assessment

Day 60: Good news on Monday morning, the doctor says that I will be able to go home on Tuesday, December 21st . I'm

62

very excited and can't wait. It appears that the prognosis for my recovery is positive. Today Dave and a crew of therapists, along with the head administrator, assess my balancing skills. They have me march in place. At first I don't do very well, but I get a little better with practice. They want to see if I can steady myself and regain my equilibrium on my own. They nudge me as I might get nudged on a crowded New York sidewalk. At first, I don't know what to do to keep myself from falling. I begin to keel over and Dave grips and holds me. Dave shows me how to bring my foot forward, to the side, or backwards to break the fall. At first, I have a lot of difficulty doing this. Still I comprehend what I have to do, even if I can't always execute it. My legs are shaking as I attempt these advanced balancing techniques. Finally, Dave has me walk backwards and forwards without my cane. I do well walking forward, but backwards is a lot tougher. Walking with my eyes closed is next to impossible without my legs shaking. When I can't see what I'm doing, it's very difficult to do anything. I am very concerned about how poorly I do on balancing and ask Dave if this will prevent my return home. He is also concerned, but feels that as long as Amy or someone is with me when I walk it should be okay.

My Education

Although I believe Chris receives excellent care in the Mount Sinai head trauma unit, what bothers me the most is that no one sits down to educate me about his head trauma and what I can expect when I bring Chris home. I never really know what is going on. I only see the social worker when it is time for Chris to be referred to NYU Rusk Head Trauma Outpatient Rehabilitation Unit. I naively think that when Chris is released from Mount Sinai he will be back to his normal self, and back to work as if this were a broken leg that has to heal. I learn the hard way. This is not going to happen.

The whole time I feel so alone and empty. Maybe I should go on the web to educate myself about brain injury, but I don't have a minute to spare. I am barely surviving myself, juggling work, my visits to the hospital, and trying to keep myself together.

The Familiar is Miraculous

Day 61: It's so great to see Ali and Dave before I leave. I owe them both so much. They take me out of the hospital in a wheel chair and advise me to use one when it is needed, especially if I am home alone. I know they are well meaning, but I don't see myself using the chair unless it is absolutely necessary. I feel that using it will be a step backward instead of forward. I worked so hard to get out of the wheel chair, the last thing I want to do is sit back down in it.

The Motivator

The therapists from Mount Sinai insist that for Chris's safety, both at home and when he leaves the house, a wheelchair be readily available. However, it is relegated to a corner of our dining room. He not only refuses to use it in the house, but he does not let me carry it down the stairs to pack in the trunk when we go out. Every time he struggles to walk from the living room to the bathroom he sees the wheelchair in the dining room. The wheelchair becomes a motivator for Chris to do whatever he has to do to not end up using it. It is a constant reminder of where he was, and he wants no part of it.

Going Home

The doctors take me off the Ritalin and some other drugs. Gabe and Billy pick me up from the hospital. They each give me a big bear hug before I get into the car. Since I am having trouble with my sinuses and dryness in my nose my homecoming must be delayed. They bring me first to Dr. Pincus, my ear, nose and throat doctor. He is very happy to see that I am on the road to recovery. He gives me some medicine for my nose and puts me on antibiotics for an infection.

The Familiar is New

The facial numbness is still there, the ears still ring, my eye sockets ache - just business as usual. It is still wonderful to be home! The familiar seems new and miraculous. I am happy and exhausted at the same time. My eyes tear right up. I am so glad to be home before Christmas. I did not think this could happen. This is the best Christmas present ever. Gabe makes a great meal for Amy and me that evening. It is so great to be with the people I love in my own little apartment. Amy, Gabe and I continue visiting until I become so tired that I have to go to bed. Sleeping in my own bed is the best feeling. Once my head hits the pillow, I know I am back home.

Day 62: It's my first morning back home. Gabe and I prepare breakfast. I try to toast my own bagel while I am talking with him. I forget to defrost it first. I guess I am trying to do too many things at once. I end up turning on the toaster without the bagel in it, and forget that the bagel is in the microwave. Once the toaster goes off I realize there is no bagel in there and I begin to look high and low for it. Eureka! I locate it in the microwave. I feel a little foolish and upset at myself. With Gabe's encouragement I try to laugh it off. I take my time and stop talking while I prepare the bagel. This helps me get the job done more successfully. I relax and chalk it up to experience. It will get better.

I do my PMR relaxation exercises later in the morning and throughout the day, which is helpful. I have the same symptoms today as in the past, but being home makes a difference. I try to take things as they come and enjoy whatever I can.

I speak on the telephone to my folks and my sister, who are together in Utica. My great aunts also get into the act. They are urging me to come home for the holidays. I certainly cannot say no to my two great Aunts; Aunt Evie and Aunt Edie are the last of my grandmother's siblings still alive. Since grams died July 30th of this year they are our primary link to this side of our Italian family-the Laurey family.

I am not great over the phone; the effort only aggravates my headaches. It's tougher for me to speak on the phone than in person. When I have trouble saying my words clearly I slow down and focus on the techniques I learned in speech therapy. As the conversation continues on my brain gets tired and my speech becomes more labored. Strange, it is almost as if my brain has only so much gas in its tank, and it just runs out when the tank is empty.

It's no surprise that the severe headaches continue; they have become a way of life. According to the doctors at Mount Sinai, the pain may last for several months or more. I just have to learn to live with them. My capacity to handle the pain varies from day to day. To a great extent, I must be resigned. When it gets excessive I take medication and do the PMR and visualization exercises. In my case, it takes some of the edge off the extreme pain I am experiencing in my head. This technique is similar to one I used on many occasions with my own clients when I worked in the Chemical Dependence Clinic in Utica. My therapist at Mount Sinai told me it used to be called DMR (Deep Muscle Relaxation). I guess a rose by any other name is still a rose.

The Day before Christmas

Day 64: Christmas Eve, I can't help it, but the spirit isn't there. No sense of wonder or anticipation. I have a responsibility, a duty to make the trip home for Christmas. My parents and great aunts are looking forward to seeing me. I especially don't want to let them down.

As I open my eyes I am assaulted by tremendous headaches. Amy tenderly approaches me to see how I am doing and proceeds to help me sit up and place my two feet in the direction of the floor as they hang off the end of the bed. Thankfully, I have made enough progress in therapy that my wife no longer has to put both arms around my waist and guide me off the bed to a standing position. I walk with my cane in hand gripping it tightly as I slowly and deliberately cross the hallway to the bathroom. I have made enough progress since rehab that I can finally go to the bathroom without my wife's help.

Taking a shower, however, is a whole other story. Taking a shower these days requires Amy to be my guide, my rock that I totally rely upon in order to accomplish this very necessary task. Before I enter the bathroom Amy sets up the plastic shower bench inside the tub. I make my way into the bathroom when she is ready for me. Amy helps me undress and when I am ready, guides one leg at a time into the tub and onto the shower chair. Since I have that wavy dizzy sensation in my head, to be safe and secure I must sit in a special chair to take my shower. The only problem is that the chair doesn't have a high enough back for me, so Amy has to come into the tub to support my body by wrapping her arms around my chest while I attempt to wash. I can't tolerate being under the running water since it further aggravates my balance. She sets the chair back allowing me to place the washcloth underneath the water as it flows down in front of me. While I am attempting to wash myself Amy is continually encouraging me and also prompting me to wash and rinse, since I am easily distracted and forget where I have soaped up and not yet rinsed. I fatigue so quickly that I must take breaks during my shower. After I finish washing up, Amy shuts off the water, grabs my towel and drapes it over my shoulders to keep me warm. After taking another breather, she checks with me to see if I am ready to get out of the tub. I tell her I am and she carefully steps out of the tub while continuing to support my back. On my signal she secures her footing and lifts me by the waist while I push myself up to stand. I am very unsteady, but know that she's got me so I won't fall. One leg at a time is raised out of the tub as Amy coaches me each step of the way. I am so exhausted by this point that I sit on the toilet seat while Amy dries me off. I sit for a long time and try to catch my breath.

I am usually able to dress and undress myself since getting out of Mount Sinai, but after a shower I struggle much more and need Amy's help. While she dresses me I have these visions of the "end stage" of my life being totally dependent on Amy as my caregiver. This is part of my living hell, my loss of all independence.

When either Amy dresses me or I dress myself, we have to be sure to pull my shirt over my head quickly so as not to block my vision for too long, otherwise my vestibular system goes crazy and I become violently dizzy and can't balance myself, even while sitting on the bed.

My brothers Paul and Bill pick Amy and me up to drive to Utica. Bill and Paul try to be upbeat, but cannot disguise their worry and concern. I don't have much to say, conserving my strength for the Christmas festivities.

The trip takes longer than usual. We stop frequently so I can pull myself together. Riding along in the car is an ordeal; my head hurts, my ears ring, and my eyes tear, in between I go into free fall. Oncoming traffic is a nightmare, although it is fairly light. It appears to me that any of these vehicles could come crashing into us at any moment. Frequent stops help me to cope. I move to the back seat, hoping it will help. It doesn't. Only the knowledge that I will soon see the people I love provides any relief.

Home at last. We are all grateful to be together this Christmas. It is remarkable to me that just a few days ago I was in the hospital. Despite the strain, I'm really happy to be here. When I entered the hospital my initial goal was to be able to come home for Christmas. Although I have a lot of work to do to really improve I have at least met this goal. I am hopeful that upon my return to New Jersey I will begin an outpatient brain injury rehabilitation program that will help me put my life back together again as it was before. All I am asking for is plain unvarnished normality. In the meantime, I'm going to enjoy this Christmas, which is the most special Christmas in my life. I am here, I am alive, I am with those whom I love, and who love me.

Christmas at home means so much to me. Coming home for Christmas is always filled with so much excitement. Wonderful homemade Italian dishes that my Great-aunt Evie and Mom put together are an important part of our family tradition. By the time everyone arrives from here, there, and everywhere, we have a pretty good size crowd filling the house. Christmas typically doesn't feel like Christmas until the young kids arrive. My brothers and I liked to tease them when they were younger and really get them going, but now all but the youngest have grown up enough and are wise to their uncle's teasing ways. My sister Laurie always comes to their rescue as do their proud grand parents.

Christmas time is always filled with great joy and laughter, story telling is a hallowed tradition and there is always an incredible amount of terrific food and holiday drinks; relatives and family friends are always popping in. It's a real homecoming, a chance to see all the people who I grew up with and their expanding families.

A Family Holiday

Day 65: A rough start for this Christmas Day. The trip to Utica has taken its toll. The headaches and all the agonizing feelings are very bad from the time I wake up. I do the PMR breathing and visualization exercises throughout the day. A little mind over matter helps manage the pain. My ears ring throughout the day. My speech comes along slowly. I find it more of a struggle to speak without "dysfluencies" as I become more tired, or when my head pain is at its peak. Despite how badly I feel it is still Christmas; a time of reverence, celebration, and reflection. It is a family holiday and I feel blessed to be with my family. I do not feel well enough to leave my parents' house for church or participate in the usual round of holiday visits.

My head pounds in the front part of my brain above my eyebrows. The medication helps, but I hope it will decrease soon without any further medicinal intervention. I would like to kick this without medication. When my head aches in any way (the numbness, wavy feeling, vice grip feeling on the side of my head), I prefer to stop what I'm doing and rely on PMR, which seems to help take the edge off. I think my brain just gets tired of thinking and concentrating and I have to rest it.

Throughout the weekend in Utica I notice I have trouble with my memory. Over and over, I do not recall Amy telling me where she will be and as a consequence I am consumed by worry. I continually forget what I am in the process of doing. I repeat myself constantly and tell the same stories to the same people. The person I have become is very embarrassing, but I try not to get too down on myself.

Christmas

I do not have any vacation time left at work but the president of my company gives me the week off between Christmas and New Years to be with Chris. I will use some of my time at home to complete a couple of end-of-year work projects. While I take seriously my obligations to my company, all I know is that I have to get home to Utica for Christmas. I need to go back in time to experience Christmases past before Chris was hurt. I have to escape, I need Christmas and family and security.

Maybe I am being selfish. I am not thinking how this trip will affect Chris and quite frankly do not care. I need family and a little normalcy, and Chris is just going to have to tag along.

Chris later admits he is going home for Christmas for me. He missed my birthday and the least he could do is to give me a little Christmas.

We go home with his brothers. The usual three and a half hour ride turns into six long hours. We had no idea that the windshield wipers would make Chris dizzy, or the other cars rushing by would startle him so much that he shakes. Feeling the car skid on ice makes Chris frantic. He screams out as if we are going to crash. By the time we get home I curse myself over and over again for putting him through such torture.

We pretty much carry him into Mom and Dad's house and into bed where he sleeps until the next afternoon, Christmas Day. Every once and a while he joins us in the family room for festivities, but he needs to take breaks and recuperate with several naps from the holiday hustle, bustle and noise. As I help get Chris ready for bed we say good night. He hugs me and tells me he thanks God for another Christmas we are able to share together.

This is truly my Christmas, not opening presents under the tree, but holding each other, holding him, hanging on to the part of him I have back. I know at this moment our lives will never be the same again, but this night makes me see things in a whole new light. I am in a way reborn and vow to make sure he is never going to be put in an uncomfortable environment again that hurts and makes it difficult for him. I need to protect him. I am given a gift that night, the realization that he could have been taken away from me. My Christmas gift is Chris.

The Return

Day 67: Back home in Jersey there is a letdown after the holiday. I come home to the same old excruciating pains. The world of work seems so far away, my surroundings seem so empty. I continue to do what I've done for the past three weeks – PMR and visualization. I do an inventory of areas that have improved and those that require the most work. I walk better with assistance of my cane. I only lose my balance a few times a day when walking in the apartment. I still need to work on advanced balancing skills and practice other things I learned in therapy. I can hardly wait to begin my out patient treatment at Rusk.

My peripheral vision continues to cause some problems. I bump into furniture and trip over things on the floor. I feel like a klutz. There are still flecks of black in my visual field, which are very distracting. I am super sensitive to loud noises. They literally can knock me off my feet, but thankfully on most occasions the noise only causes my body to shake while I momentarily lose my balance. The sound of a loud TV or music is devastating. It can lead to headaches, the wavy feeling, and ringing in the ears. I am learning to adapt to these occurrences. The PMR is always at readiness.

My New Millennium

Day 71: Amy and I ring in the New Year, though not too loudly. Our friends, Jeff and Laura, come over from Brooklyn to celebrate the New Year/New Millennium with us. It's a very sedate New Year's for me. I don't dare have a drink. Just a nice quiet evening. They bring most everything for the celebration since they know Amy and I have our hands full dealing with me. Again and again I take breaks and go into the bedroom and quietly do my relaxation and visualization exercises. I am unable to stay up and watch the Times Square ball make the descent.

Day 72: It's New Year's Day and my neck at the base of my skull is hurting like it did in the hospital. I also notice that when I speak I'm continuing to have trouble with consonant words. I am trying to slow down and not beat myself up emotionally about it, but I can't be complacent for a second. I become more conscious about my speech techniques when this happens.

In bed I pray that Rusk will enable me to conquer my condition. Whatever it takes to ease the pain and reconstitute myself, I'm ready. I can't wait to begin. It beckons like the New Millennium, my hope is intact and despite everything, I look forward to the future.

Chapter Six

Jennifer, Our Godsend

A Very Special Young Lady

Day 74: Amy picks up our niece, Jennifer, at Penn Station. She has come to stay for a few weeks. She's generously using her college break to help us out. I know she could be working over her school break making money for college, but Jennifer wants to help us. I am very happy to have her with us to handle a part of Amy's burden. I do not want Amy's work to suffer because of me. She is proud of her success in business and committed to her work. It's a blessing to have Jennifer here with us, to escort me to and from Rusk.

Life with Jennifer

Day 75: I have trouble preparing breakfast and talking to Jennifer at the same time. I forget what I am doing and the proper order for doing it. I take a teacup out of the cabinet and forget that I am getting hot water for the tea. This upsets me and I have to reassure myself. I have to believe that eventually multi-tasking will become easier.

Jennifer and I go for a walk. A few times I lose my balance, even using the cane. Jennifer is holding on to me the entire time, so I am fine. She's a sweet girl and very patient, a delight to be around. When we come back from the walk I do visualization exercises while Jennifer prepares lunch. I have that wavy feeling and my head is hammering. After lunch I return to bed to do deep breathing, visualization, and PMR exercises. I don't feel well the whole afternoon. The wavy feeling and head pain continue throughout the day and evening. It feels like my head is squeezed between a vice and a screwdriver is jabbing in my eye sockets. I'm a mess.

Day 76: Jennifer and I go for a walk again. I do really well walking with my cane until we come to a slight incline in the sidewalk. Contrary to what I expect, this is a real problem for me. Although Jennifer holds me tightly all the way down, as I approach the halfway mark, my legs begin shaking and each step I take becomes more and more difficult. In the process, my speech also breaks down. I cannot find the right words to express myself. My brain is unable to tell the rest of me what to do.

It's so depressing. I think I am doing so well, whether it is my walking or talking, and then I try to do something only slightly more challenging and everything falls apart.

Renewal at Rusk

Day 81: Jennifer, Amy and I wake up early, 6:30 a.m. Monday morning January 10th to get to NYU-Rusk Center for the crucial evaluations to determine my treatment needs. We share a sense of excitement and high expectations as we cross through the busy lobby and navigate the crowded corridors of the rehabilitation center. I spend the early part of the day going from one evaluation to another - physical, occupational, and cognitive. Although I'm very happy to return to therapy, I feel frustrated and depressed as I struggle to perform during the evaluations. I try to stay focused on my therapy goals and never give up, but it's upsetting to recognize the challenges that exist. Granted, I know I need more therapy, but it's depressing and frustrating when I see how much work I have to do. I guess I don't have a clue just how much it takes to improve. In a testing situation my challenges are much more apparent to me. I feel that I have only taken some small steps on my rehab journey.

In the afternoon I have a speech therapy session. My new speech therapist is friendly and relaxed and tries to put me at ease. Emile recommends additional speech training. She says I'm a great candidate for a high level functioning group that focuses on language skills building. This makes me feel a little better about my situation. Everyone in this brain injury group is a high functioning professional and highly motivated to recover their speaking abilities. It sounds like it would be a helpful experience. Emile says she will let me know when this group will start again.

This very full day raises my spirits, but when I return home I am exhausted. My head hurts terribly. The medication I am taking all day doesn't do anything. My brain is overloaded by the mental concentration and the physical and cognitive activity. This affects the quality of my speech, my thinking, and walking.

Our Godsend

Jennifer is a godsend. What would I do without her? How could I manage to get Chris into the city each day for his outpatient therapy sessions, go to work, and then bring him back home? I take off a week from work to be with Chris and Jennifer as he starts his outpatient therapy. Together, Jennifer and I work out a plan to get Chris to and from the hospital for his rehab therapy.

Staying Positive and Focused

Day 83: Jennifer and I go to Rusk ourselves today. I am eager for my therapy sessions. My impressions of my new therapy team are very positive. The day begins with speech therapy. Emile seems as happy working with me as I am working with her. It is important for me to have a therapist I can relate to.

Next, I have a physical therapy session. My physical therapist is Barb. She greets me with a wide smile. We have an instant rapport. Today she works with me on side-to-side walking, which is a struggle. Although the time between my discharge from Mount Sinai and my admission to Rusk is only about two weeks, it is long enough for me to feel that the recovery process is set back. Barb tells me not to be too concerned, as I will quickly make up for lost time. Beside my half hour private session with her, I take part in another half hour group session in a gym-like setting filled with exercise and weight machines. Barb is a very patient teacher as she puts me through my paces performing leg squats at a 45 degree angle on a sliding board, pedaling a stationary bicycle with my feet bandaged to the pedals, and raising and lowering my legs on two types of padded apparatus. The gym setting is very good for my morale. Group and private P.T. will be every Monday and Thursday.

Though I get a healthy workout, I still feel strong when I meet with my occupational therapist Robin. My therapy session consists of a brief discussion of my goals and a paper and pencil test of simple calculations. I am surprised by my inability to do the calculations. Robin points out the errors, which I correct on the spot. I am going to have to relearn the basics.

I meet again with Gina, a Rusk cognitive psychologist. She will not be my permanent therapist, but continues the evaluation process. She informs me that I will start my cognitive therapy sessions in a couple weeks when treatment schedules are firmed up and I get the proper insurance clearances. I really look forward to getting my thinking back on track. I can see from the testing she is doing, improvement will take time. I will not let this overwhelm me. I pledge to stay positive and focused.

Day 84: In physical therapy today Justin is pinch-hitting for Barb. I do better on my exercises that involve kneeling and sliding on a mat. I work on scanning from left to right and up and down, while maintaining my equilibrium. Scanning to the left and looking up are the most difficult for me. I really miss Barb and that added measure of moral support.

My speech therapist Emile looks over Colleen's assignments from Mount Sinai and puts me through the paces of some new exercises to help with my speaking techniques. She also assigns homework; a different version of continuous phonation, which has me take a breath before saying each word.

Afterwards, Jennifer and I eat lunch in the hospital cafeteria. It is too busy and noisy for my still sensitive system. My head starts aching badly. I also experience quite an intense wavy feeling, which lasts through the trip home and continues for the rest of the day. My fatigue is overwhelming. I go to sleep early tonight.

Day 85: Jennifer is getting into the swing of the city as a new week begins. Despite the sub-freezing temperatures and not a cab in sight, Jennifer and I persevere making the best of the journey by foot to my ENT and Neurologist appointments.

Jennifer

Jennifer is so mature for her age. She quickly takes the lead and organizes a schedule for Chris to follow easily each day. She works up a large but simple chart that Chris can understand. She helps him get back and forth to different therapies inside Rusk. Jennifer uses her initiative to keep Chris punctual for his various doctor appointments within and outside of Rusk. This is no easy task given the cold winter weather, the snow and the iced over sidewalks. Chris is still having difficulty walking and is fearful of slipping and hitting his head. When Chris is off from Rusk she works with him on his home exercises, makes his lunch, and even has dinner ready when I get home from work.

Movies at the Mall

Day 86: I wake up with a real bad headache, the worst one I have had for quite a while. I can't get back to sleep. In the early morning, about 6:00 a.m., I go to the bathroom. Afterward,

I still cannot get back to sleep. I feel better after my shower. The headaches are tolerable with the help of the medication. The morning sky is clear and the sun is shining. I smell bacon frying and bread toasting. I hear Amy singing with the radio. All is right with the world.

The weekend lies ahead of me and I look forward to it. The weather has definitely improved. Amy, Jennifer and I go to the Newport Mall, which has an outside walkway. The fresh air is exhilarating. I can't help breathing it in and sighing with contentment. Life is good. I have a terrific day walking forward, taking strides with my reliable cane. Occasionally, I lose my balance. This usually happens when there is a lot going on in the surrounding environment - loud sudden noises, fast movement in front of me, and a lot of people walking toward me. Jennifer and Amy are always close by to hold and steady me. I haven't fallen yet!

Later we go to the movies. The picture isn't much, but it's just a lot of fun chewing on popcorn next to my family watching another mindless flick. Unfortunately, I am really out of it by the time we return home. I go to bed very early.

Day 87: On Sunday, I choose to float. I rest the entire day, taking medication as needed. I am just plain tired. I snooze away the whole day like an infant in its cradle. I guess going out on Saturday, a stroll in the mall and a movie was too much for me. But that's okay, because I had a great time.

Day 88: Amy is home for the Martin Luther King Jr. holiday. It's always a pleasure to have her home. We are not home for long, since my landlord's apartment is being painted and smells to high heaven from paint and turpentine. The smell is so toxic we vacate the apartment. It is like my nose is submerged in a barrel of ammonia.

Homework at the Food Court

We go to the food court in another mall and have a bite to eat. Throughout the day I experience those wavy feelings, but am still able to walk with my cane. As difficult as it is, I think I am starting to accommodate to this wavy feeling. Like the doctors say, it will go away eventually. I hope so. I just have to accept it and give it time to pass. As usual, rehab is always on my mind and I take the time to do an occupational therapy assignment. Jennifer helps organize a table in the food court as a working space, while Amy runs a few errands. Amy may have a day off, but it is no vacation. As I work on the assignment my head begins to pound. It feels like a vice is squeezing the side of my head and my ears are ringing on and off. It drowns out everything else! I have trouble understanding the directions to the assignment. I am looking through all my papers like a wild man. I cannot make heads or tails out of the directions, which are just a little different from an earlier assignment. Since Jennifer was at the occupational therapy session with me, she explains the directions until she is sure I understand them. I feel very stupid having to depend on my niece in this way.

I know these assignments are elementary, and it troubles me that I'm having such difficulty understanding how to carry them out. I just have to bear down and stay focused on my goal. I want to believe, I mean I have to believe, that this will pay off in the long run. I am exhausted mentally and physically by the time I finish the assignment. I find it more difficult to walk steadily when we are heading back to the car; I guess it's the traffic and all the other people heading back to their cars. On the way home I tell Jennifer how frustrating it is for me when I have trouble understanding these basic tasks. I tell her how annoying it is that my head begins to ache and my forehead feels numb after 15 to 20 minutes of concentrating on a grammar school exercise.

I tell Jennifer that before the accident, I was "intellectually," at the top of my game. Hell, I could juggle ten tasks at one time, all successfully. People depended on me, both professionally and personally. Now my role has changed. The doctors and therapists believe I will improve, which is great to hear. They say it will just take time, but how long? There are times when I feel things are not moving quickly enough. It is very frustrating on a day-to-day basis dealing with this injury. I hold on to the end goal, keeping focused on the positive, but it isn't easy. I tend to assess my progress on a week-to-week basis, which is helpful, yet at the same time, discouraging.

After I finish rambling, Jennifer reaches over, gives me a big hug and kiss and says, "Don't worry uncle Chris; try to be patient. You're doing well, so just keep it up! You'll get better ...I know you will!"

Jennifer our Angel

Jennifer never treats her uncle Chris like a child. She treats him with respect, understanding, kindness, and does not judge him or think less of him. What a remarkable young woman she has become. She is like an angel sent to help us for a short time. She helps us make a difficult transition, easing us into a new way of life.

Back on Medication

Day 90: On Wednesday, Jennifer and I go to Mount Sinai to see my physiatrist, Dr. Wilkins. She's an MD who acts as a sort of go-between making sure that my neurological condition relates to the course of my therapies. After updating her on my progress at Rusk she has me walk in the hallway for some neurological tests. She prescribes the same medications that I took in the hospital. I'm not happy about going back on these medications at all, but I must follow doctor's orders. She thinks that they will help with my concentration and help alleviate some of the pain. She is also concerned about keeping my stress level and anxiety in check. According to the doctor, if we don't control this, my brain will begin to become conditioned to its current unhealthy state, regarding it as the norm, and I won't get better. She tells me to give her a call in a couple of weeks to help her keep tabs on how the medicine is working. She asks me to keep close track of whether or not my symptoms increase.

A Three-Hour Marathon

Day 91: The trip to Rusk is becoming routine for Jennifer and me, but today is a special day. At last, I have a full cognitive workup. The psychologist administers a battery of cognitive psychological tests. Gina knows my vulnerabilities and works very slowly with me. We are in session for over three hours. I am totally drained after that. I do not really mind. I'm stretching myself. It's another building block for overall recovery. Besides, I can't fix it until the professionals figure out what exactly is wrong.

No Place is Perfect

Afterwards, Jennifer and I head over to occupational therapy, where a young woman introduces herself as Tina. She is substituting for my regular therapist Robin. Today I am working on shopping list exercises that entail some sorting and basic calculations. The O.T. room is never very subdued, but today as the patient activity increases and the decibel level rises, it is increasingly difficult to concentrate on my tasks. I am totally distracted by all the commotion. My head is really pounding and my eye sockets are aching. Tina says it's okay. She can tell I am in such pain, wincing as I try so hard to focus. I try to explain to her that I'm pretty worn out by the cognitive evaluation. I have trouble understanding the directions she gives me. She clarifies and repeats them. I cannot retain some essential facts that she told me just moments before. She can see that I am feeling frustrated and she reassures me. I am having trouble focusing with so many people in the room who seem to be moving in different directions and speaking at once. I'm sure some of the other people are having the same problem. I guess no place is perfect, not even Rusk.

Physical therapy makes up for the dud occupational session. I do my half hour group workout. It feels great getting back into physical exercise. I do arm and leg lifts on a Nautilus machine. After practicing with Barb, my physical therapist, I do better walking sideways and backward. I know she is supporting me, but I can tell I am improving. I talk with her about my progress and how she makes me feel good about myself and hopeful for the future.

Right from the start Barb goes above and beyond her job description, and I am eternally grateful to her. Barb is, in my opinion, an angel who is here to do whatever it takes to see that I have every opportunity to improve.

Jennifer's Farewell

Day 93: Today, January 22nd is a very sad day. Amy and I drive Jennifer to Manhattan to catch an Amtrak train back home. She is excited to return home, but is worried that I won't be able to cope without her. Amy and I tell her not to worry, that we will make it work. We are grateful. It was wonderful having her with us. She was such a big help organizing my therapy schedule, escorting me wherever I have to go, arranging meals, and keeping my medication on schedule. She even made our bed in the morning and arranged my shower chair so it would safely hold me in the tub. She will really be missed. She has truly been a godsend. I think this period has brought us all closer together. At a time when Amy and I desperately needed help, Jennifer was there for us. I'm very grateful to her parents, Mike and Anita, for supporting her decision to come and help me. I could not have made it for these crucial weeks without her support.

Just the Two of Us

Chris and I both have a good cry when Jennifer leaves to return to home for school. She offers to take her next semester off to stay and help us, but Chris is firm. "Absolutely not," he insists, "School is very important." I am a little lost after Jennifer leaves, but at the same time, I feel prepared for what lies ahead and confident I will be able to build upon Jennifer's accomplishments. It's just the two of us now, and I have a sense of being refreshed in mind and spirit and have a feeling of renewal to take on whatever comes next.

Life without Jennifer

Day 95: I wake up early for rehab today. Amy brings me into Manhattan and hails a cab. She travels with me to Rusk. We both agree that daily taxis would break our budget. I am going to have to learn very quickly to handle public transportation. I miss Jennifer already, as much for the company as the support. It is a real mental exercise trying to find all of my appointments as well as the lunchroom without Jennifer, but I still manage to muddle through. The hustle and bustle in the hallways makes it difficult for me to concentrate on where I am trying to go. I get lost and disoriented a few times before getting to my destination.

Back and Forth

I now accompany Chris to Rusk in the morning, take the bus across town to work, and leave early to return to Rusk to help Chris back on the bus to the Port Authority. Then together we take another bus home to New Jersey. We will continue this routine until the weather improves and Chris feels comfortable making his way on his own. Between Chris's needs and the responsibilities of the office, it is hard not to feel tense and worn out. I really miss Jennifer.

My O.T. Adventure

Occupational therapy is an adventure. Robin has spoken to Amy about my transportation requirements and today I will get some practice taking the bus. I have been on very few buses over the years, since I usually took the subway or walked to get where I wanted to go. Today we travel from Rusk to Mount Sinai and over to Amy's midtown office. A route I will have to travel on my own. The exercise helps me understand exactly what I need to do to get around the city by myself. I look forward to mastering bus travel, which will bring me closer to real independence. The subway with its noise and crowds in a confined space, at least at this point, is beyond me.

Prior to the bus ride, Robin tells me several times how to use the metro card, a skill I have to relearn. Robin brings along an intern and directs me to pay for her as well. She tells me how to handle the transfer to another bus, which does not seem very hard. I make my way into the bus and slip my metro card into the machine. Robin reminds me to slip the card in again to pay for the intern. We stop at our first destination and exit the bus. Robin again reminds me a few times that when I enter the next bus I must dip my card in only once, and that this would transfer both the intern and me. Despite Robins' clear direction just before the bus pulls up, I dip the card in twice, creating a double charge instead of a free transfer. When we sit down, Robin asks me if I remembered what she told me about transferring. I have absolutely no recollection of her telling me anything. She repeats what she said. It doesn't ring any bells. It is so simple, but yet I can't remember the directions. I feel embarrassed. Robin sees that I am beating myself up, so she smiles politely as if to shrug it off and tells me not to worry. "You'll know next time what to do." I apologize for wasting her money. Robin just chuckles and says, "Don't worry about that at all, it's the hospital's dime."

Keeping My Balance

Returning to Rusk, I make my way to physical therapy. Barb gives me some exercises to do at home, which will help with my balancing problems. She says that I have to have Amy spot me when I do these exercises. The exercises involve lifting arms and legs, standing on one leg, crawling forwards, backwards, and sideways. Like many of the exercises I do with Barb they seem like child's play when she explains them to me, but are difficult and sometimes impossible to perform in practice. I feel like a middle-aged toddler.

Barb seems happy with the progress I made with the other therapist while she was away at a conference. Although it is fine working with other therapists, I really missed her and am glad she's back. I guess that's because I feel like I am developing a routine, and am comfortable working with her. I depend upon the familiar.

Later that afternoon in speech therapy I practice breathing/speaking techniques with words that begin with the consonant " M. " It's difficult, but with more practice when I'm at home, I will master the M's and every other letter in the alphabet.

My trip to Amy's office does not go smoothly. I am a little uncertain when I go out to First Avenue for the bus. I have to make sure I choose the right one. Otherwise who knows where I will end up? A bus pulls up to the stop. The doors fly open. I have trouble asking if it stops at the desired location. I stutter and sputter. The driver scowls, the door slams shut and the bus zooms away. I am speechless, angry, and embarrassed all at the same time. How could he be in such a rush that he couldn't ask me to repeat what I am saying? I find myself getting very nervous, so I do some breathing exercises to calm down.

Another bus draws up shortly afterward. Now I am ready. I know exactly what I am going to ask and do the best I can. This bus driver seems more understanding and gives me space to fumble around a little to choose my words. I get my question answered and I am happy to be on my way. Another small victory, but gradually they will add up.

Life with Father

While talking with my dad on the phone in the evening I ask a question about the reception on my TV. He tells me what I can do to fix it, which includes making an antenna. He describes what I need to do, but I am unable to figure out what he is talking about. I just can't conceptualize it. He patiently repeats the directions several times in an attempt to help me understand. The more he repeats the directions the more confused I become. I am totally frustrated and eventually I just give up. "It's not a matter of life and death," I say. He keeps at it. He really wants me to understand this. He says, "Don't worry you'll get it, let me try it another way." It is great that he is so supportive, but no matter how many times he explains it, I just get more confused. He reassures me that in time I should be able to do this, perhaps not right now but in the future. He really understands how I feel. He sympathizes and really wants to help.

A Positive Routine

Day 96: Today is a good day. I am getting into a very positive routine on the days I stay at home. I do my home exercises for speech and for physical therapy in the morning and the afternoon. The physical therapy exercises are particularly challenging. I rest throughout the day doing breathing, visualization, and PMR exercises. During the day Amy calls to remind me to take a sandwich out of the refrigerator and eat. Since my accident my appetite does not function normally. My brain just refrains from telling me to eat. My ears are still ringing occasionally and my face is still numb. In the evening I ask Amy to spot me for additional physical therapy balance exercises. Overall, I do better with my right side than with my left.

Our Routine

Over time, Chris and I develop a routine. Before I leave for work I make sure his clothes are laid out on a chair for him, his medicine is on the bed stand with a glass of water, and breakfast is prepared, so all he has to do is take the milk out of the refrigerator for his cereal. His lunch is wrapped and in the refrigerator with some type of chips and cookies set on the same place on the counter each day. I call him each day between 12:00 and 1:00 to remind him that it is time to eat lunch. Often times I call him again 20 minutes later to make sure he is eating. By the time he hangs up the phone he forgets to get his lunch out. During my second call, I have him put the phone on speaker and walk him through the steps of getting his lunch. I don't hang up until I know he is sitting at the table eating.

Some Ups and Downs

Day 98: Tony, my landlord's brother, offers to drive me to the PATH train station so that I can travel into the city for therapy. The weather is cold and icy. The ride is welcome. Once we get to the PATH train, Tony helps me out of the car and to the stairway where it is dry and clean.

When I arrive at Rusk I drop my coat off at the physical therapy office and continue on to the cafeteria. I don't want to be weighed down by the coat all day long. I guess if I am planning ahead like this my executive function must be improving. My ears are ringing from the moment I arrive and the waviness is ever present, but I am able to manage, despite the discomfort.

Leaving the cafeteria I become disoriented and have trouble making my way from the cafeteria to my occupational therapy appointment. I approach the elevator that I am supposed to take that is always packed with staff and visitors. Once on the elevator I don't realize I am on the first floor and ask a person on the elevator to press "ONE" for me. All of a sudden people behind me start yelling. A tall orderly sarcastically reminds me, "We are on One!" Others begin chiming in. I am embarrassed and very nervous and in a stutter say, "I mean-mean G-G-G, g-ground." The same man shouts out just as sarcastically, "This elevator is going up!"

I walk off the elevator without saying a word and find a stairway instead. I feel so alone, useless, and frustrated. Still troubled by this experience I don't pay attention and walk up the stairs until I reach the second floor. I finally realize my mistake. You just can't win sometimes, I guess. I turn around, and slowly walk down the stairs. I repeat to myself, "Chris, it's okay; at least you know where you are going now."

When I reach occupational therapy I tell Robin what happened in the elevator and about the problem at the bus stop. I also tell her about my discussion with my dad regarding the TV antenna instructions. She maps out the bus travel for me and I write it in my notebook, and then we walk around the hospital together so I can get my bearings. She then shows me an easier way to get around. I write down her instructions very carefully. She encourages me to tell Emile about my dads' conversation and the bus incident. When I see Emile, I tell her what happened. She says that this is "the language piece" she was referring to the other day "that I need to work on." She then shows me the test results of my aphasia (inability to use or understand words), assessment. Although among typical aphasics I score pretty well, among a normal population I am well below normal. As difficult as this is to hear, it makes sense to me when I see how much trouble I am having communicating my thoughts at times. This becomes even more difficult when I am tired, in a rush, or when I am talking with strangers. Emile assures me that this is one of the things we will work on.

Physical therapy goes well today. Although I have a little trouble balancing on my left leg when my eyes are closed and walking on the ramp, I am a little better at scanning quickly from side to side. Barb says that I have shown improvement from a few weeks ago, and believes I am coming along really well. I ask her if we will eventually be working on advanced skills like jumping and jogging. She says I will definitely be doing these things. Barb receives a message during the physical therapy session that I have an appointment with a Rusk psychologist at 4:00 p.m. I call Amy and she comes to the hospital for this appointment.

Respect my Fatigue

We meet with Rhonda, one of the psychologists. She is very nice. She tells us that it is common with some brain injuries that nothing will show up on a physical test, like an MRI or CAT scan, and that the symptoms I have are very serious. She explains that although my injury has caused major deficiencies, she feels that I will do well in treatment. She doesn't promise how close I will get to a full recovery. She indicates that some of the deficit areas I will be working on include memory, attention span, problem solving, and information processing. She says the foggy feeling that I call "feeling half empty" should go away in the months ahead. The psychologist recommends I participate in a cognitive remediation group as well as individual treatment and psychotherapy. The cognitive group will address the cognitive functions I need to get back to enjoy as "normal" a lifestyle as possible, and that the psychotherapy will help me deal with the emotional and personal issues I am experiencing. I am anxious to follow through with her recommendations. She indicates that for therapy she would probably be sending me to a cognitive behavioral therapist. She concurs with Mount Sinai that my pre-morbid level of brain functioning was superior and that now it's about average, but that we will be working on regaining whatever we can.

I never thought I was above average and certainly not superior, though I knew I could achieve most things I set out to do. Prior to this injury, I didn't think about whether I was intellectually superior. Rhonda advises me to "respect my fatigue," and be aware of taking time to rest my brain. She respects my stance that I want to work as hard as I can to get better, but emphasizes how important it is to rest my brain so that it can heal.

Day 100: Saturday morning I feel good for a change, so I handle some paper work for a project I was working on before the accident. I know in my heart of hearts I cannot proceed with my plans and ambitions in my current condition, but I am not yet ready to give up. The good feeling doesn't last long, eventually the fatigue I feel morphs into pain.

Later that day I get a call from Rosemarie, former assistant principal at my school, who is now a principal of another school. It is great hearing from her. She is as positive and encouraging to me as I would expect. She says that I sound real good compared to when we last spoke in the hospital. I agree my speech has gotten better, but most of my challenges aren't immediately visible like the pain that is nearly always with me.

She says that she believes that I will succeed in anything I do. It's great to hear her say that. I think she believes so much in me and knows how determined I am. She doesn't doubt I will fully recover. This is very flattering, and I hope I do, but if I don't she will hopefully view my success in terms of what I have already accomplished in rehab.

Some Rusk Challenges

Day 102: Although I had a great deal of pain over the weekend, I feel okay today. Hell, I almost take these crushing headaches for granted. I am ready for another day at Rusk. Today occupational therapy is a real challenge. My brain is working overtime. We review my homework. I have made a lot of errors. I read the directions several times and I still can't do a math/ordering exercise correctly. I feel very stupid after Robin reviews my work. After all, this isn't rocket science. Robin offers some strategies to help with this type of task. She shows me how to reduce the stimuli on the page by using another piece of paper to block some of the extraneous words, lines, numbers etc. She suggests that I check off or circle items that are accounted for. She also encourages me to read the directions slowly and underline the key words to help me focus on the important points. I leave there with more hope than disappointment.

Barb works on my neck in PT and teaches me some stretching exercises. She also provides me with some exercises to do at home that will help with my neck pain. She promises to take me outside on our next session. It is something to look forward to. She feels I'm coming along very well, and encourages me to have some patience with my progress. She thinks that I'm having most difficulty reacting to fast commands or fast moving things. She thinks that my reaction time is slow right now and also believes I may get anxious, which aggravates any problem.

In speech today, Emile gives me an aphasia handout to give to my family and anyone else with whom I speak to in order to alert them to the nature of my challenges. She also gives me several homework assignments. I am learning how to better formulate sentences. I tell her about how difficult it is for me to speak on the phone. "It's very common with brain injuries," she says. I just have to give it time. As Barb told me earlier today, "Just try and be patient."

Patience with myself has never been a strong point of mine, before or after my injury. I think now there are times I'm especially short of it. When it comes to my pace of improvement, I am very impatient; but maybe it's only natural. After all, living with this type of injury 24 hours a day, seven days a week isn't easy. I know she's right, I have to work on being more patient with my progress. After all, getting stressed out over it can't be doing me any good.

Chapter Seven

Relearning and Adjusting

Making Adjustments

Day 103: The first day of February greets me with the usual assortment of pain. My eye sockets and both sides of my head are pounding. I follow my home exercise regimen with the aid of reminders on my bulletin board and messages taped to the walls. Funny thing, I still don't have any desire to eat. If Amy didn't call me I guess I would starve. I eat to survive. I never have that urge.

I do the physical, speech, and occupational therapy home exercises today according to schedule. I am at the top of my game with the PT and speech exercises, but by the time I'm working on my OT exercises, I am really bushed. I completely crash after a sorting and organizing numbers exercise. It takes me 40 minutes just to put some dates in chronological order. The rest of the day is spent recuperating. Next time, I will take more breaks. Now I just sit back in my lounge chair, put my feet up, and try to relax to recharge my brain.

My ears continue to ring throughout the day. I also notice that my face feels more numb and tingly than usual and my head hurts worse than usual. No, it is impossible to relax.

Laughing it Off

Day 105: Today at Rusk I do some planning activities in occupational therapy. Robin reiterates some strategies to help me keep track of what I am working on. I must focus on instructions, isolate key words, make notes to compensate for memory difficulties, and never rush.

In physical therapy today, I do scanning exercises with Barb without my cane. Barb has me walk down the busy hallway near the PT room minus my cane. She is holding my belt from behind so I don't take a spill. She notices that when she says the word "stop," I don't bring my leg up from behind and come to a sudden halt. I suddenly stop like a freeze frame, whatever my position. I shake and fall off balance. She thinks that perhaps my brain isn't sending the message down to my legs to take another step to help me balance. When this happens I try to laugh it off but I am very frustrated. I know that I am making progress, but I cannot help being impatient. I know, however, that a little laughter is a good alternative to getting upset. Laughter and humor are the best healers. It's not always easy to find the humor in my predicament. As a matter of fact, I don't always find it, but I do try.

The Playback

In speech therapy I question Emile about my inability to formulate words physically, and express them after I have been speaking for a while, say, after talking to Amy. She recommends that I repeat the consonant sounds like "ta, da and ba" as an antidote. Emile then has me read into a tape recorder. She asks me if I know how I sound when I speak. I thought I did. I know when I say a sentence in the wrong order or when I use the wrong word when I'm formulating a sentence. She plays back the tape and asks me to discuss what I hear. I am shocked at the sound of my voice. That can't be me; but who else is it. I hang on to the consonants and trip over any multi-syllabic words. I run out of breath at the wrong times and leave words half spoken and dangling. I do not pause naturally. My reality definitely needs testing. The tape is a wake up call.

Emile's speech therapy is really challenging. After some exercises, which are almost like doing scales for a singer, Emile and I talk about how the home exercises are going - breathing, stabilization, enunciating one and two syllable words, and reading brief paragraphs. I tell her that I think they are going well. We also talk about my intonation concerns and rate of speech. My "flat sound" is another concern of mine. For some reason or another my voice sounds monotone. She encourages me to keep reading into the tape recorder. I have to read the passages aloud to develop natural stresses, intonation, and rhythm. I have to repeat my readings, play them back, and make adjustments over and over again.

A Board of Education Vise

Day 106: On Friday February 4th Amy brings me over to a Board of Education office to be examined by Dr. Richardson. Amy and I approach the reception desk with my completed registration form. The receptionist begins to pepper me with questions about why Amy filled out this form instead of me. Many people are talking very fast behind the desk at the same time. My head is crushed in a vise. I am having trouble processing what anyone is saying. Amy tries to explain that I have a brain injury that makes it impossible for me to fill it out on my own, and that I have to conserve my energy for when I see the doctor. She repeats herself a couple of times that filling out forms adds to my fatigue and causes bad headaches. Finally, the woman behind the desk seems mollified, but insists that in the future I complete every last form myself. I am exhausted by the time I see the doctor for a routine examination and even more drained when we leave.

Later that day I take a nap. Now fairly rested, I go with Amy to the Laundromat. Amy is recovering from the flu and I offer to help with the wash. This is a big mistake. All of the televisions are turned up very loud. The fluorescent lights are very bright and children are running around as if it's a playground. On top of that, the whirring, rumbling, and beeping of the washers and dryers are sucking every ounce of energy out of me. I am jumping out of my skin. Amy tells me not to worry as she helps me back to the car. Fatigue consumes me and I fall asleep while waiting for her to finish the wash. I have another "early to bed" night.

Day 109: I wake this morning with a ferocious headache. I take the medication as prescribed. When I arrive at the Port Authority I eat a bagel and take more pain medication; the regular part of my morning regimen. I am hoping for relief, which never quite comes. The trip to Rusk is happily uneventful.

Not as Good as it Gets

I begin the Rusk regimen with OT. Robin and I initially try to go over my homework assignment. I just can't get into a groove, follow the material, or express myself properly with all the noise and activity in the occupational therapy room. Robin eventually gives me a map exercise that is part of my therapy to do at home.

As our session starts to draw to its end, Robin and I start talking about my progress and how I am so far from where I want to be in getting back to my normal self. Robin replies saying, "There are many other patients in far worse condition than you." She feels I'm higher functioning than many others. Maybe she says this because I tell her how challenging and frustrating it is for me to concentrate in a room with so much noise and other distractions. I tell her how my head hurts when I try to focus and think when there are so many things going on around me. What does she mean when she says there are many other patients in a far worse condition than me? Is that really germane to my therapy? I thank God that I am not as debilitated as others.

On the other hand, I firmly declare to Robin that, "This is not as good as it is going to get for me. I am just at the beginning of my journey, I am not ready to give up and settle."

She says she is not even suggesting that I won't improve, but just wants me to acknowledge how much worse it could be. This really upsets me. I know it could be worse! I also know that it could be a hell of a lot better. I know what I was capable of before this injury and I am very aware that I'm not even close to where I was before. I understand what she is saying, but I am so focused on improving and regaining what I've lost, that telling me it could be much worse does not bring me any comfort. Down the road I may start thinking about acceptance, but right now I think of nothing else than regaining what was taken from me.

Awareness

In speech therapy Emile and I discuss "awareness." She says that she thinks that the more I become aware of my deficit areas, the more challenging it is for me to manage my frustration level. As an example, she points to my response to first hearing my voice on tape. I share with Emile my discussion with Robin earlier that day. She understands my reaction and tells me, "It is natural for someone so motivated to feel that way." I tell her that I'm working on managing the issues I'm becoming aware of, but that I won't even consider accepting any deficit or limitation, now or ever. I confide in her that I am unhappy with my slow progress; my baby steps toward normality. "It drives me crazy!" I tell her that I work so hard every day to make improvements and that I feel at times that my effort is not producing the results I expect... that I demand. She explains that I am probably at a plateau. She is looking forward to my next level. She says my high level of motivation challenges her. She knows that I follow her recommendations and that keeps her on her toes. This makes me feel good. It seems like she is always ready to raise the bar to help get me to the next level! I am looking forward to more challenges.

Day 110: The next day as I do speech and language exercises at home I notice I am becoming more aware of how I sound when I listen to the tape. I am beginning to hear not only what words I am having difficulty with, but I am beginning to notice what I am doing that causes the difficulty. Improvement to me means that I am beginning to hear how I sound as I speak, and learning to make corrections on the next group of words or sentences I speak. When I play back the tape I'm no longer shocked about how I sound.

I set aside today for practical rehabilitation exercises - phone conversations, reading, organizing paperwork; stuff I once took for granted. The result is major headaches. I take breaks by sitting, lying down, and doing breathing exercises. The rest of the day I try to be at peace and relax.

Changes

Day 112: It is a nice change today to be outside the walls of Rusk for PT. At first I walk with my cane, but at a certain point on impulse I hand the cane over to my therapist. I do well walking forward, but not so well walking backward. My speech therapy is also a little different today. Emile's supervisor sits in on our session. I am nervous at first. I want to show her all I have accomplished. I want Emile's efforts acknowledged. From my own work experience I know what it's like having a supervisor evaluate my every move. Her supervisor has me do a wide range of exercises, which seem to confirm apraxia, one of the original diagnoses for my speech problem. Apparently, she and Emile already talked about this possibility. I ask her later if this is like the aphasia she has observed in previous sessions. She tells me that apraxia deals with speech and aphasia deals with language. The supervisor follows up by asking me about my neuropsychological status, where I am in terms of getting cognitive therapy. I tell her that I spoke to the department administrators today, and they're still waiting on my insurance approval. The last thing that Emile's supervisor discusses is a change of physiatrist from Mount Sinai to Rusk. I ask her if it would be possible to keep my original physiatrist, and she says that it will make treatment planning more difficult. My therapy could be coordinated much more smoothly and easily with all the key people at the same site.

Money We Can't Afford

Changing physiatrists makes me jittery and uncomfortable. I am conflicted. I like and trust my current physiatrist, but the Rusk doctor does not take my insurance. Hell, its money we cannot afford. I find out later that day when Amy calls the insurance company that Rusk has not yet sent in a neuropsychological report and that the company can't approve the cognitive therapy until they receive it.

Later that day, Rusk calls our house and apologizes for the delay and faxes the proper papers to the insurance company and promises to follow-up by phone. The caller also tells Amy that psychotherapy, also recommended by Rusk, would not be covered by insurance. They would try to work something out.

Jumping through Hoops

Why does one have to jump through hoops to get medical care, especially when an accident is not your fault? First there is a delay in getting Chris the proper therapy care at Rusk. Then there is the constant struggle in dealing with the bills I shouldn't be receiving in the first place for the therapy that is supposed to be paid by the insurance company. I keep excellent billing records and am scrupulous about financial matters, but I still find myself having to argue my case with various collection agencies. Initially, there is no one to assist and advocate for me. Finally, I find that one person who understands how the insurance company works with the hospitals and the doctors and this makes my life much easier.

Incident at IHOP

Day 114: Since our TV set conked out last week Amy and I decide to take advantage of the good weather today to go on a shopping expedition for a television. On the way to the mall we take a detour to IHOP. I think Amy can use a break from the routine, a little outing like old times. Bad choice. There are too many dishes crashing around as the busboys dash between tables. The customers are loud and rambunctious as if at a private party. Scattered throughout the restaurant are bawling babies and screeching children. For me, every sound is amplified, deafening to my ears. I feel like I'm at a concert forced to listen to blaring music that I can't stand. To top it off, a miniature train circles around the perimeter of the dining room that whistles and chugs at scheduled intervals. Amy thinks it is so cute, but for me it is one more distraction that drains my energy. Unfortunately, we order before noticing all this noise. I decide to stick it out. I take some pills and close my eyes. I follow up with breathing and visualization exercises. Nothing works; I am flooded with stimulation and pain. I tough it out and make it through lunch, another victory. I even complete the shopping expedition for the TV. I can't follow the salesman at all. It is Amy's call. I'm just along for the ride.

Day 115: It's Sunday, I decide to lay low. Amy and I do a few things in the apartment and relax most of the day. We sit side by side in our love seat recliner and watch some shows on our new TV. After dinner we rehash the week's events and discuss some plans for the week ahead. Amy bakes some chocolate chip cookies using my mom's recipe. Just being together with Amy is a pleasure.

A Total Blank

Day 116: February 14th. It's a hectic morning. I find myself rushing to catch my bus for the city and waiting too long for another bus once I get to the Port Authority. I am out of breath and dreading I will miss my appointment. The bus I enter is filled to the brim. There is a commotion near the front with a woman refusing to pay a fare for her daughter. All the while, I become increasingly anxious.

When I get off the bus at Park Avenue and 34th street, the city streets are buzzing with activity. As I cross the street to make my way to the doctor's office a woman passes right by me talking loudly on her cell. She is giving a person the location of where she is heading. I suddenly stop and draw a total blank on where I am heading. I am concentrating so hard on where I am supposed to be going, I am unaware that I am standing in the middle of the street. Where am I going...How do I get there? I am very frightened and confused. Honking horns and people shouting at me breaks my concentration alerting me of the dangerous situation I am in.

I somehow manage to make my way to the other side of the street and lean against a storefront. I look left and right at street signs to get my bearings. I am afraid and even more confused. I am totally vulnerable without a hint where I am or where I am going. I talk to myself and try to calm down. "Relax... don't worry... everything is going to be okay... just breathe... relax...." I strain to recall my schedule. I wish that Amy were here with me. She knows exactly where I have to go. Suddenly Amy's phone number pops into my head. In sheer desperation I go over to a phone booth and dial Amy's number. As the phone rings I wrack my brain, hoping to recall where I have to go and how I am going to get there. Amy answers with her familiar crisp business greeting. I try to tell her what's going on, but my anxiety kicks in and I can't get to the point. Amy somehow understands what I am saying and calms me down, urging me to concentrate on my breathing. She asks me to report to her what I see from where I am standing. I tell her that I am at the corner of Park and 34th Street. She reminds me of my appointment with Dr. Pincus, my E.N.T. guy. Suddenly it dawns on me as quickly as it slipped my mind only moments ago. I shout out to Amy, "I have to go to 36th Street between Park and Madison." What a relief! I am only a few blocks and an avenue away. That weekend Amy and I purchase cell phones, an added security net for future memory lapses. Pay phones are getting harder and harder to find these days.

The Attention Bank

I tell my occupational therapist about this experience. I ask her why this happened when I had been to this doctor so many times before and after my accident. She thinks it is a combination of events including the bus mishaps, the stress of my appointment obligations, and an added effort to concentrate that caused me to drain my "attention bank." Her analogy to a bank helps me to understand. All of the energy it takes for me to focus on what I am doing in the moment is like a withdrawal from a bank (my brain) that is responsible for my attention and concentration. Essentially I run out of these resources, unless I make a deposit (rest and relax). She is pleased that I did not give up or give in.

Scheduling

Now that the weather is warming up and Chris is more confident about walking and taking buses, I feel more relaxed when he is going to various appointments on his own. Of course it all requires some planning. I sit down with Chris each evening and map out a schedule for him, whether he is going to rehab or has an appointment with a doctor. In the evenings, I rehearse with Chris what buses he has to take, times of appointments, and other crucial particulars. Concentrating at work on his appointment days is difficult. I wait on pins and needles for Chris's call letting me know he has arrived safely at a particular doctor's office. I get very anxious if he does not call me around his appointment time. I worry that he is lost or that he is hurt.

My concern is usually unnecessary. Most times his call is delayed by problems with public transportation.

Learning to Modify

In PT, Barb introduces me to several additional home exercises; again she focuses on stretching, extending and holding positions. Getting better is a full time job. The more therapy I receive and the more exercises I learn, the faster I will be the old me. Next, I perform backwards and lateral walking. It seems I lean slightly forward when I lift my feet and need to straighten myself up. I must "modify." Barb is happy that we find a way to deal with this problem. I talk about my head pain. She asks if I am massaging the temporal area to gain relief. I tell her that my face gets numb when I massage my temporal areas. I think it may be more intense on the right side.

The Window of Time

In speech today, Emile and I talk for quite a while about our conversation with her supervisor. Progress is the main topic of discussion, or rather my lack of progress. She discusses with me something called "spontaneous recovery." She says this happens when a body naturally heals itself. This process, when combined with therapy, usually yields the best results. She said that although there is no set window for when spontaneous recovery occurs, the change usually takes place over the first six months of the period following the trauma. So, of course the next logical question I ask is, "Where am I now?" Emile says matter-of-factly, "Maybe this window of opportunity is opening before you." Emile's supervisor asked her if I expect to recover fully. She told her that I did. She then told me that her supervisor asked if we discussed the possibility of that not happening. We talk about this possibility now, very briefly. I tell her that I want to believe that with all the effort I'm making and all the therapy I am receiving, that I will get everything back to normal. Of course, I know anything can happen, but for the present, I am holding on to the positive. Only time will tell how I do. Meanwhile, hope and faith are great motivators.

I just want to get back to the old Chris. I never really think about how intelligent or capable I am or was, I do not believe I was or will be a "genius." I know that for most of my life I was a quick study, successful at whatever I put my mind to. I have a graduate degree and a variety of certifications and credentials and was about to prepare for another advanced degree, before my brain injury. I was doing well in my job in the school system, and was being recruited to become an assistant principal. I was also developing a private counseling practice and working on my pet project, a training resource for counselors and social workers. Life was looking good, and all my hard work and effort was starting to pay off.

October 22, 1999 (day 1) changed that in an instant. So, I am struggling with what I could have had, or should have been, versus what I am right now. Since I was so successful accomplishing whatever I tackled before why shouldn't I be able to conquer this thing?

Exploring Possibilities

Later that day I meet with Joan, a vocational counselor. She says it is too early in my therapy to make plans. It makes more sense to check in with her further down the road. She encourages me not to worry so much about working right now. She thinks it's best to concentrate on my program at Rusk and give it some time to see how things gel. She asks if I am feeling some pressure to come up with a vocational plan right now. I level with her about my concerns over what I am really capable of doing effectively. The future is an unknown. She seems to understand, and assures me that she will be addressing all of these issues in the future. She also says she will be the person to act as an advocate for me once I'm ready to re-enter the world of work.

When I get home I share with Amy the downers and triumphs of this day, particularly my discussion with Emile. It is a way to explore the possibility that I may not improve to the person I was before the accident. I don't want Amy to be disappointed. I think it may be helpful for us to begin to process all of the possibilities, even the ones I don't want to face. I know that Amy is very concerned about the future, but in her goodness always tries to be positive and supportive. I appreciate her unwavering support, but she has to be tough enough to examine worse case scenarios.

Serious Discussions

Tonight I see that Chris is very serious. I know that he has something important to say. He tells me he may never be back to 100%. I don't know how long I cry. Chris holds me in his arms, tight as he can trying to protect me. I remember it was only the night before I prayed to God to please give Chris's voice back to him. I remember thinking that I could handle the wheel chair or a walker but could not bear not to hear his deep romantic voice calling me or saying "I love you." That night as I cry in his arms he tries to reassure me as I see the life we planned slipping away. There will be no assistant principal position for Chris leading to a principal position in a school, and no private counseling practice. In between my sobs I tell Chris, "but you don't understand... when I was praying to God for you to get your voice back, I forgot to ask God about your brain."

Chris starts laughing and soon we are both laughing together. He says, "As long as we are together we can accomplish anything. "It may be hard on you at times, but we can do it."

That night I become a different person. I now know many of the responsibilities will be on my shoulders and our roles will change. I know in the future I will have to be more assertive, demanding, maybe some would even say bitchy. I know that there will be many occasions when I will have to put my foot down to get Chris what he needs.

Practice Makes Perfect

Day 117: I am up early to do the physical therapy exercises Barb want me to work on. I push myself through this new repertoire, but remember to take regular breaks for rest, relaxation, and deep breathing. My head aches badly, my ears ring periodically, and my face is numb. The numbing continues to increase when I rub the temporal area of my head. The numb feeling starts on the right side, the side that usually feels worse.

Later that evening I do balancing exercises with Amy spotting me. I stand with my eyes closed for 1 $^{1/2}$ seconds and increase it to 2 $^{1/2}$ seconds, before I start to fall back. I do okay with crawling forward and backwards. I concentrate hard to crawl backwards. I also have some difficulty going sideways. The most difficult exercise is holding my opposite arm and leg up for ten seconds while I am on my hands and knees. I hold this position for about two seconds. I'm sure that the more I practice, the better I will get.

Organizing my Black Book

Day 119: No mishaps on the way to Rusk this morning, but I am more jumpy than usual. In occupational therapy Robin does some orientation exercises with me. She heard about my "lost in New York episode" and offers some strategies to help me make my way in the future. First, I must be prepared with directions and phone numbers for any regular destinations and appointments. I must painstakingly put them in the black binder I carry to therapy. This way if I am ever feeling confused or lost as to where I am traveling, I can always refer to my binder. She suggests this preparation before I leave the house, no matter what the circumstances.

Making the Rounds

After organizing my book for contingencies, as an exercise, Robin instructs me to make my way around the hospital to locate certain offices and services from a list she prepared. In this search she insists on one provision, I only ask people I do not know outside the occupational therapy department for directions. I am so self-conscious about how I sound; I am reluctant to buttonhole strangers. I tell her I'd rather try to figure things out on my own. She encourages me to discuss this reluctance with my speech therapist and prods me to develop strategies that will help me feel more comfortable when I have to approach others. Robin also suggests that I speak more concisely using short sentences. Later, I speak to Emile about developing these strategies. She will think about it for our next session.

I decide myself that I can increase my ability to interact with others by approaching people on the street or in stores in the vicinity of Rusk and ask them basic questions. For example, where can I find a specific product or service? If I can prepare questions I want to ask in advance and rehearse them in my head, perhaps I will be more confident making inquiries. Maybe it would help me stop stuttering and sputtering and get to the point.

Once the weather improves and I can get down the driveway without Amy helping me, I think I will try this in my own neighborhood. Since my accident, Amy does most of the talking when we're out together. I know this is probably not helping me, but I just feel so embarrassed listening to myself. How am I going to practice the speaking techniques Emile is teaching me, if I don't speak to people?

A Working Weekend

Day 121: I do all my physical therapy exercises and Amy and I both see some improvement. In particular, I am crawling backward, forward, and sideways really well. My balance is improving, at least when my eyes are open. I make some gains in my speech and I do well reading. I more readily focus on problem areas by playing back my recitations on the tape recorder. I know what I am doing wrong and can correct it. I discover that I have particular difficulty with the letter "B" in words, if the" B " is in between letters and not at the beginning of a word. For variety, Amy and I go on the Internet for awhile and I do some other computer work as well. While I am sitting and concentrating on the computer screen my eye sockets begin to hurt. I must remember to take breaks.

Warming up the Engine

Day 122: I wake up feeling pretty wiped out. I have trouble putting together a coherent sentence for Amy. I still persevere with my home therapy exercise program. I can't miss a day. I believe that the more I do them, the closer I come to complete recovery. The physical therapy exercises continue to be challenging. My speech is coming along. Still, I have to admit sometimes I sound like a car engine trying to turn over on a cold day. Every few words I take a breath and begin to hurry the next chunk of words. By the time I finish I am out of breath. Something has to be done.

My speech must also improve in real life situations. It's hard to ask a question when my speech is so fragmented and flat. Most people try to be nice, but I can still see their reactions. I can sense that they're thinking I am weird, inept, or even stupid. Whether it's talking to the girl at the checkout counter, or asking a salesman a question, the look on their faces makes me feel ashamed.

Day 125: Amy and I go to see my physiatrist at Mount Sinai hospital. The physiatrist is fairly satisfied with my progress. She is concerned that my cognitive therapy has not yet started. I tell her I'm trying very hard to get things in order. The physiatrist would also like me to become involved in something other than getting my health back in order, some outside outlet. She suggests that I look into something I'd like to do for fun that doesn't take a tremendous amount of concentration or energy. Her ideas include arts and crafts and taking care of a pet. I am polite and agreeable. The only thing is I am allergic to cats and dogs, and don't really enjoy being around pets. I already have hobbies like photography, but for the present they have to go on hold. I tell her that as the weather gets better it will be easier to venture out and take walks. She thinks this is a good idea, but she would prefer to see me do something outside the apartment with others in a group type setting. I'm not sure about this, but I will think about it.

I tell her that I'm self-conscious about how I speak and the reactions I elicit from others. She says that there are many different types of people out there and I shouldn't prejudge them. Some people are more tolerant than others. Again I agree with her, but I have to add that it is difficult to be on the receiving end of their looks. In my mind, it is very clear that tolerance and understanding are not the first things on their minds. I will, however, take her advice and make more attempts to communicate with strangers and not be as concerned about how I sound. Perhaps this very practice will help me overcome how I feel about talking as well as improve my quality of speech.

A Red Letter Day

Day 126: Barb is challenging me quite a bit in physical therapy, which seems to be paying off. Although I am still having difficulty with balancing, I feel I am slowly making improvements. This is motivating me more and more to continue working toward my goal. My neck and head are pulsating with pain, while there is a ringing in my ears. The scanning exercise seems to be helping, although I need to take it more slowly since the movement causes me to become lightheaded.

Although Robin is on vacation I continue to make strides in OT. I have a replacement therapist who is helping me with reading comprehension. She also challenges me to solve brainteasers. During these exercises my head begins to pound badly. Once I finish them, however, the pain subsides and I am left with a pleasant sense of accomplishment. I seem to perform better with reading comprehension when I respond to multiple-choice questions. It is more difficult to deliver original answers in complete sentences.

I am pleased with my work in speech therapy today. Reading aloud helps to improve my "fluency and intonation." Listening to the tapes of me reading a passage, Emile and I decide together when to take breaths and make stops. In order to help me sound more natural, she marks my home exercise sheets with slashes and underlines to cue me when to make pauses and emphasize syllables. Emile reminds me to practice these skills in actual conversations. Emile does some additional apraxia testing in which I look into a mirror and do different nonverbal movements with my mouth and tongue. I also repeat verbal commands. She provides me with several exercises which I can do each day at home to help me improve the coordination of the movements involved in speaking.

Emile mentions that she may change my therapy from two half hour sessions per week to a single hour session. This will enable her to see me at the beginning of the day. She thinks the change will provide more continuity.

Today is a day to celebrate. At last, I receive a schedule for cognitive therapy. I'm relieved and grateful that this is finally in place. I can finally begin to work on the deficit areas that were uncovered in my assessments. As excited as I am to begin, I'm apprehensive. I'm not sure what to expect. All I do know is that I have things I need to work on, and have the desire to do whatever it takes to improve. I guess these two things are the most important factors to help me be successful in this journey. I have to trust that my therapist is on top of his game and knows just what he needs to do to help me.

Chapter Eight

New Life ... New Strategies

Acceptance

I have been hearing an awful lot about "acceptance," lately. My therapists continually harp on this theme. They may be right, but it's too early for resignation. Improvement is my highest priority, but unfortunately it comes too slowly. The therapists and doctors say that I need to measure my improvement from month to month. Easier said than done! I need to evaluate myself every day. I must live with my condition twenty-four seven. Why not look at myself realistically? I will not allow myself to become a complacent month-to-month guy, but at the same time I have to broaden my perspective and see the big picture.

True Friends

My circle of friends has certainly diminished since October 22, 1999, at least in regard to most people I met and befriended during my years with the Board of Education in New York City. Perhaps those whom I considered friends were not friends at all, only friendly colleagues. I know that people have their own lives to lead, but the truth of the matter is that during these early days of my recovery any phone call or short note from the people at SPARK or my school would be a morale booster and motivator. I was very touched when immediately after my accident I received letters from the students of my institute and the SPARK Program wishing me well. I really appreciated the money collected by teachers and administrators that helped defray some of the cost for the cabs to my many medical appointments. With the initial shock of my accident having worn off, I feel like I am now a distant memory. I am not sure why. Maybe they are uncertain if I am well enough to speak on the phone, or maybe they don't know what to say. They may have nothing to say. Whatever the reason, it doesn't change how I feel at the moment. For the most part, with a few exceptions, the friends that remain closest to me are those friends I made in upstate New York in another life. Every time I hear from them, I get a great emotional boost.

Lost and Alone

I really appreciated receiving so many calls; even at work, from Chris's friends asking how he is doing, how's he feeling. Although Chris isn't comfortable talking on the phone, I could still tell that he was very pleased with the constant calls, cards and best wishes. Too quickly, however, the overflowing phone calls trickle. Only family and true close friends can be depended upon. It's a surprise, how quickly so many familiar voices and faces disappear from our lives, probably wrapped up in their own cares and everyday concerns.

I assure Chris that it doesn't matter that they don't call anymore. It's the two of us that count most. As long as I am holding your hand nothing else matters. Often, I find him staring off into space, maybe deep in thought. I quietly sit down next to him and hold his hand or place my hand softly on his cheek. Then he will always turn to me and smile. The unspoken brings him back to me.

I am so worried that he is slipping away to somewhere where I will not be able to reach him and bring him back. Looking into those baby blue eyes, I do not see my Chris looking back at me. I see only a lost soul trying to find its way, straining to reconnect.

I refuse to settle, this is not as good as it will get. I restrain myself, repress my feelings, and hold on for dear life, surviving. Lost, yes I too am lost. I just don't know what to do to *help bring my Chris back to me. I feel frustrated and so alone as if I am the only woman who is going through this struggle.*

A New Kind of Doctor

Day 133: I meet with my cognitive psychologist, Dr. Mark Herceg, for the first time. He is an outgoing energetic kind of person. From the beginning, he impresses me with his eagerness and determination to help me cope with my challenges. He doesn't try to be the detached MD. He cares and is not afraid to show it. He talks to me almost like a concerned friend even when he asks clinical questions. He gives me material for my binder to keep a record of my cognitive experiences. My journal will still record my reactions, reflections, and experiences in and outside of rehabilitation. There will be a lot of overlap. Rather than concentrating mostly on my outward participatory life, I will also spend time contemplating my inner life.

Mark explains that we will be focusing on improving functions such as increasing my attention span and level of concentration, as well as verbal and mental flexibility.

Today, Mark encourages my verbal flexibility and creativity by having me form as many words as possible from a combination of letters. He will start by giving me pencil and paper tasks with virtually no distractions in the room. He says later on in the month he will introduce some distractions while I am engaged in a task. He has me take breaks every twenty minutes or so to allow my brain to recharge since these tasks and my effort to concentrate takes so much out of me. I am really counting on the cognitive therapy to make a difference.

As my therapy progresses my sense of frustration increases. It seems that the more I become aware of my challenges, the more discouraged I become. I work diligently each day at improving where I am physically, mentally, and emotionally. I try to take advantage of every opportunity to

117

improve as much as possible, but the illuminating and liberating breakthrough still hasn't come.

The Reality of Chris's Injury

The reality of Chris's injury hits me hard when he begins cognitive therapy. His laid back light-hearted personality has changed. He's tense and keeps getting angry with himself and his surroundings. He flares up. He responds with short verbal outburst to the little things I do that he would once have laughed at or simply said, "Oh come on Aim." He tells me about something he is doing in cognitive therapy and I am stunned. Here is a man who could do so many things at the same time having trouble working on the most basic task with the radio playing. He becomes so distracted and frustrated that he cannot do the simplest thing. I now know it is going to be a long hard road back. I also realize that he may not get it all back.

Dinner with Friends

Day 136: I am trying to relearn my socialization skills. I am spending more time with a few close friends, attempting to "normalize" my life as much as possible. It doesn't go that well. When I go out to dinner with my wife and some old friends I find that the noisier the restaurant, the harder it is for me to direct my attention, listen, absorb, and participate in a conversation. All the noise is amplified and the movement is accelerated. What may sound to others like a simple phone ringing in the distance sounds to me like a fire alarm going off inside my head. A person crossing my path as I make my way to a table or to the restroom is a very big deal; it's a sudden and major obstacle. Dishes clattering, people talking and laughing loudly, children screaming and crying, are bombs going off. After a while I can't hear anything. My head starts to ache and my energy is depleted. It just doesn't seem worth the effort. On the other hand, the only way for me to begin to tolerate this type of environment is to expose myself to it. I am going to talk to my therapists about this and see if there might be some alternative.

Day 156: I do seem to do better in more private familiar environments with less happening, less stimulation. Amy and I go to our friend's Larry and Stacey's house for dinner one afternoon. We cook up a nice meal together in the kitchen. Conversation comes fairly easily, despite my speech issues. I do have some difficulties, but Larry and Stacey make adjustments. They turn down the TV when I have trouble filtering it out and headaches threaten. During dinner they put on some relaxing background music that they know I like. Unfortunately, after only a few minutes, I cannot concentrate. I am unable to think with the music on. They quickly turn it off. It doesn't seem to bother them at all, but I hate being the odd man out.

After dinner we watch a video. I like films but I cannot follow it and soon we are saying our goodbyes. I don't realize, at least in the moment, how quickly I tire. In a split second my body and brain suddenly start to rebel. I speak and walk like a zombie. I nearly fall. Larry helps me to the car. As I approach, I feel fatigue setting in and my body ready to collapse. I guess I over did it. I am not ready for "normal" activity. Maybe I am getting ahead of myself. I think I will try to keep better track of how I am doing in similar situations in the future. I have to learn to monitor my fatigue level.

Our Life on Hold

Chris and I loved to go to restaurants, theater, friend's houses, parties, concerts in the park, street fairs, and Sunday mass. Now much of our socializing is on hold. At the beginning of our life with Chris's TBI it did not make any sense to go out. Chris even stayed home when I went to do the laundry. Eventually we do start going to a nearby diner, but this is more of a therapy exercise then a good time. First, he has to rehearse his speech to order the food, constantly flinching at the noise of clattering dishes and the loud exchanges of other customers. He struggles to walk as we exit the diner. It doesn't seem worth it to put him through all of this misery, but his therapists tell me to keep doing what I 'm doing.

The friends we have left, every once and a while, invite us to diner and eventually we accept and agree on a date. Oh, how I miss our outings. Sometimes I feel like a caged bird. I miss seeing my playful happy Chris being the life of the party. He had a natural way about him that just drew people like a magnet. Now he is a lonely guy seated in a corner surrounded by noise and lost in an abyss of I don't know what.

Our friends do their best to make Chris comfortable and don't seem to mind when he asks several times during dinner to turn down the music. Leaving is a struggle too. He becomes so worn out trying to join in and be an active participant, his entire body breaks down and he has difficulty walking. Our friend has to practically carry Chris out to the car. The therapists say putting Chris out there in real life situations will help him. I don't see it. I only see him struggle time after time without any great improvement.

As a result of that dinner, we incorporate a new strategy for socializing. We use his watch with a "count down" timer to remind him to take breaks. No matter where we are we make sure that people know that Chris needs a quiet space where he can lie down and take a breather to restore his energy. I become more and more aware when Chris is showing signs of fatigue. I can see it, even before he realizes he's tired. I keep my eyes open, ever on the alert, always observing everything about Chris to try and protect him from himself.

My Cellophane Cube

I feel like I'm living in a cellophane cube. I can see and hear the world around me, but can't feel or taste it. I press and push against the cellophane wall to reclaim what I once had been, but despite my efforts I am unable to penetrate the wall. As I look through the wall I see my life... my very existence... the true essence of what my life was like before this injury. I can see who I am in relation to others - the supporter, the go to guy, counselor, advisor, son, brother, nephew, cousin, friend, husband and lover. Although I believe I will always have these bonds with friends and family, the equation has changed. They no longer depend upon me; I depend upon them. I'm the one who seeks help and guidance from others. Yes, I do thank God each day for the progress I am making, albeit slow progress measured over months not days or weeks. But my life is now defined by dependence on others, whether it's my wife, my therapists, neurologists, physiatrist, insurance providers, family members and friends, or even my walking cane. I'm no longer an individual, autonomous and self-reliant.

I am struggling with this overwhelming sense of powerlessness. Every ounce of energy I can bring forth is directed to focusing on regaining this power... this independence. As frustrating as it is to only be able to see and hear the other side of this cellophane wall, I thank God I am able to stay focused and goal driven. If I stop believing, I will stop succeeding. I need to believe that I will reclaim myself in the end.

Strategizing

Day 158: During a break in cognitive therapy, Mark, sensing my frustration and an overriding need to finish the assigned task in the assigned time, urges me to "take it easy." He is afraid that I will become so mentally worn out that all my abilities will be compromised. He knows that I mentally beat myself up all the time, that I'm in his words an "emotional minefield." He tells me that we will develop strategies together to help me prevent emotional and cognitive overload.

New Strategies

Cognitive therapy provides Chris, actually the both of us, with strategies to use in everyday life. Once he explains some of these to me we begin to incorporate them into our daily lives. For starters, I always have an extra pair of earplugs in my purse and a couple in the car in case he forgets his. If we go out to eat I have him rehearse what he is going to say before a waiter comes to take our order. We plan every outing with break times and always carry reserves of water. In some ways my life resembles the life of a woman with a small child. Instead of making sure I have all necessary items in a diaper bag, I check the tote to make sure I have a wide variety of new necessities.

Testing Myself

Day 168: In today's cognitive therapy session with Mark I am at last gaining insight into how my brain works and the parameters of my injury. I ask Mark why it takes me so long to process information. His explanation is simple. The information and processing center in my brain was affected by the blow to my head. As difficult as it is to hear about another area of my brain that is malfunctioning, it helps me make sense of my condition. It is important, as well as scientifically interesting to me. I think that the more I understand about what is going on inside my brain, the more I feel empowered to work on my improvement. Putting a name to things makes what's going on more tangible and less overwhelming.

Amy and I have begun to take longer and longer drives in the jeep we borrowed from my brother Billy. The jeep has been a great help in shopping, getting our laundry done, and ferrying me to doctors. I am building up the time that I'm able to handle riding in a car. It's an incremental process. I'm now up to about an hour or so in the vehicle before I need to stop. Of course, conditions like the speed of the car and the nature of the traffic must also be taken into account. I seem to do best on "the open

122

road," when there are not so many distractions and SUV's zooming by me. I really hope I can drive again, since I love being behind the wheel and miss it terribly. Amy has been a good sport about doing all the driving, but I know that she'd rather be the passenger just as I would rather be the driver.

Primary Driver

Before Chris's injury, he did 99% of the driving. I was the navigator when we traveled; reading maps comes easily to me. After the accident I became the primary driver. Not only do we have to take a lot of breaks for Chris to rest while traveling upstate, but also for me since prolonged driving wears me out. I am trying to adjust, but it is tough. I also have to be the navigator, referring to a map and looking for the signs as I drive. I miss just sitting back, looking at the countryside, and singing to the radio.

No Laughing Matter

My short-term memory continues to be a big challenge for me. Lately, I am trying to be more active at home. I am beginning to cook, clean, and do a few dishes. I have big problems remembering. If Amy, for instance, asks me to get something in the pantry while we're in the kitchen, by the time I take several steps toward it, I forget what she asks me to get. It is so discouraging and humiliating to walk about 10 to 12 ft. and not remember something so simple. It's not as though she asks for several items at a time. She asks for one thing at a time!

What I do now is repeat what she asks me to get, and try not to talk to her about anything else until I come back with the item. This actually has helped somewhat, but often I find myself on auto pilot, and go over to the refrigerator first, which is also in the pantry, no matter what I intend to get. I try to shake off my errors and laugh at myself.

One of the things I do in the kitchen is no laughing matter. Several times, I leave the water running and the gas on without realizing it. One time I knew something was wrong right away when I singed the hair on my arm. Another time I took a pot off the burner and forgot to turn off the gas. I use to regularly leave the oven on, but now I put a magnet on the oven door to remind me when the oven is on. This visual cue has been helpful in reducing kitchen accidents.

My short-term memory and attention/concentration difficulty has also made it hard to deal with my medication schedule. I have a watch alarm, which helps me remember, but after it beeps and I reset the alarm for the next round of pills, I forget that I am supposed to retrieve the medicine and end up looking into space. I am constantly thrown off course, distracted by any sound, inside or outside the house.

Day 172: In occupational therapy, Robin is helping me develop a strategy for popping my pills on schedule. I now have a pillbox with separate compartments with the dosage times written on it. When my alarm goes off to alert me to take my medication I re-set it for five minutes later as a failsafe measure, in case I get distracted in between and forget to take the medicine. The whole alarm drill is a little cumbersome, but it works most of the time.

Sticky Notes

Thank goodness for sticky notes. They are a real lifesaver. Countless times, I walk into the bathroom only to find water still running in the sink or over the sides on the floor. I come home from work and I see an open flame on our gas range or even sniff smoke. Chris needs reminders to compensate for his memory lapses and a well-placed sticky on the bathroom mirror can help Chris remember to "turn off water." Chris and I put up notes all over the house reminding him to "take a break," "drink some water," "brush your teeth," and to "eat your lunch." I often change the color and shapes of the sticky notes and move them around so he does not get too used to them. I want them to constantly stick out. Fortunately for me, Chris was always super observant. Even before the accident he could walk into a room and tell me any item that is missing or moved. I think this helps him because he notices the different colors and is particularly aware of change. His feelers are out; he reads the notes and acts on them.

He gets very frustrated when I ask him, "Don't you remember this or I told you to…" I start to write summaries of our discussions in a calendar to jog his memory and help him look back and confirm that we did discuss a particular subject.

My Myriad Problems

Another of my myriad problems is sequencing; putting things in their correct order, whether it's getting dressed or preparing a bowl of cereal. When it comes to stuff more complicated, like the unending paper work for the hospital or insurance company, I simply can't do it. Something that I was able to do blind folded before is completely beyond me. I cannot help attacking myself. I feel so stupid. I have done these things a million times.

I feel so alone when things get messed up and confused. I start to talk to myself… if only I walked through that door a split second earlier or a split second later on that October morning. I realize that this is futile, even self-defeating, but it is the way I feel. This is a real frustrating time for me. Although I try to stay positive and goal oriented most of the time, I have my moments when I lose hope or just try to wish my accident and injury away. Maybe my cognitive psychologist is right about talking with a psychotherapist. I don't think that I need to go to see anyone. My emotional life is okay considering my situation. Still, the more I see how I beat myself up and get down about things the more I think it may be helpful. I guess I'll see what arrangements Mark can make for me and give it a try.

Applying my Therapy

Day 177: Finally, the weekend is here! Amy and I go for another drive. For a change, I am going to be the navigator reading directions from a sheet of paper. Amy keeps her eyes on the road. For some reason, I goof up the directions. Maybe I skip a line, which causes us to go in a totally wrong direction. I get very tense and upset. Amy is also a little nervous herself. She doesn't have a clue what happened. After settling down and regrouping, Amy and I figure out where I went wrong and get back on the right track for our destination. As a result of this petty mishap I am totally exhausted.

This is just another example of neglecting to utilize the strategies I learn in occupational therapy with Robin. I could anticipate these problems by going over directions in advance, focusing on key words, or underlining the material so it is easier to scan. My cognitive psychologist believes that I need to be prompted to use these strategies because I have difficulty generalizing from one situation to another. It may sound kind of funny, but it's hard to remember these strategies in the moment and utilize them. It is much easier to realize the right thing to do in retrospect when I'm sitting back and analyzing what just what went wrong. I just have to get better at remembering to take a minute to figure out what strategies I can use to help me in given situations before I start a task.

Taking Breaks

One of the things I am remembering to do is to take breaks when my head starts hurting. Usually, after concentrating for about 20 to 30 minutes my head starts to hurt, which lets me know it's time for a break. By stopping what I'm doing at that time I can usually avoid crashing. Sometimes I don't think about taking a break and I really pay for it later. What I am trying to do now is to set my watch alarm for 20 to 30 minutes after I begin a task. The alarm beeps, reminding me to take a short break.

Handling Distractions

Day 179: In speech therapy the emphasis is on auditory and reading comprehension tasks. This entails following multi-step directions and note taking while completing reading tasks and listening to oral presentations. I also work on attention and concentration. Emile turns on the radio and opens the door while I am doing a paper and pencil exercise. Every therapist is aware of my attention and concentration difficulty and they all give me these types of exercises. It's a struggle to attend to the tasks at hand when it becomes noisy. I become totally frustrated when I can't concentrate enough to complete a task because of the distractions. Mark says it's hard to block out the distractions because the part of the brain that helps filter out noise has been affected. I guess this makes sense. I hope it becomes easier over time.

In addition to "generalizing," Robin also has me working on sustaining and shifting attention in occupational therapy. She interrupts me while I am doing a pencil and paper task and asks me a couple of questions, or talks to me about something outside of what I am doing. I have to force myself to shift my attention back to my original task and pick up where I left off. This is easier said than done. After I become distracted I have trouble following or even understanding the directions. Between the usual noise and activity going on in the outpatient room and Robin interrupting me, I get tied up in knots. Hopefully, I will do better in these types of environments down the road. I will have to wait and see.

Shopping as Therapy

Whether or not I actually attend formal therapy at NYU/Rusk, every day is loaded with therapy challenges. Today, Day 180 is no exception. Amy and I are off to Stop and Shop, our neighborhood grocery store to pick up a few items.

Stop and Shop is a large grocery store with very bright florescent lights and highly waxed floors. The bright florescent lights have a strong impact on my eye sockets, which begin to ache when I am exposed to them. The glare of the lights off the waxed floor adds insult to injury. I have my sun clips over my glasses to help reduce the invading light. The store is busy and I feel overwhelmed as I stroll down each aisle. I feel like retreating to the car to the reassuring sound of silence, yet I realize that hanging in there will benefit me in the end.

My cane is placed in the cart and I take charge of rolling the cart following behind Amy. As we finish shopping in one aisle Amy asks me to go and find a bottle of ketchup. She brings me to the proper aisle and watches me as I begin my search. Cane in hand, I turn away from Amy and walk slowly and deliberately down the aisle scanning the shelves from left to right and from top to bottom. I take about three strides and realize I have forgotten what Amy asked me to find. I come to a dead stop and try to think back to what Amy asked me to get, but it doesn't come to me. I am trying so hard to successfully accomplish this task but it seems that the bright lights, shinny floors, loud noise of customers chattering, rolling carts and advertising announcements blaring out over the PA system, the memory knocks right out of my consciousness.

I turn around and thankfully find Amy is still watching me. I'm sure she can read my feelings of frustration and embarrassment. I feel beaten. I approach Amy and ask her to remind me what the item is she asked me to get. She tries to cue me in hopes that it jogs a memory, but this doesn't happen. She tells me again that I am looking for the ketchup and encourages me to use the strategy of repeating the item to myself over and over until I find it. I walk away very slowly, again scanning each side of the isle repeating the word Ketchup...Ketchup... Ketchup. I am determined to redeem myself. I am half way down the aisle when the ketchup section catches my eye. I make my way over to the ketchup and select the bottle of choice. I am thrilled and cannot wait to tell Amy of my success. I turn to head back down the aisle and see Amy in the distance. As I get closer I can barely contain my excitement, and shout to Amy, "I found it Amy, I found it!"

We return home and I take a short break while Amy puts away the perishable items. She eventually calls me into the kitchen and asks if I would put a can on a shelf in the pantry that she can't reach. Without hesitation I say, "sure", and bring the item into the pantry with Amy following behind me. As I reach up to place the can on the shelf I feel my arm start to tremble and my body falling backwards. Amy is right there to provide support and urge me on. As I bring my arm down after putting the can on the shelf, my legs begin to tremble and I start to lose my balance. Amy secures me with a big hug and tells me how great I am doing. When we speak later about our day it becomes clear to me that Amy is always trying to apply in daily life the strategies and skills the therapists are helping me learn in therapy. This is no surprise to me. What is a surprise is that I don't seem to realize it in the moment. I really thought she needed my help. Little did I know she was helping me.

Shopping

I work on strengthening Chris's memory when we go shopping. The first time shopping, I ask him to retrieve three things. It breaks my heart that as soon as he turns away to look for the first item he has to turn back to me to refresh his memory. He just can't retain them. Next I ask him to get only one item. He again turns around, heads towards the aisle, quickly returning to me only seconds later to ask me what he should get. I hope I can get through my own frustration and be patient with Chris. I repeat the item to him, but this time I ask him to keep repeating what it is in his head until he finds it. I follow him until he locates the item. I notice people staring at Chris as he scans the aisles from left to right from one end of the store to the other. He looks so determined, repeating the item out loud as he searches. No doubt, they are listening too. At first I eye these people with distaste, and then I simply ignore them. Thankfully Chris is totally oblivious to their stares and remarks. He is just focused on completing his quest. He looks so happy and proud as he retrieves a bottle of ketchup. It doesn't matter to me that people are gawking and mumbling comments. What matters, is that Chris is using a valuable strategy. Although I understand how important it is for Chris to challenge his memory, perhaps for a future shopping adventure I will encourage Chris to write down a couple of items on a piece of paper to help with his memory challenges...just another strategy to pull out of my little bag of tricks.

If Chris's energy level is still high when we leave the store I intentionally go down the wrong side of the parking lot so Chris has to cross the median to get to the car. Usually there is some type of obstacle he has to struggle with. It may be a little gravel or pebbles, wood chips, or a grassy hill. I continually try to raise that bar to challenge him.

When I put the groceries away I have to use a footstool to put the can goods, paper products, and cleaning items on the top shelves of the kitchen pantry. When it is time to prepare dinner I ask Chris to reach for one of the items on the top shelf. Sure I can get up on the footstool, but I want Chris to practice reaching. At first he is reluctant to reach for the item as it is too high and asks me to get out the footstool and get it myself. I ask him to try and reach it for me. He cautiously lifts himself up on his toes while I hold on to the back of his belt to steady him. The first time isn't very pretty. With the item in hand he shakes violently as he comes down. I hold on tight to help him keep his balance. He is totally exhausted and irritated with me for putting him into this position. What bothers him the most is that such a simple task is a big drain on his energy. Helping him to the couch his weight almost overwhelms me. Still, I am determined to continue this exercise believing that the more he challenges himself with difficult tasks the more likely it is he will accomplish them. Over time, all the effort pays off. Chris is not only willing to retrieve items from the top shelf, he is also eager to help put groceries away.

Easter in Utica

Day 183: Its Easter weekend, a time of resurrection and renewal. I pray for it to happen to me. Amy, my brothers Paul and Bill and I drive up together to see mom and dad in Utica. At the outset of the visit the mood is light and convivial, family jokes and a lot of ribbing. Later, as the stresses of a long ride get to me, my own mood turns somber. It is wonderful to see my family. I haven't seen them for a while and I miss being home, but I still feel out of it.

I spoke with all my therapists about the trip home. We developed strategies in advance for a whole range of contingencies. By anticipating what might occur when I go home I will be better able to adapt to situations. It doesn't turn out that way. I guess there are some things you just can't prepare for.

The first night home I sit down with some of my family at the dining room table. There are a lot of different things going on around me at once. Some of my family are watching television and joking around with each other in the living room. Amy, my sister, mom, and Aunt Evie are doing dishes in the kitchen and catching up on weddings, christenings, and engagements. Meanwhile dad, one of my brothers and I are discussing the state of the world, which seems to be in as bad shape as me.

If the house were as grand as the amount of love the family has for each other, the buzzing activity would not cause me a problem, but the house is small and everyone in my family loves to talk and is excited to see each other. There is so much going on at one time that I can't focus in on the table talk. I remember to ask my dad and my brother to move their chairs closer to me so I am able to concentrate and block out the static. This doesn't work, so I try putting in earplugs to reduce the distractions. At one point I am leaning in so close to my dad I am inches away from his face. This is an ordinary family get together, nothing out of the ordinary, but for me it is monumentally exhausting. It is impossible to concentrate any longer. Everything enters my brain at full volume and I cannot control any of it. The floodgates in my brain are open; everything is rushing in at one time. Later, I start to look at the TV. My Aunt Edie talks through the commercials. I am having trouble following her with the babble of the TV huckster in my head. I explain my problem to her and she solves it immediately by muting the TV while we talk during the commercials. I guess it pays off to be direct and candid.

High Mass and High Decibel Music

Day 185: It's Easter Sunday and Amy and I go with mom and dad to mass at Our Lady of Lourdes. As beautiful and inspiring as it is to hear the choir sing on such a special occasion, the high decibel music is too much for me to bear. I appreciate the power and glory of the symphonic instruments and the harmony of the large choir, but it is just too loud. The sounds of the horns are piercing my ears. I have, thankfully, remembered my earplugs and put them in. It reduces some of the intensity, but the kettle drums and the high-pitched organ notes go right through me. My head is pounding. It's a shame. I enjoy this music so much.

I am having quite a bit of trouble with my balance. There are too many people moving around me in different directions during communion. By the end of Mass I am exhausted and wait with my family while the parishioners make their way out of the church. I try to relax as I look around the church reveling in its beauty and grandeur. Finally, the bustle of parishioners leaving the church is replaced with serenity. I return home and go straight to bed until it is time for Easter dinner.

Home for Easter

It is a joint decision to go home for Easter. Unlike Christmas, Chris is able to ride in the car for more extended periods without a break. It is great to see him able to interact more easily with his family; those crucial strategies Chris learned at Rusk make a big difference. Throughout our stay, he takes his breaks and rests in a quiet room to retrieve his energy. He is obviously more verbal and even laughs a couple of times. When the television is too loud I am glad to hear him speak up and request that it be turned down. During some points in the day I am thrilled to see my old Chris coming back.

Easter Mass has always been a deeply moving spiritual experience for both of us. For Chris, it is now a physical ordeal. The choir we both belonged to and loved still sings beautifully, but for Chris it is simply a loud jarring noise as he struggles to get through the mass. It is an effort for him to take communion and he has a difficult time getting back to our pew. I want to walk beside him to be that shoulder to lean on, but his stubborn independence speaks loud and clear. We wait until everyone has left the church before we make our way out to the car. Back home as I help Mom prepare the Easter feast, Chris sleeps, sleeps, and sleeps some more.

Worn Out

Day 186: The next morning I have trouble getting out of bed and even making my way to the bathroom. I have a lot of balance problems. My speech is indistinct, slow and halting. I guess I am just worn out. I stay in bed resting and doing all the relaxation exercises I learned in therapy. I don't leave the bedroom until about 2:00 p.m. The rest of the day the house is quieter, but I find it very difficult to re-energize for any length of time. This is so frustrating for me. Clearly, this visit was just too long and too busy for me at this stage. I think about how I might do in a work environment with many more people around me. It is depressing.

Waiting for the Subtitles to Appear

Day 189: Back at Rusk I tell Mark, my cognitive psychologist that it still takes so long for me to process information when someone is talking to me. Sometimes it's like I'm watching a foreign film waiting for subtitles to appear so I can understand what the other person is saying. I'm always a step or two behind. This is much worse for me in noisy and frenetic environments. Mark suggests the obvious, that I ask people to slow down when they are talking to me.

Coming to Terms

Robin, my occupational therapist, again talks to me about accepting where I am in the recovery process. In the past, I wouldn't think of it. Acceptance would only interfere with the determination I need to return to my old self. I'm much more comfortable accepting "for the time being," "for the right now," as opposed to accepting that this is the way it's going to be forever. Perhaps, if I start to accept myself in the here and now regardless of the future, I can begin to recover emotionally. I have moments when I do okay, but then there are other times when I am depressed and life is too difficult for me. I guess the more I begin to accept where I am right now, the more able I will be to work on other significant issues; both physical and psychological.

Robin emphasizes to me that my current condition has nothing to do with my level of intelligence. It's about getting information processed up to speed and being able to concentrate on tasks. She said that my information and processing center needs work. I find myself getting very frustrated when I try to concentrate and need to work on being more patient. I guess things will begin to fall into place at their own pace. Maybe I have to keep my fighting instincts in check a bit. I just want so much to get better that I think by force of will, I can make it happen.

Chapter Nine

Integrating Back Into Life

Getting to Know Myself

I hope that in the course of my journal I get to know myself better, become more aware of my inner life and inner struggle, and gain greater insight into the whole rehab process. Maybe at some time in the future I can share this experience with others who find themselves in a similar situation. Perhaps sharing my journey with others will help them navigate their own journeys of discovery.

The Bureaucracy of Recovery

I finally make the decision to transfer the management of my case to Dr. Richter, the physiatrist at NYU Rusk. I suppose it's best to have all my physicians at the same hospital so every therapy can be coordinated, but I still feel a sentimental attachment to the caring staff at Mount Sinai who helped me take my first steps after my injury. The new arrangement will expedite communication between my therapists, the doctor, and the all-important insurance company. In the past, I lost out on therapy due to misunderstandings between the medical bureaucracy and the insurance bureaucracy. Any trip in and around the city is a full-scale struggle for me, and to make that trip for nothing was a deep disappointment and a shock to my whole system.

Day 193: Mark, my cognitive psychologist, is encouraging me to join the cognitive remediation group that is beginning soon. It is a group of high functioning professionals who, like me, have suffered a brain injury. Of course, I am rearing to get involved, but it's the usual story; I am waiting for a green light from the insurance company. Although I think it will be helpful to interact with a group of people like myself who really can relate to what I am going through, I'm concerned that too much stimulation might occur with so many people engaged in a group. I am afraid of losing my focus and concentration when there is so much to follow. I also hope that I will not have too much trouble keeping up with the group. I am now better equipped to maintain my energy level in social situations, but I eventually wear out, losing my capacity to speak, walk and think. I guess I will just have to see how it goes.

I speak with Mark about group meetings for family members of the brain injured. I worry about Amy's emotional health, since she doesn't have a real outlet to vent her concerns and frustrations. She certainly has her own thoughts and questions about caring for and helping a brain injured person that she would love to share with others in the same situation. Mark promises to keep her in mind when, and if, a family group gets off the ground.

I meet for the first time with Dvorah, my new psychotherapist. She works with many clients with TBI. Dvorah is very direct with a New Yorker's sense of humor. I like her. Today, I discuss with her all the things that happened on my visit upstate for Easter. We talk about some strategies to help prevent some difficult situations in the future. She asks me what I could have done differently to make things easier. We talk about calling ahead before a visit to inquire about what's exactly going to happen to determine if it will be too much for me, and if not, what special preparations can be made.

Jumping Higher

Day 196: Cognitive therapy is very challenging today. Mark continues to raise the bar and I have to jump higher. It's tough emotionally, but that is the only way to make progress. The battleship and bull's-eye exercises test my cognitive

138

flexibility and frustration level. At times I want to scream and throw up my hands, but I desire above everything to conquer the task put before me. I think it through again and again, coming up with fresh strategies. Unfortunately, much to my chagrin, I am still unable to figure out these puzzles. Mark emphasizes that the exercises are not only about correct answers. What counts is my thought processes and overall approaches and their applicability to other situations. I have always played by the rules, but I play to win. His comment offers no consolation.

In occupational therapy, Robin works on developing strategies to help me improve my short-term memory. These techniques are still in the trial and error stage, but I think they will help. It is a pleasant surprise to actually remember to use some strategies learned in rehab. One night, I am proofreading something for Amy and automatically take a blank piece of paper to reduce the stimuli on the page. I also read the material twice to be sure I understand what I am reading. It is great to do something real outside of therapy and have success through the use of the strategies I am learning.

A Surprise Performance

Every day since my accident I pass my piano on my way from one room to the other. Using every ounce of energy just to concentrate on getting from the living room to the bathroom I hardly have any left or even desire to sit down and play. Still, it always beckons to me. Today, Day 198, Amy changes all that. I am sitting on the couch in the living room and Amy comes in and kneels down beside me. She asks me if I want to try and play the piano. She looks so eager to have me try that I agree. We make our way over to the piano. Amy helps me settle myself on the piano bench and raises the piano key cover. I just stare at the keys. I am going over and over in my mind what it is I need to do. Where do my fingers go on the keyboard? Where is middle C? How do I even place my fingers to play a chord? What songs do I even know how to play? It is all a big blank. Amy suggests that I play one of her favorite songs after I tell her I can't think of any. I don't tell her about all the things that keep rolling around in my head.

Finally, I place my right hand on the keyboard and attempt to strike a note... a chord... something to produce sound. I am concentrating with all my might. I want to play this song for Amy but my brain won't talk to my fingers. Amy tenderly places her hand over mine and together we strike my first chord. It doesn't sound anything like the chord playing in my mind. My body begins to shake and my head begins to tingle. I am done...end of experiment. Amy seems happy that I try to play, but I am sure she is wondering if I will ever be able to play the piano again. I don't blame her; I am thinking the same thing myself.

A few weeks later Amy hears a song on the Rosie O'Donnell show that she likes and decides to purchase the CD. It is a Celtic music CD that includes several beautiful relaxing ballads on it. She makes me promise to learn to play one of the songs on the CD when I feel up to it.

Gradually, I am making progress each day re-training my fingers, ear, and brain to play the piano and decide to make an attempt to learn this special song for Amy. It will be a small way to thank her for everything she does for me and all that she has been through. After listening to the song several times I head over to the piano to pick out notes on the keyboard. Much to my surprise I am able to play the melodic line of the first 15 seconds of the song with my right hand. It isn't perfect, but it doesn't have to be. I keep on going over this part of the song until I feel I have a good handle on it. I play for about ten minutes. This is a huge accomplishment for me. I carefully get off the piano bench, stand up, and slowly make my way back to the couch where I soon fall fast asleep. When Amy comes home I never mention that I am learning this song for her. My goal is to surprise her when I finish.

After about a month of several mid-afternoon practice sessions, the time has come to surprise Amy. I call her into the piano room and ask her to sit down next to me. I start to play the beginning of that Celtic song she loves, or at least my version of it. As I strike the last chord I look up at Amy and see tears in her eyes. She is so happy. Her eyes tell the whole story. When I finish we hug. I hold her in my arms as she cries some more. I am just thankful to be able to present this gift to Amy.

My Maestro

It worries me that Chris's finger dexterity is so poor and his coordination is so compromised. I persuade him to sit at the piano and try to play a little music. I remembered reading an article, I don't know where, showing how piano playing could be therapeutic for people with arthritis so I took it a step further. Maybe it could help Chris move his fingers more easily.

He sits very stiffly with his fingers on the keys ready to strike a chord, and nothing happens. I start thinking that maybe he forgot how to play. Seeing the confusion and determination on his face, I gently place my hand over his and press one finger at a time to strike the notes and then press all three fingers at once to produce a chord. We strike the chord and that is it. He is done. I have to help him up from the piano bench and back to the couch where he falls asleep. I'll try again another day. I am not going to give up hope on Chris's wonderful piano playing. With a little patience on my part, I am sure my maestro will return. A month later, I come home from work and hear a lovely song on a television show. The next day I purchase the CD with that beautiful track and ask Chris if he could learn to play that song for me. He doesn't think he can, but I ask him to try. Several weeks later when I come home from work he says he has something to show me, but not to expect too much. He starts playing the first couple of bars from the song on the cd and I am so moved that tears come to my eyes. He secretly has been working on this song for me. What an amazing gift. My maestro has returned.

The Baptism

Day 219: The weather is mild and I actually look forward to the long drive to Lowville, N.Y., where Amy and I are participating in a baptism ceremony. We are godparents for her stepbrother Paul and his wife Dahlia's daughter, Glen Morgan. We are only going to stay for the church service. I am not up to going to the family picnic that follows. As much as I enjoy good times with the people I love, I know I can't handle it. I am proud to be a godparent and revere this rite of passage, but all the sounds echoing through the church wear me out. Being around this many people in a large public building distracts and drains me. The giggling sound of young children playing with their dad's car keys as they hammer on the wooden pews, and people talking to each other during the homily, make it difficult to concentrate and participate.

After we leave the church we decide to stop by Amy's sister and brother-in-law's house before heading back to Utica. After a short visit we say our goodbyes to Mike and Anita, but as we are leaving Amy's two older sister's show up at the house for a surprise visit. Amy is so happy to see them, so after a quick glance to each other I give her the, "Ok, let's stay a little longer" nod. Amy really doesn't get the chance to see her family that often, so if I can make it just a little longer I know it will mean so much to her. As happy as I am to see them, they are a little loud and too high-spirited for my vulnerable condition. My whole system begins to break down. As I feel my energy begin to ebb, I quickly hobble out of the room. I retreat to another part of the house to talk with my brother-in-law, Mike. Unfortunately, Amy's two sisters follow me out. No escape! I decide to retreat to the bathroom for a cognitive time out. While I am in the bathroom I lay down my own strategy. I will visit with Mike who is now in the backyard. By the time Amy and I leave I am completely wiped out. I know I am pushing myself, but I also know Amy enjoys being around her sisters. I am able to sleep in the car on the way to my parents' house. It is a chance to regroup.

Becoming Godparents

We are asked to be godparents for my stepbrother's child. We both have mixed feelings about it. I immediately think of the event, dressing up, seeing family and friends, the reception, the whole special occasion, the fun. Chris thinks about the formal role of godparent. Could we fulfill our duties and responsibilities as godparents should anything happen to Glen Morgan's parents? I didn't even think about this. I speak to my stepbrother and his wife and explain our concerns. They understand, but insist that all contingencies are provided for and they are sure that we are equipped in ways that count the most to guide and take care of their child. Chris feels much better after their vote of confidence.

After the baptism we do not go to the reception but stop by my sister's house to say hello. It is a nice quiet visit until my two other sisters drop by. Overjoyed to see them I forget about Chris and fall into the cackling, laughing, chiding relationship I have with my sisters. I forget all about the strategies to keep Chris on an even keel. When I realize that Mike, my sister's husband, has taken Chris outside for some peace and quiet, I return to my protective mode and ask my sisters to quiet down.

On the way home I apologize to Chris, but he is already so fatigued I can't really discuss the matter further. I decide that it would have to wait another day. I do resolve in the future to be more of an advocate for Chris and to keep all these crucial strategies in mind to help him. I learn a valuable lesson today.

Billy Wants his Brother Back

Day 221: Driving back home to New Jersey my brother Billy tells me how well I am doing. I thank him and reply that there are still some "humps" to get over. He acknowledges that I still have "a lot of work to do" and then bursts out, "I just want my brother back." He is making a powerful statement. I respond succinctly, "I want me back too, Billy, and I'm working on it." I know, and he knows, that it's not clear how much I will get back, but we both know that I'm going to do everything in my power to get as much of my old self back as possible.

He proceeds to tell me about a dance student of his who suffered a traumatic brain injury. He says her symptoms are similar to mine, and that after a year or so she now feels "pretty much back to normal." I say, "That's wonderful for her, and hopefully I'll get there too." We both agree that we have to give it time.

I Want My Husband Back

I sympathize with Bill's comment, "I just want my brother back." I want my husband back! Maybe my reaction is selfish, but I live with Chris every day and will live with his condition for the rest of my life. I have to deal with so many changes every day. Family and friends see Chris occasionally or speak to him over the phone. Only then do they get a glimpse of what I deal with every day and it's easy to forget his true situation. I suppose his brother and other family will also have to deal with this for the rest of their lives, but not to the extent that I will. I also want the old Chris back, but the reality is that he will likely never be the exact "old Chris" again.

A Wish to be Productive

Day 222: Amy and I see Dr. Richter today. Things go very well. I feel comfortable about the transfer from my other physiatrist. We also talk about my future. I'm interested in being

144

a productive member of the work force again and hope that there will be opportunities available to me. I'm too young and not rich enough to retire at this point in my life. I want to work and be a part of society.

He informs me that people with my type of injury sometimes return to work, but that I may not return to the exact type of work I did before. He's very knowledgeable about the New York City Board of Education and the school environment. He concludes by saying: "We'll cross this bridge when we get to it." I share with Dr. Richter how my head and eye socket pain increases when I try to read and how the words seem to jump off the page. I also tell him that when I walk, what I see are images that constantly flicker, similar to watching an 8mm film. Dr. Richter talks to us about a referral to the State University of New York (SUNY) Optometric Center head trauma unit for an eye exam. He also refers me to the Rusk Vestibular Rehabilitation Unit for an evaluation.

Book Talk

Day 226: I hear from my grade school friend, John Gray, this month. He calls to thank me for the congratulations card I sent him for earning his master's degree. Great to hear from him. He offers me some words of encouragement adding to my desire to continue the grueling work of recovery. He also urges me to consider sharing "my story" with others, either verbally or in writing. He says that there is a big need for stories of inspiration and hope. I tell him that other people have encouraged me to write about this experience. I'm not sure what's involved in writing a book, but maybe I'll look into it. Right now I'm just concentrating on getting better.

Pacing

Pacing.... Pacing... Pacing! This is the central theme for the past few weeks. I am conscientiously working on being steady and modulated. I used to be able to do several things at the same time very well. I would always be working or thinking about work or some project, no matter where I was or what I was doing, I was always thinking, planning, mulling things over. I never stopped working, even when I was sleeping. Now, suddenly I'm being encouraged to pace myself, by taking breaks and doing one thing at a time. This is a whole new concept for me.

I tell my therapists that I can pace myself, that it is a breeze. However, it is one of the biggest hurdles to get over. I have been on autopilot for so many years, my nose to the grindstone, working to get ahead, always striving to do my best at whatever I do. Now I realize that I know very little about pacing myself. I certainly don't believe I have this pacing thing under control yet, but I will continue working on it.

My big problem is that in order to pace myself I have to know how long I will be involved in the task I'm doing. This is particularly true when the tasks rely on my cognitive skills, such as reading, writing, and pencil and paper exercises. Often I become so engrossed in what I'm trying to accomplish that I totally forget how long I am working. Then the fatigue sets in and the headaches start. I try to set my watch to beep every 20 minutes, but the alarm itself proves problematic. Finally, Amy and I go out and buy a watch with a special alarm on it. This helps a great deal. I set the alarm for twenty minutes. It counts down and then beeps repeatedly. This works great as long as I remember to reset the alarm, which is easier said than done.

This whole pacing thing comes to a head during a cognitive psychology appointment on June 15th, Day 238, when Mark puts his foot down and insists I take regular breaks, although the task takes only twenty minutes to complete.

Working for twenty minutes on a task is not normally a big deal, but since my injury a 20 minute task feels like I am pulling an all nighter. The fatigue and headaches I get are so bad I just want to curl up and end it all.

To help with this pacing thing, Mark has me do an exercise. The goal is for me to remember to take breaks during my task, and not to worry about getting the answers right or completing the task. It's a sort of puzzle that involves spotting objects in a drawing that didn't exist in America 200 years ago. I am to circle them on the paper. I look for as many as I can. It seems easy at first, but soon I am biting my lip in frustration. It is hard enough to find the objects in the picture since many of them are disguised within other objects, but it is another thing to determine what actually existed 200 years ago. This really gets me irritated. I am so distracted that I lose my concentration. I cannot clearly recall which items belong to which time period. This is what really bothers me. I get very angry with myself for not being able to complete the assignment, despite Mark's initial statement that the goal of the exercise has nothing to do with the correctness of my answers or even finishing.

I am really very depressed. This is grade school stuff and I can't complete it successfully or remember basic information. I let it all out. Mark thinks I am trashing myself. I agree with him. Again he tells me that the point of the exercise is for me to learn to take breaks, which could speed up my progress. Finishing is not the point.

I pride myself on finishing whatever I start and it irks me not to. It probably goes back to when my brothers and I were young and we were working with my dad on the house, both inside and outside. My brothers and I worked by my dad's side until the job was done. There was no stopping. Many a night we spent with flashlights and umbrellas in hand waiting to get the sign from my dad that we were finished.

I tell Mark that in many ways I believe that this work ethic is so ingrained that it is hard not to fall into this trap even under these circumstances, but that I will work on it. Mark says that I don't realize how well I am doing. I know I am doing better, but I'm not satisfied with where I am. I work so hard to get better because I'm afraid of standing still or even retrogressing. I guess I'm thinking a lot about how I was before and how I am now. I just feel as though my brain is in quicksand. The more I struggle, the harder it becomes to think.

Mark indicates to me that I've got a lot of things to discuss in psychotherapy with Dvorah. I confide to him that I usually process those meaningful events in my life on my own. This isn't intentional, I just sometimes don't think about discussing them when I'm in psychotherapy. Something happens, time passes, and it's not an issue anymore when I get to therapy. Mark suggests I write things down to bring to each session. Maybe I don't process these experiences as well as I think. This may explain why I continue having these terrible reactions when things don't run smoothly. I assume these are natural reactions, considering everything that has happened. I will start taking notes and see what therapy can do.

Interpersonal Pacing

Day 243: Mark encourages me to work on what he calls "interpersonal pacing." For example, if someone asks how therapy is going, I should respond with a reasonable amount of information without so much detail. He notices that I tend to "run on" even when he asks me the simplest questions. Maybe I strain so hard to answer so exactingly, because knowing my own limitations, I tend to overcompensate in an effort to be clear. Anyway, it leads to a cognitive overload and my head is soon pounding. I become very fatigued and frustrated. Still, I am not really aware when I am obsessing about details.

Mark and I work on setting priorities as a way to help me establish and accomplish goals. He gives me a series of several paper and pencil tasks that focus on making priority determinations. These are cognitive trial runs for real life situations. I take some of these exercises to complete at home.

Lunch with Mario

Day 247: Mario, my buddy and counseling colleague from my school, comes and visits me in New Jersey. It is nice to see him. It gets me outside of myself. We go to the Olive Garden restaurant for lunch. The food tastes great, but the music is way too loud. I assert myself, asking the waiter to lower the music. I feel great that I am able to do that! No luck, he barely turns down the music so I am struggling to concentrate on our conversation. I am not going to ask the waiter again, so I try to suffer through it. Mario notices I am struggling, so he asks him a couple more times to turn it down. The waiter eventually turns off the speakers in our dining room. I feel a little funny about it, but am nonetheless very happy. At last, I can carry on a conversation without too much trouble. Eventually the restaurant becomes very busy with children crying, dishes clattering, and adults' voices booming. It is way too much for me. Every time this happens it's disheartening and disappointing, because I enjoy going out to restaurants so much. I shrug it off with a laugh and say to myself, it will be a piece of cake in the future, no problem.

Mario and I end up going to Lincoln Harbor in Weehawken to take in the sun and gaze across at the beautiful Manhattan skyline. We talk for a while and then he drives me home. I enjoyed catching up with all the school news, who is up, who is down, and who is up to the same old tricks. I hope we can do it again soon. For a change, I feel like a functioning human being, not a patient or client.

The Black Binder

Day 248: My black binder and multi-pocket folder that I carry with me to each therapy session is getting too heavy to drag around in my bag. I am having so much trouble that I ask Amy to help me reorganize them. We decide to remove past therapy sessions notes and homework assignments from my binder and multi-pocket folder and leave only the notes and assignments I do for that week in the binder. We create folders at home for all past notes and assignments. I really think it's a terrific idea and can't wait to share my brainstorm with my cognitive therapist.

Day 250: Well, let's just say that Mark did not share my enthusiasm. He's concerned about the plan and says we can try it for a week and see what happens. He obviously knows something I don't, but I can't put my finger on it. I ask him what the agenda is for today and he says, "It is the same as last Thursday." Well, as simple as that sounds, I can't remember what happened last Thursday even though the agenda has been the same for the past few weeks. I just draw a total blank. I try to refer to my newly devised system for the answer, but the previous weeks notes are not in the binder. I look up at Mark and he reads my mind. I tell him I can't remember and that I don't have last week's session notes in my binder to help me out. "This is why you need your binder," he admonishes. I agree, but "I should at least get an "A" for effort." I tried to problem solve on my own. He doesn't disagree, but makes his point that routine is important.

Routine is my protection. It keeps me from losing control and panicking. Needless to say, I quickly retire my idea and go back to lugging around the original binder and multi-pocket folder.

Ingenuity That Didn't Quite Work

When Chris tells me that his binder and multi-pocket folder for therapy is too heavy to carry I say, "Let's take a look and see how we can make some adjustments." With my support, he reorganizes the binder and multi-pocket folder. When he walks in the door and explains what happens in cognitive therapy and how he does not have the pages to refer back to, I understand the problem, but quite frankly I am annoyed that his therapist did not give Chris a pat on the back for using his ingenuity to solve a problem, despite the fact that it created another problem. Perhaps this wasn't a great strategy, but at least Chris took initiative, which is something he does not do that often. I am very proud of him.

Some Self-Evaluation

Overall, I think I am improving in each of my therapies. I am still working on priority setting and pacing myself both in therapy and at home. My treatment team meets regularly to discuss my case so they all know what I am working on and they each can incorporate uniform strategies and objectives into my therapy sessions. The strategies that I learn and relearn are essential for anybody who survives a traumatic brain injury. These strategies are my lifelines and I must use them in order to accomplish any task. The degree to which I accomplish a task and the rate of speed at which I complete them has dramatically changed. Knowing now how difficult it is to carry out the simplest tasks without referring to or being reminded of these strategies puts into perspective the disparity between where I was before my injury and where I am now.

I am pleased with Rusk and the progress I am making in physical therapy. According to Barb, I am showing a lot of carry over from session to session. I'm real happy about that, and so is Barb. It is such an empowering feeling to do something easily that was once a struggle. A week ago, I was unable to walk up a slightly grassy incline, even with Barb's assistance. As I would reach the base of the incline and start up, my legs would get all tied up as if my left foot didn't know what my right foot was doing, which caused me to lose my balance. I worked on this at home with Amy in a nearby public park. Slowly but surely repetition pays off. Eventually, I am not only able to make it up a small incline, but I take on steeper and steeper inclines with less and less help. Let people jokingly hum the Rocky song when he races to the top step of the federal building before he wins the championship. I now find myself humming it with a big smile on my face as I gain another victory. I have much more to conquer, but things are coming along.

Day 250: I have a new occupational therapist, Adrienne. She and I hit it off right from the start. It doesn't hurt that she is a graduate of my old alma mater, Utica College. When I tell her that I not only attended Utica College, but that the campus acted as my backyard growing up, she could hardly believe it. Honestly, neither could I. As it turns out she graduated two years after my sister, Laurie. "Isn't it a small world," I can't hold myself back from saying to her. It is real neat to talk to a perfect stranger who knows, first hand, where I grew up. She clearly recalls the street that my house was on, which abuts the entrance to the college. I tell her it is likely that my grandmother watched her walk to college each day, as she would always step out onto the porch to report on any passersby. Adrienne will work out fine.

Speech therapy is progressing nicely. I am now reading poetry from the children's book "A Light in the Attic," which Emile feels will help me improve my intonation and inflection. I am picking up the techniques, but need to work on applying and sustaining them in casual conversation.

It seems strange, when I read prose or poetry my speech is smooth and fluid with fairly good stress and intonation; but when I communicate without the written word in front of me, it is very choppy and inconsistent. I am, however, improving thanks to Emile and these exercises.

Positive Support

Psychotherapy with Dvorah provides me with positive support. She keeps me focused on the here and now, particularly regarding my interactions with people close to me. She is great at helping me gain perspective.

It is tough, even upsetting, dealing with some family members and friends who don't seem to comprehend what I am going through seven days a week, 24 hours a day. When they ask "how are you doing" and I try to tell them the hard truth, the responses I get are the same, "You are doing fantastic, you're great" as if nothing has happened to me; as if the things I struggle with on a daily basis and the impact these struggles have on me are no different than anyone else without a brain injury. The truth of the matter is unless you have a brain injury, it is impossible to know what I am dealing with and will likely deal with for the rest of my life. No one can understand the emotional impact a life change of this magnitude has on a human being. When I hear their bland responses to my condition I feel as though I am not really being heard. It is as if they are pushing me off, minimizing and denying the realities of what is. Understanding how someone with a brain injury feels, acts, internalizes, and processes information and experience is not something that most people will ever be able to do. I don't like to hear that I am doing "great" or "fine." It is very frustrating and unhelpful. It is still only half the picture, the surface at best. From the perspective of the person with a brain injury, we know that we are not fine; that everything isn't like it was before. I think it is more helpful when a friend or family member says to me, "It looks like you are coming along," or "keep up the good work". This is positive, yet realistic, in terms of what is happening.

Even the doctors don't know exactly how to explain what is happening in an injured brain. If you are not walking in my shoes there is no way to know what it is like or to really understand what those with brain injuries go through. It takes a huge amount of energy for me just to walk and keep my balance at the same time. Walking around a noisy unpredictable city or a shopping center filled with eager consumers constantly challenges every neuron in my brain as I strain to filter out the piercing noises and the momentum of rushing crowds. A simple conversation demands that I consciously call upon strategies to shape my thoughts and words to be coherent. It is often agonizing. Doing more than one thing at a time is a struggle and minor noises and events become major disorienting distractions. In the inevitable chaos of the daily grind I lose my sense of direction and even stop looking both ways at intersections. Not to mention the residual effects of any activity and the major fatigue that hits me like a locomotive. It feels as if every ounce of blood is drained from my body and I want to do nothing more than retreat to a quiet safe place. If you are not wearing a visual aid, like some kind of cast, or tapping a cane, or in a wheel chair, most people are unable to see a disability without a physical cue. Seeing is believing, and not being able to see a brain injury makes it even harder for people to understand. I am not even sure I totally understand it myself.

After therapy I meet Amy at her office and walk a couple of blocks to the State University of New York (SUNY) Optometric Center for an appointment with a specialist in head trauma, Dr. Neera Kapoor. She is extremely upbeat and conveys a strong sense of commitment. Her examination is very thorough. She gives of herself and her time. It seems that my injury has accelerated the naturally occurring deterioration of vision. I will have to rely on reading glasses sooner rather than later. She provides me with a prescription for reading clips that I can attach to my regular glasses. She believes that my visual perception problems are related to the difficulties I am having with my vestibular system. She joins the chorus recommending vestibular therapy and will talk to Barb, my physical therapist, and Dr. Richter about setting this up. Meanwhile she provides Amy with a program of vestibular therapy exercises for me to do at home with Amy's assistance.

Day 252: Dvorah is working with me on pacing myself socially and asserting myself when necessary to avoid overexertion. She seems to have an incredible ability to hone in on the emotional struggles I experience daily and genuinely understands, as well as anyone can without a brain injury, exactly what it is like to be living as a brain injury survivor. Her pragmatic approach to dealing with what life presents has an incredibly positive impact on me. Above all, Dvorah gives me permission to take care of "me" and not focus so much on feeling guilty about not being capable of taking care of others, which had been my role as long as I can remember. She shares a handy formula for life with me. I should frame it and put it on the wall: "What is mine, let it remain with me, what is someone else's, let it leave now. Let me take any information I need, and then let the feeling depart."

Dvorah Makes a Difference

Dvorah really makes a difference. Chris is better able to function in the real world, whatever the situation. What is even more important, she is helping him to develop a real willingness to participate in that world. Dvorah helps him accept the reality of his injury, which also enables me to live with the hard truth that he may not get any better.

She helps him understand that most people will just not understand or appreciate the extent of his injury, and that only those who do will be more sensitive to his needs. I notice now some of the old Chris coming back, and I also see a new Chris being born, whom I can adore and love for the rest of my life.

Dvorah encourages him to believe in himself again. I witness a new birth of an adult with a different mindset. His spirit is intact, capable of loving and being part of society.

Family Matters

Amy and I are supposed to attend her niece and nephew's graduation party, but we think it may be too taxing for me. Besides the trip upstate, having to deal with so many people at once is way too much! They are wonderful people and I am sure they would try hard to make me feel comfortable, but I am just not up to the challenge. When Amy cancels, one sister is graciously persistent. We have to take care of ourselves first. It is reassuring that Amy and I are on the same page, although at the same time it makes me feel guilty.

Social Events

I know in order for us to attend social events I have to depend on our newly learned strategies. I call ahead to restaurants for a quiet table in the corner away from the clatter of dishes and crowded group tables. We usually dine in between the lunch and dinner crowds. We plan and prepare in great detail for family gatherings - baptisms, birthdays, weddings and funerals. We decide well in advance whether or not to attend the reception or the service. We find out how far the drive will be to any function, what the weather should be like, the number of people attending, and the availability of a quiet place if Chris needs a break. All this information helps us to decide if we are going to accept an invitation.

Our families are getting used to the inquisition and I think they understand. Not all may, but this no longer concerns us. My first concern is Chris's wellbeing and his ability to function in a particular social situation without negative consequences.

With each new event Chris attends, I believe he pushes himself harder to be involved. I am also well aware that Chris's love for me is an even more important factor. He does not want to deprive me of the socializing that I treasure. Perhaps there is still a piece of him left that longs to go out and kick up his heels. I hope so.

Another Assessment

Day 258: My first vestibular assessment by Beth, a member of the Rusk staff is today. I begin the assessment by standing up and doing a scanning exercise. Soon after beginning this exercise I have to lie down. I am feeling very lightheaded. Beth brings me a cold pack for my forehead. I am clammy and pale. I have the dry heaves, which is very embarrassing in the middle of the physical therapy department. I think that doing this exercise aggravates my system, which is already upset from a new medication I am taking. The evaluation cannot be completed.

Odes to Common Things

During my psychotherapy session today, Dvorah lends me "Absence and Presence," a book of Pablo Neruda's poetry. His writings are so powerful and rich. This book brings me to another place. A collection of intense, emotionally powerful photographs taken by Luis Poirot compliments Neruda's poetry. One that particularly strikes me is a close up shot of a window frame with the ocean in the background. It is positioned in such a way that it forces the viewer to feel as if he or she is leaning against a wall looking out a window towards the majestic sea. There is a huge magnifying glass on the table in front of the window, distorting a portion of the ocean view. It has a very strong emotional impact on me. It symbolizes for me the present and the future. Right now the present is one big blur. I can sort of make out parts of my life that are in flux as I experience rehab, but it is still a blur overall. I don't have a clue where I will be six months or six years from now. I try not to think too much about it. It is much more helpful for me to find clarity and stay focused on what is happening right now in the present. The future is clear to me as to where I would like to be, but I have to persevere and stay determined, fighting through the blur to the eternal sea.

Orlando and Back

Day 267: Prior to the accident Amy and I had arranged for a time-share week in Orlando with my mom and dad and we have no intention of canceling it. The trip to Florida is airplane hell for me. My luck, I end up with a small child behind me. It never fails. I just keep on asking God to be merciful and keep the kid quiet and tranquil! No such luck. Soon after the takeoff, the child becomes restless and is kicking the back of my chair. For anyone this is annoying, but for me it is a form of torture. The more he bangs the back of my chair the more frantic I become. It feels like the kid is playing soccer inside my cranium.

Finally I have enough, and work up the nerve to turn around and give the mother a polite but pointed glance in hopes that she would see this as a signal to restrain the child. This polite approach doesn't make a dent. The kid keeps on kicking and kicking... So I take action and turn back toward the woman and say, "Miss, your child is kicking the back of my chair and it is a real problem for me. Normally, I would put up with it, but I am recovering from a brain injury and it feels like your child is slamming his foot into my head!" I am not sure this is what my therapists meant when they encouraged me to assert myself, but that's what I did. I think I may have been a little rough on her, but what can I say, I am a little bit rusty in the assertiveness department. The woman subdues her youngster, apologizes and tells me that she "can hardly imagine what I am going through." She wishes me "a swift recovery." How about that! A perfect stranger gives me an honest humane response when she hears what happened to me. The outcome of asserting myself couldn't be any better. I am able to have a restful trip for the remainder of the journey.

We meet up with my parents who came in on another flight. By the time we get to our hotel I am totally drained and ready for a nap. I keep in mind my therapists' and doctors' advice to be very aware of pacing myself during this trip. I must try to avoid getting overtired since that leads to problems with my speech, my ability to walk and balance, and terrible headaches. I am anxious to avoid cognitive overload. We take half-day trips to Epcot Center and to the Kennedy Space Center with resting days in between. It is not just the demands made on my energy to do the rounds of these amusements, but a toll is taken just to prepare for the outing. From the time I rise in the morning I have only so much gas in my tank to expend for the whole day. If I am not careful I may end up using all the gas in a single conversation or single activity. It's very bizarre just how quickly I become fatigued. I get intoxicated with fatigue and everything slows down, like I am living in a slow motion movie. I feel as though my body and brain are underwater, while the world around me is still moving at its normal rapid rate. The only thing I can do is go to sleep to recover my energy. If I don't my head begins to feel all rubbery and my brain begins to tingle. It's an eerie prelude to the pounding headaches.

As well as I am doing, I fail to pay attention to doctor's orders and I overtax my system at the Animal Kingdom. Eventually I pay the price. Leaving the park, Amy and my dad rush ahead to retrieve the car, while I have a melt down. My legs aren't working right and my cane isn't much help. My speech fails. The noises of the park are literally tossing me around and throwing me off balance. I am way over stimulated. I feel like an erector set with the bolts loosening at the main joints. I just keep focusing on the parking lot while my mom does her best to keep me from falling over.

On the flight home, instead of the "kicking kid", I deal with a female card shark who has a compulsion to regularly shuffle and rap her cards two times against the flight table attached to the back of my seat. This is actually more irritating than the kicking kid. After several unsuccessful polite turns, and about 30 minutes of fuming, I make another effort with a more direct request. Actually, it is a little more like a polite demand. I ask her to please stop banging the cards on her tray table and tell her why it is so important to me that she desist. She's a middle-aged lady with a full-figure, but acts like a small child with her hand in the cookie jar. She replies indignantly, "I'm not hitting the cards on the table." I don't know if I am more upset or flabbergasted by her failure to come clean. Does she think I am some type of idiot? Since she is acting like a child I think it is best to respond to her in the same fashion. I emphatically repeat my request. My voice is sharp; it is clear that I mean business. I think between my delivery and my precise "don't mess with me lady" attitude, she gets the message. Needless to say, for the remainder of the flight, she is quiet as a mouse. My ability to assert myself on the flight is reassuring. I am building confidence. I don't know how this assertiveness will play out on the streets of New York or with friends and family in their living rooms. I will have to wait and see.

To Go to Orlando or Not to Go

I know I should cancel the Orlando trip, but it was planned a year ago and all tickets and reservations are paid for. I am not sure if I am being selfish, but I really need a break and Chris is determined to fulfill his obligation to his Mom and Dad. One thing we learn from this trip is how important it is to plan, prepare, and strategize. Even before we get on the plane, Chris has a difficult time handling the airport security process. The loud noise and the abrupt movements of people lifting and shoving their luggage onto the scanning device, the beeping of the scanning equipment, and commands from the security officers are so overwhelming for him that he has trouble walking and talking. I observe someone being helped who is in a wheelchair and I make it my business to convince Chris that this is the best way for him to get through the airport screening the next time we travel.

The flight is terrible for him; he has a child kicking his seat. I offer several times to change seats but Chris declines. He wants to be by the window so no one could possibly knock into his head as they walk along the aisle. Eventually, Chris is so worked up about the kid kicking his seat I am worried that he will snap and create a big scene. Chris, however, keeps his cool, asserting himself by explaining the situation to the child's mother. Luckily the mother is very sensitive to Chris's injury as she suffers terribly from migraine headaches. The rest of the flight Chris sleeps like a baby. A friend told me that the airlines save the bulkhead seating for people with disabilities or special needs. I store this information for the next time we take a trip.

The rest of the trip is like a penance for me. I watch Chris's energy deplete to zero, his speech falter, and his legs become shakier while trying to enjoy some of the Orlando vacation spots. Seeing him like this so often is like a knife to my heart. I know he agreed to go on the trip for my sake and his parents, but we will definitely have to discuss any future trips well in advance, plan ahead and make all kinds of adjustments to make it easier for Chris. This first big trip since Chris's accident opens my eyes to the many obstacles he will face when we travel. I am determined to remove these obstacles. The next time we fly I will speak to his doctors and therapists to discuss different ways to safeguard Chris. I know one thing for sure, that Chris would have greatly benefited from wheelchair assistance.

Chapter Ten

The Quest for Independence

Specialty Seating

Day 277: Here we go again. I am on the M-16 bus heading over to Rusk for another day of therapy. As it approaches Sixth Avenue the bus gets very crowded. Thankfully, I board the bus at the beginning of the line so I am guaranteed one of the seats reserved for the disabled. I prefer to call this "specialty seating." Anyhow, as the bus fills up I am feeling more and more uncomfortable as most people who enter the bus don't seem to notice my feet are connected to a living breathing person and step on them with impunity. Despite the bus driver's repeated requests to move to the back of the bus to make room for the new passengers boarding, none are moving. The people entering the bus begin to aggressively yell at the other passengers to make room. I am glad to have my earplugs in so that the noise is at least a little muffled.

As the bus approaches Fifth Avenue, a woman with a thick Russian accent and a hefty male companion trample over my feet and the woman squeezes into a seat next to me. Just then an old man lugging a huge oxygen tank on a luggage cart struggles to get up the steps of the bus. Once he makes it, he scans the specialty seats hoping to find a free one. All of the seats are filled and not one of the seemingly able-bodied passengers offers to give their seat to him. They just stare at the poor man. I am so disgusted and appalled by their insensitivity. If only I were capable I would give up my seat in a minute. Unfortunately, in my condition I know that I would not be able to stand without the risk of losing my balance and falling. Suddenly, the Russian woman sitting next to me starts shouting in a gruff voice at me, "Get up...you... you...monster, get up!" All of these people, including her, shamelessly remain glued to their seats while she is ordering me to move. At first, I am too shocked to react. I don't know where I get the nerve to finally take her on. Maybe it is all the assertiveness stuff that my therapists are pushing. I turn around and look her straight in the eye and with as much energy as I can muster, I tell HER to get up. For added emphasis I raise my cane in the air, which she apparently hadn't noticed. The guy she is with looks over at her. He blushes, not saying anything. She mumbles something in Russian that I am sure is not very complimentary, but she does not follow up on her tirade, which makes me happy. She instantly forgets about the poor old man forlornly standing with his oxygen cart. Finally a woman with a touch of gray in her hair gets up and gives him her seat.

Everything Will Come Together

I am distraught and mentally drained. I have only a few blocks to re-charge as I make my way to Rusk from the bus stop. I am glad to go to Physical Therapy; the physical exertion will help me forget about what happened.

Today, Barb and I are working on the first stages of jogging. I start with a quick side-to-side movement. I am able to handle the mechanics of this movement for a brief time, but soon my legs get all tangled and I lose my balance. Barb says this happens because my brain runs down too quickly when I try something new. I notice that my legs also have trouble keeping up with my upper body so I start leaning forward from my waist up as I am performing this task. Barb believes that the messages going from my brain to my legs are not getting there fast enough yet. She encourages me to be patient. "Everything will come together in time."

Sequencing and Prioritizing

I continue to work on sequencing in cognitive therapy. Sequencing really depletes the brain. As I do the exercises that Mark has prepared it is increasingly difficult to sustain concentration to complete the task. This being said, I have improved the amount of time I am able to work on a task with minor distractions, such as a radio playing very quietly in the background, to about 30 minutes. Granted I end up exhausted, both mentally and physically, but it feels great to be improving my time. I also work on prioritizing. This is easier said than done. Mark urges me to choose the most challenging task and do it first, so that I use my mental resources while I am still fresh.

She Made My Month

I had quite a surprise this evening. Out of the blue, a former student, Kaysha, calls me at home. She apparently stopped by my old school to see me and was informed, inaccurately, that I suffered a fall. She isn't given any other information. Very concerned, she decides to track me down. It is a delight to hear her bubbly voice. Throughout my years in the school system I aspired to be a positive influence and support for the students I counseled. During our phone conversation, we talk about my counseling program. Kaysha says that I really helped her find her way in such a big overwhelming school. My SPARK program became the family that she and the other students wanted and needed. I am touched by her heartfelt words.

Making a difference in these young people's lives always compensated for my low salary and the sometimes challenging work environment. I also believe I have left a positive "imprint" on my students that go way beyond mere immediate impressions and short-term learning. With love, care and perseverance I worked to leave "imprints" that would help young people develop over time.

Graduation Day

Day 309: Emile has completed her individual speech therapy work with me. I guess I am graduating. Like most good teachers Emile inspired me and spurred me to action. I will miss her. She refers me to a pragmatic speech group. She believes this group will really help me develop my speech skills with regard to the social purpose and interaction of language. She enumerates the wide range of topics it will cover.

What a list. I can see that based on where I am right now this group can be very beneficial, putting me in situations that are difficult and challenging. I know that this is precisely why Emile has recommended me for this group. I will aggressively take on this challenge, but it is scary to throw myself in with a bunch of strangers and work on the significant challenges that have become an enemy to my sense of self. It is hard for me even to accept that I am a patient undergoing all this individual therapy, but now to reveal my limitations to a whole group of people makes me feel very insecure and vulnerable. It is one thing to quietly attend all these individual sessions where I am anonymous and not exposed to the outside world. It is something else altogether to be part of a group and revealing my frailties to strangers. I know that the other group members will have similar issues, but it is frightening and threatening to put my stuff out there, despite any potential positive outcomes.

Before this accident I believed my speaking voice was really good, a finely tuned instrument, which provided me with the ability to speak with confidence. Now my confidence is shattered and even the most basic communication is a struggle. I never gave it much thought before my brain injury, but when I think back I realize how I could command attention from others when I spoke. I am not sure if it was the content, the voice quality, or the passion that drew my listeners in, but it was magical when it happened.

Day 318: Wednesday, September 6th, today is my first day in the Pragmatic Speech Group. I'm a little anxious, but it helps to be in the familiar precincts of Rusk. I will be coming once a week on Wednesday for a half an hour. At the outset Isabel, the group facilitator, distributes some information sheets to help us understand the process of speaking and communication, the nature of our particular deficits and strategies to overcome or minimize our deficits. It's a lot for me to absorb. She starts out by saying that the group will focus on "maximizing our ability to handle verbal exchanges in the real world," which leads her into the mechanics of information processing, followed by a discussion and use of practical techniques for improving comprehension such as note taking or just asking the other person to slow down.

When I get home I read in a handout that we will also try to improve the "executive functions involved in communication, emphasizing the roles of initiation, anticipation and goal setting while guarding against hyper-verbosity and inadequate elaboration." We will even examine "the basic mechanics of conversation" such as eye contact and head turning. Hey, I didn't think I would have to work on that.

As in many of the groups I facilitated, we all introduce ourselves, giving our names and telling what we do, or in my case, what I use to do. Most of the other people in the group are older. I am the 39 year-old baby of the group. When my turn comes I can barely blurt out my name. This is not going to be easy.

The following Wednesday Isabel talks about verbal organization and the problems brain injured people have in this area. I recognize myself when she talks about not being concise. I know I sometimes run on and never get to the point. I also have problems putting my thoughts together. Isabel asks for volunteers for a role-play. I have no thought of raising my hand. The other people in the group are clearly higher functioning.

Some have already returned to their jobs. I cannot keep up with all the talk. Just when I feel like I have gotten a hold, I loose my train of thought and get muddled. By the end of the group my head aches and my energy is gone. I remain seated, trying to pull myself together.

Almost a Year

Day 345: It's October. Almost a year has passed since the accident and the injury. It is a terrible event and no matter how hard I try I cannot fully come to terms with it. Of course, it won't disappear. So I submerge myself in cognitive strategies to handle it. I work on generalizing, prioritizing, and anticipatory skills. I make some good headway on using these strategies in my everyday life. Every new experience is an eye opener for me and increases my awareness of the importance of using strategies like these to achieve a greater degree of independence in my daily living.

Despite my overall growth and improvements, I still consistently have a great deal of trouble responding quickly in the moment to situations. For example, I find it very difficult to come up with alternative approaches to a problem situation that is facing me. I no longer automatically think in the abstract. My new world is a very concrete one in the present. It is something else I took for granted that I have to relearn.

It is much more difficult than I could imagine. In cognitive therapy Mark is trying to help me think more creatively. I must come up with different stories to relate to a picture. Right now I am able to come up with one or two, but the actual goal is to develop five stories. When there is a distraction present it is much more difficult to think abstractly, but once I get a thought in my head I am able to write it down. Mark is not sure if I will ever be able to totally filter out distractions, but he is trying to help me manage this as much as possible.

At the end of a really productive session Mark reveals to me that despite my recent progress my therapy program will probably draw to a close in December or January. The therapy team would like me to continue with more therapy for two or three more months, but it doesn't seem that the insurance company is willing to approve it.

This really ticks me off. I am working like a demon, challenging myself constantly, filling every moment of my waking life with effort. My therapists believe that adding more therapy can be more than helpful; that it can change me and change my life. Still the insurance company that dictates treatment refuses. This is so backward! Why should I not get as much therapy as I need? I keep turning this over in my mind. I can't help it. I didn't ask for this. This injury happened to me and the very institution that is responsible to take care of me is cutting me off before the proper time.

According to my therapists I am still showing signs of improvement, so I am still benefiting from treatment. I guess this just doesn't matter. The insurance company's balance sheet comes first. It goes without saying that I am thankful for all the treatment the insurance company has paid for, but I don't think it is fair to hinder my progress by ending therapy while it can still make a difference. If I were able to pay for more therapy myself I would, but there is no way this is possible.

As a result of the insurance company's decision each therapist now concentrates on specific realistic goals to accomplish before the insurance company grim reaper cuts off my benefits. They are preparing me, conducting a sort of closure. I know what I ideally would like to accomplish, but I have to come up with pragmatic goals with the therapists for this short time frame. They offer to prepare home programs for me to work on my challenges after my therapy is over. They all know how hard I work and believe that I will take full advantage of the task and exercise programs they prepare.

The Group

Day 354: It's October 12th. I begin to attend a cognitive remediation group. It is supposed to last for six months, until April. It is also meeting at Rusk. That is reassuring. I am hopeful, but I still feel more secure in one-on-one therapy situations. Although I know the value of groups as a professional, I don't feel like making a fool out of myself in front of a lot of strangers. Now I know first hand how some of my more reluctant clients felt.

This group is fairly structured. At the outset, there is the appointment of a note-taker and timekeeper. The group leaders introduce themselves. No titles, they keep everything on a first name basis. Having considerable experience as a facilitator myself, I am pleased with their approach. Unnecessary formalities can inhibit group participation. They talk about the structure and the ground rules, emphasizing respect and confidentiality. Mathew sets forth our agenda. The group is specifically for higher functioning brain injured individuals to help them manage their emotions more effectively. Am I high functioning? Sometimes I don't think so.

In the first twelve weeks the group will focus on emotional self-control and self-regulation, while in the second twelve weeks it will address flexible thinking and planning. In addition to the large group meeting, the group will split into mini-groups that will meet with a facilitator one additional day a week. The second 12 weeks will take this process a step further. I will complete a "clear thinking" worksheet based on a real life interpersonal conflict. The worksheet is designed to analyze my reactions in depth, whether they are physical, behavioral, cognitive, or emotional.

Day 382: November 8th, and despite my initial reservations, I am beginning to find my experience in the cognitive remediation group beneficial. It is helping me understand so much about my brain injury and how I can more effectively solve problems and minimize interpersonal conflict with others. The weekly assignments are fairly difficult to complete at times, which surprises me since I feel I should have an easier time with them given my counseling background. Yet again, my background does not make a major difference in the degree of frustration I often feel when trying to complete these assignments. Today in the group, we discuss a problem-solving scenario about a brain injured person trying to deal with a problematic situation on a crowded subway car. Even though I cannot yet travel on the subway on my own, I can really relate to the scenario. I regularly confront inconsiderate people on public transportation like the guy in this scenario who is unwilling to move his bag to make room for the brain injured protagonist. In the scenario, he is eventually shamed into moving his bag by the brain injured person, who forcefully states his case, revealing his handicapped transportation card. I wish that I could keep my cool and say and do the right things under the pressure of these kinds of circumstances. I still find it hard to participate in the group, but it is good to hear the others vent about this true to life scenario and offer suggestions from their own lives on how to handle it.

My pragmatic speech group session doesn't go so well today. I am disappointed with my performance. I find in many ways that the other participants in the group are higher functioning than I am. They are more verbal and quicker. I am still working on my basic speech issues, while the others in the group seem to have no problem choosing their words, modulating their voices and processing language. Many of the group members seem to readily express themselves on almost any topic. It takes a lot of energy for me to enunciate a simple declarative statement. I must hold on tight to keep up with the other members of the group. I do everything possible to stay in the race.

Day 389: Today I am finally taking the bull by the horns in my pragmatic speech group and take the risk of engaging in the group discussion. Despite the ongoing struggle I have organizing my thoughts and finding the right words to express myself, I at last figure out that the only way I am going to improve is to jump in and go for it. Yes, it's a terrific effort to get my thoughts organized and delivered, and I soon find that the group members are very understanding and allow me the time to get my words out. Afterwards, I am exhausted, drained by the group participation, wiped out cognitively and physically. By the time I get home, my head is just banging away and I can barely stand. I have no appetite at all.

A Crucial November

Day 394: Mark is pulling it together, ranging over abstract and creative thinking, the generating of ideas, mental shifting and the further development of anticipatory skills. I have to go beyond the concrete and think beyond the situation in front of me. Mark is trying to prepare me for the end of therapy when I will be on my own. These particular skills are real brain busters. They take a lot out of me. I have to force myself to attend and concentrate. In occupational therapy, Adrienne focuses on organizational skills, mental flexibility tasks, and abstract thinking. As much as these skills are so challenging for me, I can see their benefit. Meanwhile, Barb continues to work on advanced balancing skills in physical therapy. Pressure is exerted both on my therapists and me to cover as much ground as possible before I leave. Pacing becomes secondary to rush … rush.

Day 402: November turns out to be a very critical month for me in another way. The Board of Education medical office informs me that I am to have a neuropsychological exam at their doctor's office in midtown Manhattan. Since I am unable to tolerate a full day of testing, both emotionally and physically, the doctor arranges a series of short appointments. He is a very compassionate man, and as honest and realistic as he is compassionate. He takes the time to meet with Amy and I after the testing is over. His findings are very depressing. He doesn't pull any punches. He gives it to us straight. I choke up and tears flood my eyes. This is the moment of truth. Although I think I am prepared for the worst, it is crushing. In a nutshell, he says that the test profile strongly indicates I am not able to return to work, now and perhaps, ever. The busy school environment with its multiplicity of demands would defeat me. My career as a Guidance Counselor is over. He went on to say that I may continue to improve, but taking into account that over a year has passed since my injury it is probable that the majority of my recovery has already occurred.

I feel like I have been punched in the face. I understand in my head what he is saying, but in my heart, I am not ready to accept his verdict. I have been working so hard to improve. How is it possible to say I have reached a dead end with few prospects and little hope? I know that I am not back to normal, but the only thing that keeps me plugging away and not giving up is the certainty that I will recover, if not exactly to the point I was before the accident, than pretty damn close. All I need is some more time.

The doctor takes his time answering all of our questions and seems to understand how I feel. He tries to reassure me and cushions my disappointment by saying that I will likely be productive in another career, in another time, and feels that occupational exploration may be helpful.

No, this is not enough. I feel like he is placing a band aide on a cut that requires stitches. It may slow the bleeding for a short time, but it's not likely to hold. I know that I am not ready to take on any type of job right now, but that's not really the point. I just wish I could turn back time to the fire emergency and know enough not to walk through that door at that moment.

Amy and I left his office, and by the time we reached the elevator, we both broke down in tears as we held each other in an attempt to comfort one another. All my hard work seemed all for nothing!

Day 405: It's three days since my Board of Education Neuro-Psych testing and we receive the dreaded letter from the Board of Education indicating that they were retiring me. The reality of the extent of my injury overwhelms me.

In Shock

I am shocked to hear the Board of Education doctor tell Chris that given the test results, he can never return to guidance and counseling, the work that means so much to him. I know how much he loves his job, in particular the opportunity it gives him to "make a difference." The doctor's words make my heart stop beating.

Chris is the best of the best. Together we were laying the foundation for Chris's big career move. Everything was set to happen. In a short time he would have completed all the educational requirements to become an assistant principal with a position all lined up. Chris was also looking forward to setting up his own private counseling practice.

Chris was so sure that it was only a matter of time before he would return to work, never giving up hope for a minute. I can only imagine what he is going through. He must feel as if the lid is closing on his coffin. Despair is written all over his face. Our world is crashing down around us. Can this truly be happening?

Amy's Birthday

By December, I am having an easier time following the group process in my cognitive remediation group and am more confident of my ability to speak and express myself. Gradually I am becoming more aware, conscious of my emotional response to events in my daily life. Through the interplay of the group, the group's weekly assignments, and the log I keep on interpersonal experiences, I am learning how to manage my reactions. I am becoming more self-critical and am better able to evaluate my behavior and plan ahead. I share with the group my successes and failures.

Day 406: My sister and her boyfriend are in town for a weekend visit. We make plans to meet up with my brother Paul to take Amy out for a belated birthday dinner. It is supposed to be a dinner for five, so there won't be too many people for me to handle at one time. This is a big step for me to make. I really have a low threshold for people. Paul calls me on his cell phone to finalize a plan. While we are talking I can hear a lot of commotion on his end of the line. It is very distracting to me. He asks me to hold on for a minute and when he comes back, he tells me he is at his girlfriend's house and adds, "It would be a nice gesture to invite her along for Amy's dinner." Paul is usually very accommodating. He must know that this is pushing it to the limit for me to deal with more people; particularly in a restaurant with a high noise level, crowds, cross talk, that ceaseless activity that drains my cognitive energy. I figure for him I will make an effort to handle it.

He puts me back on hold for a couple minutes and when he comes back on the line he asks me if his girlfriends' sister and parents may join us. As much as this wouldn't have been a problem for me in the past, particularly since I enjoyed get-togethers with a wide variety of people, I know that these additional people would push me way beyond my capacity. I get a weird feeling as my throat constricts. My heart beats faster and faster and my chest tightens. My head also starts aching. I am conflicted. I don't want to put him in an awkward position with his girlfriend's family, but I also don't want to put myself in a situation that would cause me to lose my bearings and become exhausted. The added stimulation runs a risk. When this happens my brain shuts down and my speech falters. I have trouble finding the right words and I have trouble coordinating my walking. The last thing I want is to embarrass myself in a crowded restaurant.

I assert myself with Paul. I tell him I really can't manage that many people at one time, particularly in a loud busy restaurant. Paul replies, "Well Chris, you gotta challenge yourself sometimes." This gets under my skin. He doesn't seem to understand what it takes each and every day for me to function. Just getting out of bed can be a challenge.

I love my brother very much, but he doesn't see me often enough to know the extent of my limitations. I don't blame him for not understanding. Despite my frustration, I keep my cool and say in a steady voice, "I challenge myself often and being with just the six of us in a public place is, in itself, a challenge. I ask him to give me a call back once he sorts out his plans. I reiterate that I simply cannot take the stress of so many people at one time. He calls back almost immediately and informs me that her parents would not be coming.

He does however, show up with his girlfriend and her teenage sister. I am sure she is nice, but that's not the point. Paul can see the look on my face, which I know is something I have never hidden that well. He pulls me aside and he insists that someone has to watch her and that if they didn't take her with them they would not be able to come. I could give him a blistering earful. Instead, I take a step back and ponder the emotional regulation stuff we continually go over in my remediation group. My voice is steady as I speak. "I hear what you are saying, but I am not happy that your problem has become my problem." Paul needs to respect where I am right now should a similar situation crop up in the future. He seems to understand what I am saying. We give each other a hug and join the group for Amy's birthday dinner.

Healthfully Selfish

Day 408: During my cognitive remediation group today, I realize that even prior to my injury I did not truly assert myself. I generally avoided conflict, particularly interpersonal conflict. Now, it is essential that I assert myself so that my personal and very specific needs can be met as often as possible. It is a matter of successfully compensating for my challenges and vulnerabilities. I have to make certain demands in order to make it through any event and enjoy it at the same time. Sooner or later people are going to have to understand who I am now.

In the words of my former New York acting coach Alan Wynroth, I have to learn to be "healthfully selfish." This has never been clearer to me than now. Before the injury, I thought about it only as a catch phrase; it did not apply to me. Now it is essential to incorporate being healthfully selfish into my daily living as a means of survival. These days I have to put myself first. This does not mean that I intend to disregard other people's feelings or good intentions. I do have to attempt to shape the conditions around me to help me continue to improve cognitively, emotionally, and physically. It is imperative that I think about what my needs are first. If I can engage in activities successfully, I can build upon that success. Otherwise, I am likely to become discouraged, which will impede my motivation to persevere and progress. I have never really related to my family in this way and I don't know the kind of impact it will have. I do, however, view this approach as a positive change that will help me manage life more efficiently with less stress, upset and confusion.

Still a Shock

Day 408: Finally the time has come. Although I have been expecting it to happen for a while, it is still a shock. It is not a great way to begin the New Year, January 2001. My insurance coverage has regrettably run out. Although all of my therapists say that I would benefit from months more of therapy, the insurance company disagrees and is unwilling to extend my eligibility. Each of my therapists has developed a home program for me so that I can continue to make strides on my own. They know I am a workhorse where my therapy is concerned and go that extra mile for me. I am still attending the cognitive remediation group, the pragmatic speech group, and individual psychotherapy, so I feel like I still have some support.

This is Why We Have Insurance, Right?

We are taught from a young age, get a good job and you can have security and benefits like medical coverage. You work hard, pay your monthly premiums and feel protected. Besides, the occasional visit to the doctor for a cold or something equally insignificant, you figure you are fully protected should something serious happen; a catastrophic illness or an accident. Then a terrible injury happens, so no problem, right? After all, this is why you have insurance in the first place, right?

Chris is showing progress with his rehabilitation but the day has come where his insurance will no longer pay for his therapy. How is this possible? The insurance company has no right to play God and make the decision that Chris is not able to benefit from any further therapy. Cognitively he is not even close to being his normal self, not to mention his physical problems with walking and balance. I am very very angry when the therapist tells me he is being cut off. She knows and I know that he needs more time. How can they tell Chris and me that this is "as good as it gets" and just drop him. Once my anger subsides, I realize that I need to take more time off from work to observe Chris at his therapy sessions. As I monitor Chris and his therapists, I pay close attention to the exercises he is performing so that we can continue working on therapy at home. Some of the exercises he can do by himself while I am at work, but there are others that require my support and assistance.

Later as he progresses at home, I call Barb, his physical therapist at Rusk, and she generously continues to provide me with more challenging exercises. To help challenge Chris I also purchase a Total Gym from a neighbor. My gut feeling is that this machine, along with a treadmill my sister Mindy gives me, will be wonderful tools to help improve his balance and coordination, and increase overall muscle tone. Although Chris is hesitant, we take things very slowly so he can not only get accustomed to the new exercises Barb gives me, but so he can experience success. I am usually exhausted when I get home from work, but I push myself to stay positive and up beat and become Chris's substitute therapist before preparing dinner.

Driver's Education

Day 442: I am lounging in the living room when I hear the dining room chairs being moved around. Before I know it Amy comes over to me and says," Chris, I want to try something." She looks so excited and proud about what she wants to show me, I can hardly refuse to check it out. As we walk into the dining room, I notice one dining room chair turned away from the table and two objects on the ground in front of it. Amy helps me get seated and tells me that we are going to pretend that I am in the driver's seat of a car and that the objects on the floor are the brake and gas pedals. I hesitate at first to try out her "car," but knowing how much thought and effort Amy puts into her attempts to help me, I give it a real try.

I place my feet and arms in the driving position and Amy begins a narration to help me visualize being on the road. We start off by her simply telling me to put my foot on the gas and head down the street. She says, "a red light is coming up, so start to put your foot on the brake." As I continue driving down this imaginary road she suddenly says, "look out, a dog is crossing the street in front of you." I make a sharp turn as if veering out of the path of a pedestrian. My arms and legs begin to shake and I start to fall off the chair. Luckily, Amy is there to hold me and keep me from falling. We both take a breath and look at each other and break the tension with a joke.

Day 446: Amy and I see Dr. Kapoor today. We tell her about my "driving session" that I did in the dining room and how I would like to try the real thing when she feels I am ready to take on the challenge. She arranges for me to take a driving readiness test at the SUNY Optometric Center and I pass it with flying colors.

Driving 101

While Chris is anxious to get behind the wheel, he is not sure he still possesses the ability to drive again. I don't know for sure but think we should somehow test his driving potential. I am worried about his reaction time and his tendency to startle and how it will affect his driving. Chris is determined to drive again and is very insistent, but before I take him out in the car or even speak to a medical professional, I set up what I call a driving simulator in our dining room. I place a dining room chair in the middle of the dining room with two wooden blocks on the floor in the position of the gas and brake pedal. I have Chris sit in the chair as if it is the driver's seat, pretending to hold his hands on a steering wheel. I ask him to turn right and turn left as if he is really driving, making sure he remembers to put on the turning signal. Okay, he is doing fairly well, so let's see if he can follow my instructions. I speak very slowly, telling him that he is driving to the store, and that a stop sign is coming up. His foot shakes a little as he switches to the brake. I tell him to make sure he looks both ways and drive straight to the store. With a sense of urgency in my voice, I tell him a dog is crossing the road, "Hurry and stop or you will hit the dog." His foot shakes reaching for the brake pedal and at the same time he tries to swerve quickly turning the pretend wheel and nearly falls off the chair, as his body trembles out of control. By this point, he is exhausted and we sit and hug each other for a while as we joke about the near fatal "simulated" hit.

When we see Chris's brain injury eye specialist Dr. Kapoor, I tell her what I am doing to test his driving ability. She schedules Chris for a driving aptitude test and it is clear from the results that under the proper circumstances he is ready to get behind the wheel.

Problem Solving

Day 463: January 18, 2001. Today I participate in the first cognitive remediation group of the New Year. It's like being back at school after the long Christmas vacation. There are plenty of smiles, handshakes, and hugs to go around. Sharon and Mathew seem almost elated to see us all back for group. I guess we really missed one another. I have a sense of purpose being here like I had at work. Well, I guess this is my job for the time being. Something is better than nothing. A terrific list of strategies for emotional self-regulation is passed around and stimulates some excited conversation.

I think the strategies that are most meaningful to me involve anticipation of trouble spots, setting limits for myself, and not over committing to activities. I have to leave myself an "out." On a more practical plane, I should take regular naps to keep my emotions on an even keel. I feel like I have learned a lot today. I just have to put it into action.

Some Place Calm and Peaceful

Day 470: Another weekday morning and I am on my way to the cognitive remediation group at Rusk. As usual, I sit in the specialty seats. I am eating a bagel and watching the world go by. My sense of ease is suddenly interrupted as a man, woman, and a crying toddler enter the bus with a huge Cadillac size stroller. This mammoth vehicle can barely make it down the aisle, but it doesn't stop the guy from trying. As luck would have it, the man squeezes into the seat between me and his significant other holding the toddler. The man is balancing a crutch in one hand and the stroller in the other. He is so busy trying to quiet down the kid that he keeps pressing the stroller wheels against my knees. I become real tense and my shoulders stiffen. My teeth clench. My chest tightens so much I am struggling to breathe. I feel trapped in the bus with no room to move. There are so many people on the bus that there is not even any room for people to stand. Everyone is pressed together like sardines in a can. I am fuming, thinking to myself that this guy doesn't know that I exist and is worse than inconsiderate. My limited energy is ebbing and my anxiety is getting the better of me, when suddenly it comes to me. I take a few deep breaths and try to visualize being someplace else; someplace calm and peaceful like the Caribbean islands. I close my eyes and say to myself that this is a temporary situation.... It's not that bad… It's not the end of the world. I repeat these things to myself over and over again until I calm down. As I calm down I empathize with the man. This poor guy is trying to balance an oversized stroller and a crutch, while calming his toddler down. That's got to be real difficult. I figure out that by moving as far over on my seat as possible, the stroller doesn't bang into my knee. Man, this stuff that we are talking about in the group actually works. I am amazed. Here I am, a person who used to facilitate groups that helped people to modify their behavior and alter their perception of situations, yet it all seems brand new. It's very different to utilize these ideas as a patient or client rather than implementing and promoting this type of process as a professional. It's much more challenging and rewarding when your own well-being is on the line.

Later in the group when I talk about this experience, I cannot help being proud. I handled it very well. Yeah, I had started to unravel cognitively and emotionally, but when I stop and put the brakes on, I am able to access and apply some self-regulation techniques, which are the meat and potatoes of the Rusk group. By using the "positive self-talk" technique, deep breathing, visualization, and empathy I am able to successfully deal with an otherwise deteriorating situation. I am doing just fine. Faces around the table, mostly older than mine, glow with warm smiles. The praise is generous. I am really going to miss this group when it ends in April.

Shooting Hoops

Day 550: Amy, Paul and I take advantage of a wonderful April-Spring day to walk up to our community outdoor basketball court. It is a bonus not to have any one else on the court bouncing balls and being a distraction. Although I mostly watch Amy and Paul duke it out one on one, they ask me to go to the line for some shots. Amy stands behind me as Paul hands me the ball and retrieves it for me. It is so much fun, just kidding around on the court.

Since Amy and I have been practicing jumping in place over the past couple of weeks, she suggests that I take a shot while jumping at the same time. I am not so sure about this one, but I know Amy and Paul are there if I run into trouble. I try it a few times, missing the shots. I feel like my pockets are filled with heavy concrete when I jump, and when I land I almost lose my balance.

Finally, it happens. As my feet leave the court for a microsecond, I release the basketball from my hands toward the net. Not only do I make the basket, it is a swish. That's right, nothin' but net! Man that feels great. Amy and Paul share high-fives with me as we all cheer. Much to all of our surprise, I make a couple more shots successfully, but I do need to sit down to recoup. I will build on this success.

Out and About

Chris and I try to take a walk every day now that the weather is warming up. This is a good time for me to raise the bar and work with Chris on his physical therapy. To prepare him for a few jogging strides I have him take long robot-like steps. He is only able to take a couple of long steps each day but eventually I have him add a little bounce to his step to create a jog. From that point, I hope he will gradually begin to run. We also work on hopping. It is not only hard for Chris to lift his feet off the ground, singly or together; but it is also difficult to manage to land with a body that does not stop shaking. Sometimes I swear we are both going to lose our footing and take a tumble. I try with all my might to steady him and keep him secure; I praise him continually.

His brother Paul comes by and suggests we go "shoot some hoops." What a great day for fresh air and sport. I know for Chris's sake that I can turn play into a therapy session. Paul and I play a little, while Chris sits on a bench and watches. Soon we have him on his feet and are urging him to take a shot. Before he knows it he is at the foul line. I am anxious to see him let loose and throw the ball. He brings the ball up over his head and tries to aim. He shoots and the ball doesn't even get close to the lower part of the board. Paul encourages him to try again and again, but he doesn't even come close to the hoop. He is ready to give up, but since we are working on jumping today, I ask him to add a jump before he shoots to get some additional height. He is hesitant but decides to go ahead. I ready myself for his shaky landing. Unbelievable! He makes the shot. Paul and I are dumbfounded and ecstatic at the same time. Trying not to show too much surprise, Paul tells him it's "beginners luck" and jokingly bets he cannot repeat. You can see on Chris's face that he is now a little more confident and before I can get into place to steady him, he jumps and "swish," nothing but net. Our loud high-pitched praise throws Chris off balance. Paul forgets about

184

retrieving the ball and runs over to help me catch him. Chris is exhausted but embraces Paul with a big smile on his face. We help him over to the bench to rest and Paul and I play a little "one on one". We glance over to see him still smiling. What a proud day for him. Another step towards the top of that mountain... nothing can stop him.

Chapter Eleven

From Anger to Acceptance?

Facing Forty

Day 575: Another milestone is coming up. This May I will be forty. There are so many broken dreams that are highlighted by this prospect. In my weekly session with Dvorah I try to clear away this debris to get it out of my system.

I tell her that I am turning forty years old this month. It isn't so difficult in itself, but what's hard to accept is how my career goals have been short-circuited by this accident. This is what eats at me. I tell her, "I resent, at times, other people's success while my ability to succeed is taken away from me with a swing of a door... just when everything was in reach."

Dvorah asks, "Who are you angry at?" I respond, "Who am I angry at?.... I don't have the time to be angry! I just want to get better so I can get back to work!" As my session winds down she tells me that I have to move beyond the anger to resolve my feelings. "You have to address them before there can be any resolution." She encouraged me to journal about this over the coming week.

After leaving the session the question she asks sticks with me. All kinds of thoughts roll through my head. Am I really that angry and not aware of it? Is it that noticeable to others? Perhaps, I am so intent on getting better I have had no time to explore my emotions. The only thing wrong with this is that these emotions may be interfering with my recovery. I am so afraid of getting depressed and demoralized I ignore this negative self-destructive energy. Maybe I have to corral all that emotional energy I have inside and refocus it. So, here it goes, full throttle and all out in the open.

The Anger

Day 576: Dvorah's question is gnawing at me... Who am I angry at? I take out my journal and with pen in hand, begin to express my perspective on this emotion we call anger. First of all, I think anger expresses many repressed emotions. In talking about anger, it is only fair to include the darker emotions that are usually well hidden and ride on the back of anger. These are feelings of disappointment, frustration, anxiety, loss, inadequacy, resentment and envy. These feelings are repressed and become the matches that ignite anger.

For all of these months since the accident, I am so focused on fighting back, climbing out of this cold, black lonely hole that I close off from a true awareness of my emotions. I believe that now with most of my rehab over I see where I am. I feel thankful for improvement in many areas, but I am not satisfied at all with my overall progress.

I am very disappointed. I always give 150% commitment to whatever I do. I always approach situations with maximum expectations of myself and the outcomes of my labor. I believe that all the hard work of rehab should be rewarded and I should regain what I have lost.

I am very grateful to God, my many therapists, my family and friends for their support and the improvements I have made to date, but the rate of my improvement has slowed and my progress is not very rapid in relation to my daily efforts. The medical experts tell me that there will be some additional improvement over time, which is encouraging and helps me to get up and meet the daily challenges, but this "day to day" struggle takes a heavy toll on my mind, soul and body. It weighs me down. What happens if I lose hope?

The Losses

I have a profound sense of loss. I was on the verge of a career breakthrough when the accident happened. By now I would be an assistant principal receiving close to double my counselor's salary. I was on my way to developing my own training institute and laying the groundwork for a private practice. Things were, for the first time in my adult life, starting to gel. After the accident, I was not ready or willing to put my goals and ambitions aside and merely put all my energy and resources into getting better. Then the board of education pulls the rug out from under me and recommends retirement. I am not totally surprised, but I hold on for dear life to these once real possibilities. They disappear. Suddenly, my ambitions, goals, and sense of purpose are taken away from me. Suddenly, the light is extinguished.

Prior to the accident I enjoyed a very full social life. I use to get so charged up interacting with groups of people, whether family members, friends or perfect strangers. More than that, my heart and soul are fueled by performing in public. I am a true extravert, feeling a rush in front of any audience, public speaking, acting, singing, playing guitar or piano. It positively inspired me and was a source of strength. I used to be the kind of person who enjoyed life to the fullest, always game for something new from deep sea diving in the Caribbean to cross country skiing in the Adirondacks.

New York, New York, the city that never sleeps. It's a cliché but it's true. I used to love the energy of the city. It invigorated me. Now, that same city zaps out of me the power it once gave me. The bright lights, crowds, intense noises and smells, fast moving objects, fast talking people, are now a recipe for disaster. I miss getting off on the urban energy.

Silly Little Innocent Adolescent Things

I miss the silly little innocent adolescent things my wife and I used to do together, just the two of us hanging around the house. Somehow it used to be magical chasing Amy around the rooms tickling her until she can't run from me any longer and laughing at each other till our stomachs ached, or playing swords like the "Three Musketeers" with those cardboard tubes from the Christmas wrapping paper. It was exhilarating picking her up and twirling her around when something wonderful and exciting happens; or for no reason at all except to let her know I love her.

Despite how drastically life has changed since my accident, my wife and I are in love just as much, if not more than before. We are the statistical exception. Still the daily challenges of dealing with my condition take a toll. We have been dating since 1979 and have been married since 1983. After all these years you just know how someone thinks and feels despite what they may or may not say. I can see in her eyes the impact this is having on her. Amy and I don't talk about the "dark side" of this injury too often. It is just too painful. I think Amy always tries to stay as positive as she can about the prognosis, despite what the doctors tell us. I believe our deep love for each other and our years of support for one another will enable us to transcend this experience. For richer, for poorer, in good times and in bad, in sickness and in health. Who would ever have thought?

Just a Passenger

My independence is another casualty. I acknowledge that I have come a long way from those dreadful days confined to a wheelchair at the Mount Sinai inpatient program, but I miss doing those things I used to do without even thinking about it. I miss driving. It didn't matter where I went, it could be just to the corner grocery store or the gas station. I just loved being behind the wheel. Now, I am just the passenger. Come to think about it, I am "just the passenger" in most everything we do. I used to provide Amy with support, comfort, strength, and encouragement, and now I can't even provide these for myself.

Everything I do, from the most simple to complex task requires Amy's assistance. The truth is that I am no longer a fully contributing partner to our relationship. There can be imbalances in relationships, but this is ridiculous. I try to raise my morale by viewing my current condition as temporary. Hopefully, I will improve and be able to take some of the burden off Amy's shoulders.

On the Sidelines

Resentment and envy are constant companions. Yes, I am sometimes resentful of the accomplishments of others. I know this is wrong and goes against so many of the teachings I grew up with. Nevertheless, it is the truth. I feel like I am a bystander, watching my contemporaries seize opportunities that I can only dream about. Maybe I am happy for their successes but I resent my inability to engage in my own pursuit of success, particularly my professional goals. I am not a sidelines sort of person; I hate being outside of things and on the periphery.

The way I define success today is very different from the past. My measure of success is how long I can concentrate on a task before my head begins to ache and feel tingly and numb. I measure my success by how long I can socialize before fatigue and exhaustion overcome me and I need to find a quiet place to chill out. I consider myself a success if I am able to complete my day's schedule of home therapies without incident.

Frustration is what occurs just before I get angry. How I behave out of frustration, thankfully, is beginning to change since my participation in the cognitive remediation group. The feelings of frustration still rear their ugly heads but I handle them better.

In the first days following the injury, during my time in therapy, I was totally consumed by recovery. I was sure I would get everything back that I lost. Over time another reality set in, one that I have difficulty still accepting. I am beginning to realize I might never be the same man. Still I stayed focused on improving. Early on in my rehabilitation, I blocked out the idea that I may not fully recover. It was too much to take. I just focused on getting better and getting back on the old career track.

Denial works for a while, as do most defense mechanisms. I think it helped me survive emotionally. Denial seemed to be an affective tool while in crisis during the initial stages of the rehab process. Maybe I was just putting off the inevitable. Anyway, once acknowledged, the impossibility of full recovery began to haunt me. I began to dwell on the negative, I despaired. Feelings of loss, resentment, and disappointment bubbled up from the depths of my being.

Straight Talk with God

So, who am I angry at? I have said all along that I know Thomas didn't intentionally strike me with the steel door, so how can I be angry with him? After all, accidents happen, right? But truthfully, I am angry with him. Why did he have to push the door open with such force at that exact moment as people are filing out? He had to notice the other people. Now he is going on with the rest of his life, going about business as usual, while there is nothing in my daily routine that is at all usual. I have been working and will continue to work on the challenges that confront me each day as a result of this brain injury. I worked so hard at my school as a counselor, advocate and friend to the students and this is what I get?

Thomas is not the only one on my list. God is also on my list. After all my personal investment in helping others I find myself asking God, "Why did you let this happen to me?" I was doing such good work for young people. I was not nearly finished. I was just getting started. You have not only changed my life, but also Amy's life in one swift swing. Why couldn't You watch over me? Yeah, I'm not stuck in a hospital bed with a paralyzing brain injury, for which I am thankful. But my life has changed forever, and I have no idea what I can expect from the present or the future.

As much as I have made improvement, I want more, much more. I am doing everything I can do, but I want more help. Yes, I have heard from many people that You never give us anything we can't handle, but I want to do even more than the minimal "handle it," I want to overcome it. Being angry at You does not mean that I have lost faith in You. I am thankful for feeling Your presence in my life, but I need more of it right now.

A Miracle in Reserve

At one time I thought that I accepted my situation. Far from it, I actually just bottled it up and stuck it on a shelf way in the back. I honestly don't believe I will regain everything that I have lost, but hell, there's always a miracle in reserve. I feel that there are times when I accept where and who I am, but then there are other times that all of the frustration, resentment and anger get the better of me, particularly when I am going nuts trying to accomplish the smallest task, or losing it when I am involved in some small social activity.

Perhaps the best healer really is "Time Itself." Time may not totally heal this physical wound, but it may hopefully heal me emotionally. I certainly hope so. I am getting tired shaking my fist at the Almighty.

Day 596: I share some of the exasperation I put into my journal in my session with Dvorah. She urges me to continue questioning and confronting myself. She suggests that I ask myself about each emotion individually: "What do you have to teach me? Do you still need to be here? Would you like me to free from you or is there still something I need to learn from you? "

A New Criterion

Later as I ponder these questions, trying to puzzle out Dvorah's thinking and purpose in presenting them. I wonder if the emotional reactions I experience are necessary in order to recognize and be happy with my accomplishments. I think that these reactions are understandable and okay to express. Perhaps the more okay I feel about these emotional reactions, the less impact they will have on me over time. Like Dvorah says, "Let these emotions present themselves, but don't hold on to them. Let them pass through you." Who said, "You cannot experience pleasure unless you have experienced pain?" I can truly relate to this statement more now than at any other time in my life. As much as I may release these heavy emotions in the future, they seem to be a motivator for me right now. I don't want to feel the heavy burden that comes with these emotions so I try to use them as motivators and strive toward acquiring new strategies and accomplishing tasks that were unmanageable a year or so ago. Choosing a goal and trying to accomplish it is what gets me going each morning. Yes, success is measured differently for me right now, but it is important for me to recognize that whatever I accomplish, no matter how little it may appear, is in fact success. I think this broadens my view on what it means to be successful and will help reduce my sense of loss, frustration and disappointment.

Depositions

Day 623: Amy and I head into the city for a legal deposition for my case against the Board of Education. The lawyer is a woman, a hard as nails kind of woman. She hammers me with questions in the confined spaces of a small office. There is hardly any letup, regardless of my condition, which she must be familiar with. She keeps me going for most of the day until I am groggy with fatigue and my head is pounding. I am still glad to get things moving.

Day 637: It's a hot July day, humid with the promise of rain, and it's back to another lawyer's office for part two of my deposition. This lawyer is more humane than the female attorney. He takes his time and lets me take my time. I am calm enough so I don't stutter too much and don't find myself having to repeat everything. He asks me several questions about the therapies at Mount Sinai. After a full review, running down the list, he asks me what I specifically did in physical therapy with Dave.

Suddenly, as if in a dream, I flash back to the first time I saw Dave in the physical therapy gym. He rolls me forward in my wheel chair between the parallel bars and helps me stand up, while holding onto the bars. My body feels like a loose erector set. He asks me to take a step toward him. I remember him looking at me and repeating several times "Come on Chris, take a step toward me." I know what he wants me to do, but can't make my legs do it. Finally, he picks up my legs one at a time and places them ahead of each other. The lawyer questions me again which brings me back to the here and now, "Chris what did the physical therapist actually do for you?" I thought for a moment and felt my eyes watering up and said, "He helped me learn to walk again."

In the Swim

Day 644: Amy comes home from work and immediately says, "Come on Chris, we are going to go swimming." I am not thrilled about this idea. I have not been in a pool since my brain injury. But Amy is very persistent, so I reluctantly get my suit on and we head to the pool. To my surprise, no one is at the pool. Amy carefully helps me down the ladder into the water. I just stand in the water holding on to the side of the pool for dear life. The texture of the water affects my vestibular system and

195

makes my brain feel wavy, numb, and tingly as it did in the early stages of my recovery. With no relief in site, we decide it is time to get out of the pool. She helps me back up the ladder where I rest on a nearby lounge chair and soak in some of the warm sun until I am ready to make my way back to our townhouse. I am exhausted, but feel a wonderful sense of accomplishment and ask Amy if we can try it again tomorrow.

It is a little easier getting into the pool the next day, and I am able to stand for a longer period of time before the dizziness overwhelms me. During the next several weeks we continue to go to the pool. Amy helps me work on my muscle coordination and balance by having me stand on one foot as long as I can. She is right there to stabilize me as soon as I begin to sway off balance.

Weeks later, I am holding onto the side of the pool and kicking my legs as Amy supports my body in a floating position. As soon as I master this, she supports me in the water with her arms cradling my stomach as I practice kicking my legs and moving my arms at the same time.

Day 687: Finally, SUCCESS! I swim my first lap on my own in over a year and a half after my injury. In the process, I reclaim another part of myself.

Swimming Again

Chris and I loved to swim and snorkel. We both were members of our high school swim team and lifeguards together in college. In the past, it was always easy for us to jump in a pool and start swimming brisk laps for a little exercise. Moving out of our small apartment in Jersey City into the new townhouse in Secaucus, I am really excited to get a look at the community pool. Immediately, my mind starts working. Maybe I can get Chris into the pool. Swimming could be therapy both for his body and his spirit. At first, Chris isn't too enthusiastic about the possibility. All he can see are the loud children, whooping and

196

hollering, running around, jumping and belly flopping into the pool. I urge him to relax, reminding him, that he was a kid once and did the same kind of stuff.

One afternoon I get home early from work and notice that no one is in the pool. I quickly go into the house and in my best drill sergeant voice issue an order: "Get your swimsuit on, we are going to the pool, no ifs, ands, or buts." Surprisingly, he only resists a little as I start to take his clothes off. With a half smile, he pushes me away, saying, "Okay, okay, I get your point. I can put my suit on myself." Chris, cane in hand, and I make our way to the pool. I don't expect him to jump in swimming, but I do have some ideas how to gradually get him into the swim.

I help Chris down the ladder and we simply stand in the water. I hold him by the waist. He says he feels like there are waves constantly pushing against him and the pool filter noise reverberates like a jackhammer in his head. We only stay in the water for about ten minutes. It is obviously time to get out. His legs shake trying to take one step at a time up the ladder. I start to think, maybe, I made the wrong decision.

We sit in lounge chairs for a little while and soak up some sun. Not a word passes between us until he says, "That felt great, I'll be ready when you get home tomorrow if you want to try this again." I nearly fall over and simply reply, "yeah, sure." Each day we go back it gets easier for him to stand in the water and I begin to think of some exercises for him to do. I have him hold on to the side of the pool and lift one leg at a time. He still needs help out of the pool, and we always rest before we return home. When we get back he usually collapses into the living room chair and sleeps while I make dinner.

By the end of the third week at the pool he is more confident getting in and out. One evening we meet a friendly neighbor named Sean. He notices Chris is doing special exercises in the pool and questions him about the nature of his condition. In his labored speech Chris explains that he is a brain injury survivor and spends every other day at the Rusk Institute in the city. Life is full of coincidences. It turns out that Sean is a physical therapist and right on the spot starts to give Chris other exercises to do to improve his balance. They are difficult at first but Sean holds him and encourages him to keep trying. Chris is very excited when we get home, but his exhilaration ends in disappointment when he hears on the radio that it is going to rain the next day. He worries that he will forget how to do the new exercises.

By the fourth week in the pool, Chris feels comfortable enough to let me help him float on his stomach. We slowly add the arm movement for the breaststroke and by the end of the week we add a kick. We practice, practice, practice his strokes over the next couple weeks. His effort pays off big! He swims the whole length of the pool with me by his side in case of an emergency. I am so thrilled for him that I can barely contain my excitement. When he finishes his lap the big smiles we give each other tell the whole story. I give him a big hug and tell him how proud I am of him.

The move to the townhouse development in Secaucus is the best thing we could do for Chris. It really contributes to his improvement. The complex has a beautiful walkway with bushes, trees and flowers. On our walks, he practices walking backwards, little hops, and the beginning stages of running. You name it, I always think of something challenging for him to do besides ordinary walking.

We have wonderful neighbors who, once made aware of Chris's accident, make a real effort to keep their kids very quiet when we visit. They are patient when Chris tries to speak or has difficulty finding the right word or stutters trying to get it out. They do not judge Chris, and I can tell he finally believes that he can be a part of the world again. Secaucus in the spring and summer is medicinal and magical for Chris. He finds his smile and I think his soul finally reconnects.

Here Comes the Bride

Day 689: It's September, a time for setting out on new adventures. I enjoy the prospect of going up to Utica for my sister Laurie's wedding. Amy and I spend a lot of time planning and preparing for any difficulties we might encounter over that weekend.

We decide to stay at a bed and breakfast inn in Utica rather than with my mom and dad. It is something we always wanted to do since Amy and I first drove pass the place and gazed at its beautiful castle-like exterior on the way to visit my great aunts. Staying at the B&B turns out to be the best decision we make. It feels like a sort of retreat as soon as we enter the building. I am filled with a sense of calm and well-being as soon as the door closes behind us. This is just what I need to recharge between the ceremony and the wedding reception. My friend Gabe and his wife Anne also stay at the B& B. They are good company and their familiar faces bring me a sense of security.

The ceremony and reception are wonderful. My sister is a beautiful bride and my dad gives her away with poignant dignity. The food is particularly good and I top it off with a festive sip of champagne. While I thoroughly enjoy myself, it is totally wearing. Between a couple hundred friends and relatives, the band and the toasts, and all the hand shaking and hugging, I am having a rough time managing things as the evening progresses. Eventually my brain gives out and stops talking to my body. The result is overload. My head hurts, I can barely speak, and my gait is very shaky. Gabe and another friend, Neil, help me exit the frenetic reception area and guide me to a pre-arranged quiet space where I can hide out for the remainder of the evening.

Despite my fatigue, I am able to get myself back together to have one dance, a slow dance with Amy. I have not danced with her since Jeff and Laura's wedding. Even though I merely stand in place while she holds my hands, it is both a very happy and sad moment. Yes, I am pleased to accomplish what I set out to do, which is to get enough rest so that I can have this last dance with my wife. While we are holding each other we are speaking volumes without saying a word. As our eyes fix on one other I know we are both reflecting back on how much our life has changed since my brain injury. We are filled with joy that we are able to be here together for this wonderful celebration knowing that the results of this accident could have been much worse, yet at the same time we are thinking about the rough road that still lies ahead. As our eyes begin tearing up we hold each other even more tightly in an effort to reassure each other that everything will work out.

May I Have this Dance?

Since Chris's injury, we have been to a couple of weddings and it is always particularly sad for me not to enjoy a dance with Chris. I miss more than anything Chris holding me in his arms waltzing me around the dance floor. He always said he couldn't dance and when we dance it is not the standard showcase steps you see on television ballroom dancing, but it is me, Cinderella, in my Prince Charming's arms and I miss it terribly. He is a terrific dancer. He can rock and roll and disco with the best of them, but his real forte is the slow romantic dance. I never feel as secure and loved as when he holds me in his arms and slides me across the dance floor.

Recently, at our friend's Jeff and Laura's wedding, while everyone is whirling around the floor and we stay seated at our table in the corner, Chris asks me to dance. I am flabbergasted and start to lead him to the dance floor, but he stops me and says, "No, right here." He pushes his chair in and opens his arms out to me. We dance there in our tiny corner. It is more of a sway with little tiny baby steps, but, oh, it is heaven. It lasts only about five minutes and he is so tired I have to help him to sit *down. We both have tears in our eyes; tears of sadness for what we have lost and tears of hope for a new beginning.*

The last wedding of the year is his sister's. We are both in the wedding party. Laurie, Chris's sister, ever thoughtful and considerate, makes special arrangements for her wedding to help Chris fully participate. As we approach the restaurant for the reception I hold him tight as we enter the ballroom knowing that the noise of the DJ and enthusiasm of our family members can throw him off balance.

After the usual toasts the music begins to play, I cannot help jumping up with the bride and bridesmaids and begin dancing. I look over and see Chris smiling, he seems fine, just glad I'm having fun. As the music gets louder, I see our friends Gabe and Neil help him from the dais and lead him out the door. I follow and sit with them for a while. Chris tells me to go back in and have fun. He is comfortable in this quiet room. I feel very guilty leaving him but he insists, so I bring Neil's daughter out with me to dance and I make sure she is having a good time too.

I keep going back to look in on Chris resting in a big armchair. Before I know it, it is time for the last dance. I look out over the dance floor and see Gabe and Neil bringing Chris over to me. Chris says softly "I couldn't miss the last dance with you." He holds me in his arms and we sway. He even takes a couple of steps this time. I can feel his heavy weight on me and know he is tired but he wants so much to dance the last dance with me. Tears come to my eyes during this magical moment that is over too soon. I help him sit down to rest. When we return to our romantic B&B we slowly walk up the stairs to our room and I help him undress. He is asleep before I can hop into bed. My prince, what a wonderful night!

A Delicate Question

Day 690:   The next morning we stop by my parent's house to say goodbye on our way back to New Jersey. The house is packed with family and friends. My engine is running down from the night before, so I make my way to the dining room table to sit down and take a breather for a few moments. As we say our farewells my eleven year old nephew comes up and gives me a hug. He asks me with great solemnity and sincerity, "Uncle Chris, are you going to be handicapped forever?"

The room suddenly becomes very still. You can hear a pin drop. Everyone seems as shocked as I am. I am taken aback and don't know what to say. I am so surprised that he uses that word that is not an every-day word for a young boy. Honestly, I don't ever refer to my injury as a handicap, although I know that it is. All I know is that I have to do better than an awkward silence in response to my nephew's very legitimate question. He is waiting for and expecting an answer. In an attempt to put friends and family at ease and respect my nephew's honest question, I somehow get my wits together and say, "Well, I am working real hard to get better each day, and hopefully I will." That response seems to satisfy him. He walks away unaware of any discomfort he has caused, nodding to himself as if he found out what he wanted to know.

When I tell Dvorah, my psychotherapist, about this incident she says, "He asked what most people probably want to know." I think she's right. Who wouldn't want to know what the future holds? I am not sure if people heard my response or understood the impact of my nephew's inquiry, but I know one thing, I am working on improving as much as I can as each day passes.

Chapter Twelve

The Realization

Lost in a Labyrinth

Day 699: It is September 11, 2001. The clock radio wakes me. The radio personality is talking about the havoc at the World Trade Center. His voice sounds frenetic. I am still pretty out of it and I am sure that he is referring to the 1993 bombing. I wonder if today is the anniversary of that attack. Amy calls me from her office and tells me to turn on the news. I am stunned to see a tower toppled by an airliner. Amy says she will call back if she is able to and tentatively adds, "If anything should happen..." I stop her mid sentence and say, "Nothing is going to happen, just please be careful and get home safely."

I am as unsure as she is at this point what will happen next, or whether she will come home without incident. I pray not only for her safe return, but also for the Trade Center victims and their families whose lives are tragically changed forever. I receive several calls from my family upstate as well as from friends in Europe who worry about Amy and me. I can only tell them that I am okay and am hoping to hear from Amy soon. I feel so helpless sitting on my bed and watching the events unfold on TV, not knowing if Amy is safe or in danger. It is reassuring that her office is in midtown Manhattan far from the scene of carnage, but until I see her face to face I am still uneasy. Thankfully, she is able to get home to Jersey later that afternoon by a commuter boat and my brother and I drive to pick her up.

But what about those people who will never see their loved ones again? I ask myself a lot of questions that evening and many more in the upcoming days. No doubt, because of my background in counseling and my position in the school system,

I would have joined a crisis response team from my Manhattan School district; helping students and their families cope with the trauma of death and destruction. Given my current condition, I am unable to contribute. This frustrates me so much. It hurts to know I am unable to help others at a time when so many need assistance. About the only thing I can do is pray for all the suffering families as well as our government leaders who will require knowledge, insight and moral courage to make the right decisions in response to this attack. I wish I could do more.

The Tragic Day

On this dreadful day, this tragic day, I think I may never see Chris again. I call him at home and ask him to turn on the TV, and as he describes to me in stark detail what he sees I immediately think the worst. In the midst of my farewells I say, "Just in case something happens I want you to know"... He interrupts me and reassures me that nothing is going to happen and tells me to just get home safely. Then the phones go dead. The thoughts that go through my mind, my fear and anguish can in no way compare to those who were trying to contact loved ones who actually work in the World Trade Center buildings, but the feelings of loss, emptiness and horror weigh heavily on me.

As an emergency measure an e-mail is displayed on everyone's computer at work announcing a meeting to discuss evacuation plans. I envision more attacks and being trapped on this island with no escape to the boroughs or New Jersey. I wonder who would take care of Chris if I were to perish. I worry how Chris will survive without me by his side.

Once my office develops a plan for all employees to leave safely we file out of our midtown hi-rise building and everyone begins to walk in different directions. Some head towards the Brooklyn Bridge where loved ones will be there to pick them up. Many, like me, walk towards a ferry landing where boats are waiting to carry passengers to New Jersey. After a three-hour wait I board the ferry to Weehawken, New Jersey. I place myself close to an exit should our boat be hit by a missile or something. Again my thoughts run wild. I know I can swim the distance to the Jersey shore if I have to. I am able to make one more call to Chris on my cell phone. He has already arranged with his brother Bill to pick me up at a nearby gas station. There are several buses lined up to take people to Giant stadium, but I only have a short walk to where Chris and his brother Bill are waiting.

When I see Chris and Bill pull up I feel like I haven't seen them for years. We ride home in total silence. We all are thinking of the events of this day. When we get home I sit down and watch the news. For the first time I see the images Chris described to me on the phone and I sob. That night we stay close to each other thankful that we still have one another to hold and to love.

A New Group

Day 713: Although I sometimes miss the camaraderie of my group at Rusk and the support and routine of regular physical, occupational, and speech therapy, I am not eager to attend a brain injury support group for family members and survivors that meet monthly at Kessler Institute. Amy, on the other hand, is determined to attend. It takes place early in the evening but I think it is too late for me to handle the strain. I am afraid by the end of the meeting I will be physically exhausted. I am not at my best by the time evening rolls around. I don't want to embarrass myself in a room full of people. I defer to Amy. It's her choice. She really has not had the benefit of all my time in therapy learning about traumatic brain injury and its many related issues. She probably also has a need to relate to others in her situation.

The meeting is okay. I just listen to other people comment and contribute. It is hard for me to keep up with the give and

205

take. It feels like I am receiving a signal via satellite from another country; the delay is so significant. By the time I think of a response to what someone says the topic has changed. Everyone is given a chance to share their names and how their injury occurred with the whole group. I am glad Amy speaks for me. It is very necessary, since I am really struggling just to get my words out without stuttering or losing my train of thought.

It is strange to have such difficulty, aren't I steadily improving? I guess it's one step forward, two steps back. One of the members of the group makes a very good point. I nod in agreement. There is far too little information about TBI and its effects available to the general public. It is a major health problem and most people don't know it exists. Members of this organization and others like it regularly receive newsletters from a few Brain Injury organizations, but that's where it stops.

It is alarming to me just how long people have been coming to this group. I meet people who have been attending meetings for three years, seven years, and even over twelve years. I guess I avoid looking too far into the future, while trying to manage my own injury. I hope by coming to this group Amy and I will gain additional support and broaden our ability to more successfully plan our lives and move beyond the group support process.

It is becoming clearer to me that the lifestyle changes we are making are much more permanent than temporary. I am starting to think that this group support may be long term. This is an eye opener for me. Being with so many brain injured people, not so different from me, still working on the same issues year after year jolts me into a difficult realization. Will anything ever change? I have a vision of never ending futility. I think, on some level, the bigger picture has escaped me. In some sense these meetings of survivors and their families is enlightening. Seeing my peers in action takes me outside the vacuum in which I have been living in since my injury.

I wonder if, in my desire to continue to work on improving, that I keep myself from understanding that this will be a lifelong undertaking. The bottom line is that I need to begin accepting where I am and hope that I can continue to improve, but I think I may have not really absorbed the "rest of my life" part. I think that deep inside I feel that if I try hard enough I can defy all odds and beat this thing. This awakening forces me to do a reality check. I am not saying that I am giving up working on making improvements, but perhaps I need to start to look at this lifestyle I am thrust into as a more permanent way of life.

On our way home Amy and I are pretty quiet. I think about how many years people have been coming to this group and how they are still trying to deal with the daily struggles from their brain injury. The realty hits me hard. I turn to Amy and softly say, "I don't think I am going to be able to fix this one, Aim." She reaches over and touches my hand and says reassuringly, "Don't worry Chris, we will get through this together."

Getting My Own Help

Finally, there comes a time when I think I am ready to burst from all of this stress. I have no outlet and this life is really starting to get to me. My only time to myself is when I go grocery shopping or do the laundry. One day I look into my employee assistance program, one of my company's benefits. I make an appointment to see a therapist. The program only allows two sessions. I would like to continue seeing her, but medical insurance will not pick up the bill. The therapist does give me some valuable advice. She suggests I join a brain injury support group for caregivers. It seems so obvious, why didn't I think about this myself? I begin to search for one. I am directed to a support group for caregivers and brain injury survivors at the Kessler Rehabilitation Center in East Orange New Jersey. When I mention this group to Chris he is reluctant to go with me. Chris makes it clear how difficult it is for him to follow a conversation with one person, let alone several people speaking in a group setting. He also feels that he has had so much therapy, both individual and group, that he does not know if he is up for any more. I remind him that this is not therapy and that it is more for my support that I really want and need. He seems to understand and agrees to go with me, but he is very apprehensive.

I finally discover that I am not alone. Other people share similar situations that I am currently going through. After the meeting I approach a mom who is a caregiver for her adult son and ask her quietly, "How do you stop from crying?" She holds my hand and says, "You don't, but when you are done crying you somehow turn those tears into strength." I am amazed at how much this mom and the other caregivers in the group help me start to deal with my inner turmoil, at a time when I feel that my very sanity is at risk.

At each monthly meeting Chris sits quietly and listens. We discuss the meetings on the way home and I ask Chris why he does not participate. He says he cannot keep up with the conversation and often feels lost. There are times when he figures out what he wants to say, but by the time he finds the right words the group has moved on to another topic. It takes six months before he speaks in group. The group quickly learns that if Chris is interrupted or distracted he may lose his train of thought, so all are very quiet when he speaks. I am so proud when he takes these first steps and speaks out on different issues. Soon people are even coming up to him after the meeting for advice.

Back in the Driver's Seat

I can't wait to get back in the driver's seat. I can smell the sense of independence that I long for. I swing the door of our townhouse open and Amy and I go down the stairs to the carport where our car is parked. I am psyched and cautious at the same time. Amy opens the car door and I adjust the car seat. I start the car and adjust the mirrors while Amy hops in on the front passenger side. The plan is simply to drive around the complex for a little while.

With a slow and deliberate glance over at Amy I see her confidently looking back encouraging me to start going. With my foot on the brake and the coast clear in the rear view mirror, I put the car in reverse. Slowly releasing my foot from the brake pedal, I begin to back up while looking over my shoulder. I am very focused, but at the same time I feel my head start to go numb from concentrating so intensely. This doesn't stop me. I continue backing up. By the time I clear the carport I feel washed out. My brain is exhausted. As much as I want to take a drive around the complex, we decide it is best to pull back into the carport. The road trip will have to wait another day. I feel down and defeated, I barely left the carport. Am I giving up? Have I failed? Amy is right there to reinforce what I have accomplished. She tells me how confident she is that the next time I will drive much further. Today is just a part of the relearning process, and it has to start like everything else I re-learn, with baby steps.

Amy's Surprise Party

Day 728: October is coming up soon. It's Amy and her twin sister Anita's 40th birthday, a milestone birthday. My Amy deserves a special celebration. She has been through so much since my injury. I am thinking of a surprise party for Amy and her sister. My whole family loves the idea and are eager co-conspirators. On the sly, I speak to Amy's older sister Mindy who always loves a good party. She gets the word out to everyone in Amy's family, while I concentrate on securing a party location and getting my clan together.

Day 746: Everything comes together wonderfully today. Amy and Anita don't suspect a thing as the hostess leads them up to an innocent looking door. Inside, the room is a rainbow of birthday balloons and multicolored decorations. The festive space is overflowing with assembled family and friends. Suddenly, there is one loud reverberating shout: "SURPRISE!" For a moment, Amy and Anita stand stock still, in shock. They are soon radiating smiles as they accept individual congratulations and the applause of the multitude. I look at Amy and get a catch in my throat. My college sweetheart turns forty, in so many ways she has not changed.

Amy and I sit away from the enthusiastic crowd in a comfortable corner with the least amount of noise and distraction. The music is mellow and low decibel. I, of course, wear my earplugs the whole time and do not try to navigate from table to table to greet people. I conserve my energy and let everyone come over to Amy and me to visit.

Happy Birthday

I am one of the few people my age who seem to really love my birthdays. I am blessed that I share this day with my own twin sister and it is very special. Since Chris's injury, my birthdays are quiet low-key affairs. But this is my fortieth, a milestone birthday, and I am anxious to share the day, at the very least, with my sister and her husband. Since Chris is better able to handle socializing and the environment of public places, I ask Chris if we can have a quiet restaurant dinner with my sister and her husband back home in Upstate New York. He thinks it is a great idea and promises to call Mike, my sister Anita's husband, to check it out and finalize the arrangements.

We decide to drive to Utica to stay with Chris's family. We meet Mike and Anita at a shopping mall and drive together to the restaurant. As the hostess brings us to our table I hope it is going to be in a quiet section of the restaurant. Chris is always uppermost on my mind. We follow her through the entire restaurant until we are all the way in the back, in front of

210

another door. I think this is wonderful that we have a private room for us so that Chris will be fine during our dinner. As she opens the door, Anita and I enter the room first and I have never in my life been so surprised. There is a group of about 30 friends and family smiling and shouting happy birthday. I don't think any birthday could ever top this one.

The Broken Computer

Day 761: Dad calls to see how I am doing. I tell him about my formal retirement hearing with the medical review committee for the Board of Education coming up on November 14th. Dad pauses for a minute and asks me if I think the Board of Education would let me try a different type of job instead of retiring me so that I would be able to get my pride back.

I know that dad is trying to be helpful, but the pride comment really bothers me. It seems like after all this time he still doesn't get what's happened to me. This injury is not something that gives me any choice. My brain doesn't work as it did before. If I were able to handle my guidance job or any other position, I would be doing it. My retirement pension is no bonanza. No one is doing me any favors. I respond to him with an analogy. I tell him to think of my brain as the CPU of the computer. "If you drop your computer, it probably won't work right after that. The hard drive may no longer be able to communicate with the motherboard, which is a big problem for the computer. Basically, the computer doesn't function as it did before it was dropped. If you were to look at the computer sitting at the workstation you would never know that something is wrong with it until you tried to do something with it. It looks like it always did before you dropped it, but the reality is it doesn't work the same way. That's me Dad," I explain, "I look like I can do anything, but the reality is that I am unable to do a lot of things, no matter how much I am willing to try."

I can tell that my dad is crestfallen. He says how sorry he is that this all had to happen. I make it clear that I haven't given up on myself, and that I work every day hoping for improvement. "This is my job now," I emphatically state.

No Family Christmas

Day 804: It's Christmas day and I am very sick. It isn't the flu but it feels like the flu. It knocks me for a loop and I can't hold down food and my nose doesn't stop running. The headaches are as bad as they ever were and I even have that feeling of free fall. I cannot walk straight. My balance and speech are erratic. No family Christmas this year, just Amy and me and an artificial tree. It's a struggle to stay upbeat and focus on my recovery exercises. Every day I must consciously motivate myself, constantly urge myself on to new efforts. Complacency is the kiss of death.

Day 810: We spend a quiet New Year's Eve 2002 in front of the TV. Amy and I toast one another with classic Coke, I don't dare have a drink. I long for my drink of choice, a shot of single malt scotch. I am too weary to stay up for the stroke of midnight and the Times Square dazzle. The thrill of the New Year is gone.

Knowledge Empowers

Day 818: Amy accompanies me to see Dr. Kapoor, who goes beyond my eyes and reading problems to help me deal with other aspects of my condition. I always feel more optimistic and sure of myself after a visit with Dr. Kapoor.

I mention to her how sick I have been over the holiday. She tells Amy and me that brain injury symptoms for survivors can intensify with ill health, but will probably lessen as the brain injured person gets better. She adds that these reactions are also triggered by alcohol consumption, physical activity, and stressful environments or situations. She helps me gain more insight into

212

my condition by discussing the neuro anatomy of the brain and how my injury relates to it. She explains that axons, the messengers of the neuron, are likely sheared off or stretched by my head trauma, which blunts the ends of the neurons in different areas of the brain. Sometimes the messages that are sent through the axon do not travel to the neuron as they previously did, or it may not be as clean a connection as it was before the trauma. The information takes a longer time to get to where it needs to go. For me, this helps explain why it takes longer to process information, or why I sometimes can't think of a word to finish a sentence, or have muscle tremors when I reach too far for things. Our discussion increases my overall understanding of what's going on in my brain. The more I work on challenging my brain, the more likely I will be able to rebuild new connections that will help me improve.

Perfect House Guests

Day 1055: It's Labor Day Weekend and Gabe and Anne come down from Toronto for a brief visit. They are the perfect houseguests and great company. I miss the social interactions of a full-time job and enjoy having people around. Gabe also pitches in to do some of the cooking and also helps me with my own kitchen chores. We all have a wonderful time during their stay. We eat a lot of Gabe's hearty Italian cooking and share so much laughter together. Gabe and Anne are both very conscious of my challenges and seem to consider all my various needs during our time together. It helps me to really enjoy myself without the cognitive drain. When Gabe and I are preparing food for dinner he gives me one task at a time, and is thoughtful enough to let me work quietly on my own without small talk to distract me. When I get derailed from a task, distracted or lose my concentration, he quickly gets me back on track. Their stay is a really positive interlude.

Ordeal at Kessler

Day 1063: Amy drives me to Kessler to determine if I am eligible to participate in a six-week balance/gait study she hears about from one of the caregivers in the Brain Injury support group. Prior to acceptance into the study group, I receive a very intense two-hour evaluation. I am totally worn out, both cognitively and physically by the time I leave.

One of the evaluation techniques involves harnessing me into a balance machine, which reminds me of a carnival fun house. After stepping into a large cocoon shaped structure, the therapist straps me into something resembling a parachute harness. I am instructed to stand up and keep my balance as long as I can while the walls rotate around and the footing changes. The platform I am standing on shifts forward and backward. The test makes me nauseous and upsets my stomach. The activity wreaks havoc in my brain. As the floor and walls move my entire body shakes violently, uncontrollably. I become angry and depressed. I flash back to the days right after the accident when I actually walked like this. It is terrible. Tears of frustration and despair well up in my eyes. I feel like I am back where I started.

The therapist notices I am upset. I confide my sense of desperation. She says that this is to be expected. These evaluation techniques are designed to determine my baseline, which will be used at a later point to determine my degree of improvement. She encourages me indicating some of the things we can work on together that will contribute to my further rehabilitation. The doctor, who is observing the process, challenges me to turn my frustration into positive energy, to help me stay focused on improving. This makes a lot of sense to me, but I hope I can keep this in mind during the study.

E-Mails From the Past

Day 1066: Another school year begins without me. I try not to feel too depressed, but I thoroughly loved working with my students. Now, I am not only deprived of a living, but my natural vocation.

Happily, I receive a batch of e-mails and some phone calls from former students of my SPARK peer-counseling program. I will certainly try to contact each and every one of them. It is incredibly gratifying to hear that they are excelling in the real world.

Graciana, a former student of mine, and an active participant in my SPARK peer-counseling program for several years, learned well. She is now an Assistant Dean of admissions in Boston where she councils and recruits underserved populations of children and their families. I am thrilled to hear about the type of work she is doing and her many accomplishments. Marguerita, Graciana's sister, is working at a residential program for runaway youth based in NYC in the Human Resources Department. Sofia, also Graciana's sister, is an assistant teacher at a prestigious school in Greenwich Village. Feliciana is employed at a marketing company that does contract work for the pharmaceutical industry. Darlene works at a real estate agency in Buffalo, New York, and Robert works for the New York City Transit Authority.

What I did professionally, particularly the work I did with the students in my peer-counseling program, defined who I was and what my mission was at that time. I poured my heart and soul into this program and to hear that my former students are doing well fills me with satisfaction and pride. I am not suggesting that either myself, or my program are totally responsible for who they have become. Still, from all that they have shared with me, it seems that my program has had a positive impact on how they manage daily events and who they are today. Hearing from and about my students is very important to me, especially now that I am no longer an employee of the Board of Education. When I look back on my life I want to feel as if I made a difference, made a positive impact on the students

I have worked with. It has always been so much a part of me to give of myself to others with the hope that those individuals would go on in life and be successful, whatever that means to them.

Chris Makes a Difference

Chris receives e-mails from some of his former students. They just heard what happened to him and feel it is important to share what a powerful influence Chris was in their lives. Their encouraging words touch Chris deeply. He says to me, "Wow, I guess I really did make a difference." How fortunate for these students to have met him. He gave them skills, spirit and hope. He clearly touched the lives of so many young people. How proud I am of him for daring to care.

The Touch

As the leaves on the branches of the trees begin to turn bright red, yellow and orange and the October sky is a brilliant blue, Amy and I decide to take a seven-day autumn break in the Catskill Mountains. During our time here I tell Amy that I have been really thinking more than usual about what lies ahead for me. Where am I going to be one year, two years down the road? Is this as much progress as I am going to make?

Day 1098: I wake up out of a sound sleep about 5:30 a.m. The room is pitch black and silent. For some reason I can't explain, I have a sense of expectancy. It is a comforting feeling. I feel as though there is a Presence behind me cradling my head in her hands. I am suffused by a warm feeling, a human touch, running from my temple area down each side of my chin. The "touch" seems familiar to me. It feels like my grandmother is holding me. I begin to think about when she was alive and the many quiet moments over the years sharing my deepest feelings and innermost dreams with her. I would lay my head on Grams' lap. She would always tenderly stroke my hair and face while we shared our thoughts. It was always very loving and reassuring when I would have these moments with my Grams. She always finished any conversation saying: "Don't you worry; everything is going to work out. Just don't worry." No matter what we talked about, this is always how our talks ended.

As I shift my eyes to my left, I see a milky white image at my side leaning over the bed. My head starts tingling. I feel an overwhelming sense of peace. I just gaze at this image and am not frightened at all. I am lighter than air as these tender hands hold my head. At first I can't figure it out, or make sense of what is happening. Then it dawns upon me. This tender touch, is Grams. After a couple minutes or so, the image starts moving toward the curtains and slowly dissipates. I lie still for another minute and take it all in. My head and upper body still feel tingly. I am exhilarated, filled with an overwhelming sense of peace, joy, confidence and renewal. I don't recall ever feeling this way before, especially, not all at once. I really think that Grams is here to tell me what she had on so many occasions when she was alive; "Don't you worry, everything is going to work out. Just don't worry."

Chapter Thirteen

Life Appraisal

Taking Stock

Time is a very strange phenomenon for me. No work and very little social life give my life a kind of uniformity. The dates that I write down and try to remember are appointments that revolve around my health and injury, mainly with doctors and lawyers.

At Peace at the Seaport

Day 1247: Its Spring 2003 and March brings some surprisingly warm and beautiful weather. I am glad to have good weather when I head into the city for an appointment with one or two of my many doctors. When I go for appointments I meet my friend Mark, who lives in Manhattan. Like me, he is unable to work and enjoys the company. After my monthly allergy shots, Mark suggests that we head over to South Street Seaport to grab a sandwich and take some rays on the pier. It's a great idea, but I am concerned about taking the subway. I don't generally travel on them since the accident. For me, the high decibel noise and crowds are overwhelming and even dangerous. With my buddy Mark at my side and it well past rush hour, I take the chance.

Well, it goes great. It is such a glorious day; spring has definitely arrived early. People are out in short sleeve shirts soaking up the sunshine and the nautical sights of the Seaport. The wide sail of a clipper ship is ruffled by a breeze as small boats and big barges navigate the river. Mark and I are at peace as we sit eating our sandwiches. I don't know why but I feel cleansed, refreshed. We don't say anything, but before long we are sharing a sense of guilt. Here we are basking in the sun and hanging out like kids cutting classes, while our wives have their noses to the grindstone at their respective demanding jobs.

Mark and I were good friends prior to his stroke and my traumatic brain injury, but we have become increasingly closer as our lives took similar turns. We are both unhappy with our life on the sidelines, enduring a difficult period of recovery and readjustment.

Mark and I joke with one another all the time (mainly at our own expense), but today we get very serious. We have worked super hard over the years and are proud of our work ethics. "We would be working now if these terrible things didn't happen to us," I tell him with my voice rising; "There has to be a real reason for this." Mark shakes his head in agreement. "Maybe these things happened the way they did so we could be here for each other," Mark responds quietly. I now let it all out and confide to Mark my dream that increasingly verges on an obsession. I want to, I need to tell my story to transform the pain and struggle into something positive, a book that will renew the lives of other people who have experienced a brain injury and other life changing events. Mark is almost solemn as he promises to use his experience as a writer to assist me. Perhaps together relating my journey, we will be able to reach and help even more people than I could counseling for the Board of Ed. We shake hands enthusiastically. I look up at the sun and smile "You know Mark, I think we are really on to something… You never know!"

Anger Management

Day 1313: Tonight, we have a guest at the brain injury support group meeting. It is a Doctor from the Kessler Rehabilitation Center, an expert on anger management. He is here to help us develop strategies to deal with our own aggressive behavior and handle our anger. I cannot help responding, at least in part, as a Counseling professional.

His A-B-C theory reminds me of the RET techniques I used with clients when I was a chemical dependency counselor.

During the session he asks us to think about experiences with anger. I immediately think back to a couple of days ago.

For two and a half years or more after my injury Amy was not only my primary care giver, she was the primary decision maker. The decisions I made on my own were extremely limited, not by design but by necessity. Whatever energy I possessed was reserved for rehab. I couldn't parcel out energy for anything else. Basically, Amy was making all of the decisions for both of us and I didn't mind at all. I start improving and become more aware of what is going on around me. I am able to take a more active role in the decision making process.

The only problem is that Amy has become very attached to her role. Amy often makes decisions on her own and I am not at all aware of them until I encounter the consequences good, bad or indifferent. I ask her why she doesn't run things by me before making her decisions. She looks at me with this dumb-founded perplexed look. "What do you mean, I've been the only person making decisions for quite a while now", she says. "You seemed okay with it, so what's going on, why does it suddenly bother you?" True to form, I start yelling at her. "I might be brain injured, but I'm not a moron. I am capable of making a decision you know." I get very hot under the collar. "After all, my opinions and ideas should be worth something. I know how things can be done too."

The trouble is that Amy doesn't know that my brain's capacities are expanding; new connections are starting to kick in. I guess I don't totally realize it either. It kind of snuck up on me. After we take a step back from the arguing, we are able to talk about what is happening to me and how we can thread this into our approach to decision making. I still, more often than not, yield to her the right to make the ultimate decision. The process of coming to conclusions, weighing pros and cons usually takes too much out of me. Due to my memory challenges, once we make a joint decision it is best to write it down somewhere so that there is a record of what it is that we have decided. I tend to forget these things, which makes for some interesting, if not contentious conversations about decisions that I simply don't recall. Sometimes when I don't remember being part of a decision, I'll simply ask her directly, "Are you sure I decided on this with you?" We usually get a little laugh out of my question, and she typically confirms that we did discuss it by showing me the note about the decision we wrote in the calendar. For the most part this seems to work, but sometimes I just simply can't remember, no matter how many hints and cues Amy provides.

The Decision Maker

Since Chris's accident I am the one making all the decisions for both of us. We have switched roles and now I decide what to do and what not to do. Given Chris's cognitive and emotional issues, I rarely discuss my concerns and responsibilities with him. It is such a struggle for him to try and understand. Sometimes he leaves a decision up to me but wants me to let him know about any final outcome. I take this new role for granted, that is until Chris starts to complain that I am taking over and not discussing key issues that affect our lives together. I respond with confusion and *disbelief. What is going on?*

Chris and I have a huge blow-up. He is so upset over me making decisions on my own, that he is out of control. I try to explain to him that it was sort of agreed upon a long time ago following the injury. Chris is oblivious. During a heated exchange, he says "I'm not a moron you know, you can ask me a question and I will give you an answer." I have no idea what Chris is going through, his words come totally out of left field, and I'm shocked. Suddenly I realize that he is at a point where he wants to try and help more with the important decisions that impact our life together. We agree to go back to discussing everything before making a decision.

Unfortunately, even after we explore options before making a joint decision, Chris upbraids me for not having discussed it with him. Chris insists that we never spoke about it and another argument swiftly develops. I am so very frustrated. With all we have been through together, Chris doubts my word. What is coming next?

I am very angry, but I grit my teeth and agree on the condition that I write a note on the calendar to indicate what we discuss and our decision, so if we are at odds again we can look at the calendar for confirmation that we did indeed come to a particular decision. It is a pain to do, but I have no choice. Just when I think everything is settled, Chris is at it again about another decision we discussed that I luckily just put on the calendar. As Chris questions what I am saying, I point to the calendar. He looks at it, sees the notation and blushes slightly. He apologizes and makes some type of joke about himself.

Advice to Caregivers

At the end of our anger management presentation at the brain injury support group meeting, an elderly couple whose daughter is brain injured, approaches me. They are concerned about their daughter's commitment to her rehab. They wonder if she is giving it her all. During our conversation they communicate a sense of dismay and disappointment. They feel I am far more successful in focusing on rehab than their daughter. I am uncomfortable with the comparisons, but I smile politely, knowing what they are going through. They go on to say that perhaps my counseling background is an advantage in coping with this type of injury. I respond that, "my background may have been helpful for me in many ways, but I think what has been a more powerful influence is my character, my upbringing and the support I receive from Amy and other family members."

I simply don't give up. I am careful to add that success is based on a continuum and that everyone measures his or her own personal level of success differently. "To me, success is being able to concentrate ten minutes more during a conversation or taking less time to find my words in a group setting, or just speaking over the phone without stuttering. Success for your daughter may mean having more muscle control in her legs than she showed a month ago in physical therapy. I don't know what she will use to measure her success, but it will be something personal to her." I finish telling them that it is possible that she needs some help in becoming aware of her successes. I also make sure that they know how far I am from being my old self. I encourage them to just keep on working with their daughter and hope for the best.

I remind them to find time to take care of their own needs and to take good care of one another. A caregiver can carry around a lot of guilt and worry which sometimes prevents him or her from taking even a short break from the grind. I confide to them how Amy almost lost her sense of self and personal identity as she became consumed by her caregiver role. I also relate how my mom and dad struggled to balance their own lives and their caregiver duties when they took care of my ailing grandmother and two great aunts.

I think it is essential for caregivers to nurture and revitalize their spirit and souls so that they can be even more ready to meet the demands of the person they care for. Caregivers must recognize their own humanity. It may be hard to admit but their resources, both emotional and physical, are limited. In order to continue providing support the caregiver needs to be supported.

Amy received this advice from our brain injury support group members early on. They emphasized that she must take care of herself to properly take care of her husband. Shortly after that first meeting she approached me and we talked about her allocating some time for herself, while making sure I was covered. It was an eye opener for me. I finally realized that she had neglected herself to cater to my own needs. I felt terrible. I know it was because of a situation that I couldn't change, but that did not relieve my guilt. I could not conceive of the impact it had on her, just as she could not totally understand what it's like living with a brain injury. But I know now that it is important for her to have some time for herself and we will find a way to make sure that happens.

Maintaining My Emotional Equilibrium

Day 1440: In February 2004 I resume psychotherapy with Dvorah. I have been struggling emotionally for the past several months. It is time to re-establish contact with her and take a hard look at what is going on inside me. I know when I need help.

I am struggling with more than my injury. I struggle to balance my needs against the needs of my family. Over the past summer I have become over involved in their lives. Gradually, practically without noticing it, I again find myself back in the family advisor role. It is a position I have neither the energy nor fortitude to handle at this time.

The truth is, nobody forced me into my former supportive role; nobody twisted my arm, nobody made me get involved. I guess I just fell into it, an unconscious move on my part to want to help. The difference between before and after my injury is that I am no longer able to juggle two or three or four things at one time. Now I can only be fairly successful if I handle one thing at a time. Well, somehow, I forgot about my limitations and now find myself up to my neck, over-extending myself and don't see a way out. My rehabilitation is the loser. I am going backwards. As a result, I am emotionally tapped out; I am physically and cognitively drained. I can't think straight anymore. I simply have no more to give right now. Sure, on the surface it may seem like I am doing okay, but the hard truth is I tend to ignore how I am actually feeling. I push myself like a weight lifter training for the

Olympics; adding more and more weight each day trying to exceed myself. Well, my barbell has dropped straight on my chest and I feel myself suffocating underneath it!

So, I back out of some of my commitments, which, of course, makes me feel only more guilt. The guilt leads to depression, which scares me. How did I allow this to happen? What was I thinking?

I make it clear to Dvorah that I feel responsible for what has happened over the past several months. Mea Culpa. I had a choice. I didn't have to get so involved. I guess I really believed I could do all these things successfully. Dvorah indicates that given my personality, it makes sense that I feel guilty, but what everyone needs to understand is that "you are still healing." She says it makes sense that I need time to restore myself and help my brain heal further. I never thought about things this way. It has been over four years since my injury and it is still healing? This is a good way to look at things. I guess it is important to do everything I can to allow myself to heal. Dvorah thinks that not only must I adapt to my new circumstances, but so must my family. I have to find a new balance. The guilt and anxiety I have been accumulating inside is slowly washed away during our session.

Relief

I am relieved when Chris decides to resume therapy with Dvorah. Chris is so changed; I don't know how to help him. We have had more arguments this past year then we have had in all the years put together before Chris's injury. His emotional outbursts towards me are getting out of control. I think I am a very patient person, but I too have my limits.

The weeks of therapy help Chris tremendously. He is less anxious and less liable to fly off the handle. Dvorah helps him understand what his limitations are and makes it clear that he

needs all of his energy to take care of himself. She helps him take
control of his life. What is good for him is good for the two of us.

A Factory Second

Terry, one of my friends from the brain injury support group, has returned to school for his certification as a rehabilitation counselor. Given my own professional background, he asks if he can interview me for a class assignment. I naturally oblige. When we finish with his exercise, we talk about our brain injuries and how the outside world doesn't seem to really understand how we can have so many ongoing challenges when we look fine. It suddenly dawns on me, "It feels like being a factory second." Terry agrees. Everybody knows what a factory second means. You go to the outlet center and pick through the dinner plates, soft goods, and refurbished electronics equipment in search of the piece that looks to be in as perfect a condition as possible. Only when you bring it home and observe it more closely do you notice the flaws. I am far from ready to be discarded ... I am still a work in progress.

June 2004

Day 1571: It is June, that time of year, when in my past life my students move up a grade, graduate or make plans for summer school. For me it was always a busy time for meeting with students, taking stock and summing up; a time for closure. I also tried in the past to do that for myself. I am the kind of person who likes to know where I am going.

I have come quite a way in four and a half years since my traumatic brain injury. From re-learning how to walk and talk to developing new strategies to assist in doing daily tasks without too much of a struggle, I have slowly crawled out of that dark place I was thrown into. The doctors tell me I may show incremental improvement over a longer period of time. So, I guess it is best to assess any positive change from year to year at this point. Granted, I am far from where I was before my injury, but I am continuing to work with the hopes of showing improvement no matter how incremental or how long it may take. In regard to my cognitive functioning, my challenges remain very apparent to me and to those who know me well. I am able to do one task at a time pretty successfully, providing I am in a quiet, controlled environment with little or no distractions. Multi-tasking remains elusive, but I continue to work at it.

Reading comprehension, attention and concentration remain a challenge. If I am reading a passage of material I worked with prior to my accident I may be able to understand it, although I may not be able to recall what I have read. If I am reading something new, it is less likely I will understand what I am reading; particularly if I am trying to read something from one of my graduate texts that have long complicated sentence structure and a big vocabulary.

In terms of relating to others, understanding and being understood, I make more of an effort to ask people to repeat themselves or to slow down when talking to me so that I follow what they are saying. I am less likely to apologize for making this request.

My vestibular system is still problematic and I remain hypersensitive to noise and quick movements. I bring my cane with me when I leave the house, as I still am easily startled and prone to lose my balance. Having the cane handy enables me to steady or catch myself when this occurs. I also try not to leave the house without my sunglasses, or sun clips, should I enter a building or office where artificial light, particularly fluorescent, can cause my eyes and head to ache.

Fatigue remains a constant challenge. I pace myself and prioritize my activities which go a long way to help me conserve my energy. These strategies are not foolproof. There are times when I completely run out of steam and fall into bed. Still, I am much more aware of the causes that lead to exhaustion and work hard, with Amy's help of course, at not getting myself to that point where I poop out.

Social activities are a real "brain drain". So, Amy and I pick and choose which ones we feel won't be too overwhelming for me. This means we regrettably have to decline some invitations, but it is better to decline an offer and stay as healthy as I can than take two or three days to recover from an exhausting outing. Yes, there are times when this approach will make Amy or me feel disappointed and down for a while, but at the end of the day we always agree it is the best decision for right now. Who knows, maybe I will be able to tolerate more stimulating social events down the road.

Amy remains my primary care giver, thank god. I consider myself very fortunate that my wife has remained my strongest support, my most passionate advocate, and soul mate. Her patience, compassion, fortitude and love has been the foundation that has supported me through my recovery journey. All too often, we hear how other couples in which one or the other has suffered a brain injury wind up in divorce court. I am truly blessed that our relationship remains strong. Most of my family members have a good understanding of my particular needs. They are quick to assess if any special arrangement needs to be made when we get together, and are always willing to do more to make our visits as enjoyable as possible.

I am so grateful to family members and friends who genuinely want to understand all they can about my brain injury and are always doing everything they can to help me be successful. This is a process for everyone, not just for me; they continue to strive to increase their understanding about the nature of my brain injury and how it is shaping the new person that is evolving.

After learning about my journey, many people tell me that they don't know how I keep going, remain motivated and committed to improving. They say, "If this happened to me I would have given up."

I believe that most of us are unaware of the true extent of what we can accomplish and what we can endure. People underestimate the inner strength of the human spirit, and the depth of the reserves that can be drawn upon from deep within our souls and psyches. Our unique ability to overcome seemingly impossible obstacles comes from a dynamic mixture of attitude, determination, emotional strength, and resilience. The key is to be open to change. We must be willing to embrace the circumstances of life changing events, and not just be open to, but actively engage in the process of re-defining our life as we begin and continue through the journey of healing and re-growth. No matter what else is stripped away from us, this powerful spirit and fortitude will always be within us. No matter how far we are pushed, no matter how invasive the despair and desperation may become, ordinary human beings just like you and me can and do transcend tragedy. I understand that my tomorrows will look much different than today, but I embrace that with all the optimism I can muster because I believe – with experience to prove it – that all things are possible. As my journey continues I will continue to move forward…and I will never give up.

Epilogue

October 22, 2011 - day 4372. Today marks twelve years of living with a brain injury. It is an understatement to say that this journey has been, and continues to be an ongoing learning experience for both me and Amy, as well as for family and friends. This journey has provided insight into a world of re-discovery, re-direction and has re-defined the way Amy and I perceive our relationship and the world around us.

Our move to the Valley of the Sun has proven to be a wonderful environment for me. The climate and slower pace of Arizona is, however, only partly responsible for the strides I have made in my recovery. With Amy's unwavering love and support, and me continuing to utilize strategies that help me manage some challenges that remain, I have learned to live again.

Soon after our Arizona arrival in May 2006, we stopped by the Brain Injury Association of Arizona where Mattie Cummins, the Executive Director, greeted us with a warm smile and asked how the BIAAZ could help support us. We inquired about attending a support group in the Northwest Valley. She mentioned there is currently no brain injury support group in the Northwest Valley, but that a rehabilitation hospital is actively looking for a seasoned facilitator to run a support group. Since I had a lot of experience running groups in my counseling career, Amy gave me one of those, "Hey you can do this" looks. After further discussion with Mattie, she introduced us to the CEO of the rehab hospital where we became the group facilitators for the new Northwest Valley Brain Injury Survivor and Caregiver support group. Through the continued generous support of Beth Bacher, the CEO of HealthSouth Valley of The Sun Rehabilitation Hospital and her staff, this little support group has grown from 22 survivors, caregivers and family members back in October of 2006 to well over 100 families today. Each and every survivor, caregiver, and family member we have met over the years has made an imprint on mine and Amy's lives and has enriched our souls.

In addition to facilitating monthly support group meetings, we began a social planning committee. This passionate group of people has been instrumental in creating social opportunities for our support group members to reintegrate back into the community.

Amy and I also present at civilian and military survivor and family conferences for those who have been impacted by brain injury throughout the State. We openly share the experiences we have encountered in the capacity of survivor, caregiver, and as a couple learning how to live again after experiencing a life changing traumatic event. We also present at professional workshops and training seminars, all in the hope of helping others realize that tragic events, while life changing, do not have to be life ending.

Drawing upon both our professional experiences prior to my injury and our personal experiences since then, Amy and I designed a Peer Mentor policy and procedure manual for the Brain Injury Association of Arizona. We also developed, and have facilitated a 10-hour training workshop for Peer Mentor volunteers. This project is dear to both of our hearts, and we are thrilled to be able to do our part in preparing these special volunteers to make a positive impact on the lives of those they mentor.

ço ço ço ço ço ço ço ço ço ço ço ço

Given my prior background as a professional counselor, our life experiences, and our passion to continue helping those who are facing times of transition, adversity and other life changing events, we have embarked on yet another journey to assist those facing life changing events through the founding of ASPIRE PLACE LLC, a Personal Life Adjustment Coaching and Consultation Service. Our life adjustment coaching and consultation services are offered to individuals, couples, families, businesses and organizations.

Our work with Aspire Place has given me the opportunity to explore the internet and social media in a way I might not otherwise have. In an effort to assist others through their own life adjustment, I am helping to develop Aspire Place's networking tools including www.facebook.com/aspireplace, and on twitter @aspireplace.

Whether it is through our coaching, consultation or training services, or through motivational or other public speaking engagements, we ASPIRE to assist others as they journey through their own unique challenges of self-exploration, and support them as they redefine their purpose, reclaim direction, and renew a sense of hopefulness.

ASPIRE to move forward![SM]

Our Ten Top Strategies

It has taken several years of struggling to outwit, accept, and finally live with my brain injury. We hope that by sharing our journey it becomes a valuable resource for others who find themselves in similar life changing circumstances. It does not matter how you were hurt. It could have been from a traffic accident, an athletic injury on the playing field, a warrior wounded while protecting our country, acquired your brain injury from a stroke, aneurysm, or brain tumor; or just a person like me who happened to be in the wrong place at the wrong time, you can still live a meaningful and purposeful life after a brain injury.

Learning to live with brain injury is an ongoing ever changing process. It means always being willing to try new adventures, creating helpful strategies and adjusting them to meet your ever evolving needs. It also means asking others for help when you need it. Some of the most valuable lessons we have learned about living successfully with brain injury have come through the process of trial and error, and they are the ones that really stick and have proven to be the most viable and practical aids in my recovery journey.

As much as the strategies and tools we list in this section can be beneficial to those with brain injuries, they may also benefit individuals who have acquired cognitive challenges through other medical conditions. Some of the strategies listed below can also benefit caregivers, and anyone interested in improving personal health and wellness.

Our views and conclusions about living with brain injury are by no means the final word on brain injury rehab and recovery and may not be right for everybody. This is a starting point, a general guide. These strategies, tools and aids provide a compass to move you forward in your own recovery journey.

1. <u>Going Home</u>

Transitioning back home after a hospital or rehabilitation stay can be an exciting time for the brain injury survivor as well as for the caregiver and family members. However, without helpful information, support, and proper planning the excitement can quickly turn into anxiety and frustration. As the caregiver, you may feel very overwhelmed during this transition, and it is understandable. You are about to embark on a journey that may not have a clear path and you may not have the tools you need to best help your loved one in his/her recovery process. Hospital staff, healthcare agencies, medical doctors, and other organizations you are dealing with may often assume that you know everything you need to know about your loved one's brain injury. These professionals may assume that you and your family members are ready and capable to do everything you need to do to meet all of your loved ones needs. Yet, this is likely not the case. This is a new and unique experience, unlike any other that you have faced.

As you begin to make the transition from hospital/rehab to home, above all else, "Don't be afraid to ask questions!" The more information you receive from therapists, doctors and nursing staff, the more prepared you will be to care for your loved one. With so many concerns running through your mind, staying on top of your loved ones care can be overwhelming. Being organized at the beginning can be helpful in managing your stress level when the medical staff starts talking about "discharge," leaving you little time to prepare for the homecoming:

Purchase a divider notebook or binder with tab dividers, and label each section as listed below. Include a pencil pouch to hold all medical business cards, prescriptions etc. For Smartphone users, you can utilize a variety of phone functions to create a similar tool.

Section 1: Therapy: Speech, Physical, Cognitive, Occupational, etc. (use this section for specific questions that come up, and for specific observations you notice during your loved ones therapy sessions).

- What do I need to do to assist my loved one with his/her daily care?
- If lifting or supporting is required, how do I do this in a way to not injure myself or my loved one?
- What types of tools or aids could I purchase to help my loved one with daily living tasks? (Purchasing weighted silverware to help him/her more easily hold utensils if they have diminished grip strength or assist in stabilizing tremors while eating).
- What type of durable medical equipment or daily living aids will my loved one need at home? (Wheelchair, walker, shower chair, grab bars, bed rails, etc.).
- What can I expect when I bring my loved one home?
- What specific exercises can I work on with my loved one at home?

Note: Whether or not outpatient cognitive therapy is prescribed, if your loved one is still struggling with cognitive functioning there are variety of computer software programs and internet sites that may be helpful with these challenges. Here are a few websites: www.lumosity.com; www.sharpbrains.com, www.braintrain.com; www.positscience.com. Here are a few software programs: Brain Spa by Ubisoft; Brainiversity by

Brighter Minds Media, Complete Brain Training by NeuroActive Program. Search online vendors such as amazon.com for these software programs as well as many others.

Section 2: Social Worker/Case Manager:
- What healthcare assistance, community resources and supports are available? (i.e.: medical and non-medical home health care, transportation assistance, respite care for caregiver, support groups, financial assistance, community agencies such as your Statewide Brain Injury Association)
- How do I obtain copies of medical records and scans?
- Will my health insurance cover prescribed out-patient therapies?
- Given my loved one's injury, should I consider filing for either Social Security Disability or Social Security Income benefits on his/her behalf? How do I start this process?
- Are there therapists who can work with my loved one at home to continue his/her rehab? (If outpatient rehabilitation is being prescribed)
- If an assisted living facility is recommended, how can I obtain a listing of those facilities who understand brain injury? Is there an agency that can help me with this search?
- Do you have any written material that can assist me in learning more about my loved ones brain injury?
- Who do I call if I have additional questions when my loved one is home?

Section 3: Follow-up Appointments:
- If given follow-up appointments be sure to ask what type of specialist they are and their contact information.

- Confirm that the specialist accepts your loved ones insurance.
- Be sure to call before the appointment dates to determine if you need to bring any medical records.

Section 4: Medications: It is not uncommon to be overwhelmed by the variety of medications your loved one may be prescribed. Ask the discharge nurse if they might be able to help you set up a daily schedule on when to administer each medication. By eliminating the "medication guess work" it is one less thing you have to worry about.

Other Things to Consider:

Whether your loved one has private insurance, is on a State insurance program, or enrolled in Medicare, learn your patient rights. Contact the insurance company and ask to speak to a case manager or advocate to discuss patient rights and discharge planning. Your insurance provider may be a helpful advocate if you feel your loved one is not ready to go home.

In addition to any type of law suit you may be pursuing, there may be additional legal matters to address such as: Guardianship, Conservatorship, Special Needs Trust, Private Fiduciary Services, Health Care Planning, and Medical and Financial Power of Attorney. Although some states have self-service centers to help prepare the necessary documents for many of these legal matters, the overwhelming task of being a caregiver and completing legal forms may be daunting. You may want to consider speaking with an estate planning attorney to help you understand your options.

2. **Managing Fatigue**

For many brain injury survivors fatigue is a constant; always just on the horizon. Noise, stress, over-stimulation, overwork, intensity of light, and distractions can produce debilitating fatigue. Taking breaks and pacing yourself is a "Must" for the brain injury survivor, particularly for those who are struggling with physical and cognitive challenges. Taking a break does not mean shifting to another task. It means just that...stopping what you are doing and finding a quiet place where you can restore your energy.

Using your digital watch or Smartphone Apps can be helpful tools in managing fatigue.

- Know your limit (how long you can work on a task before you cognitively or physical crash). 10 minutes...15 minutes...30 minutes?
- Prevent yourself from crashing by setting an alarm on your device alerting you at 5 to 10 minutes prior to your "limit." It's time to take that break!
- Take several breaks throughout the day as needed. It could be a 10 minute break or a 30 minute break, or even longer. It all depends on your fatigue level. Your brain will let you know when it is recharged.

3. **Reducing Noise and Light Sensitivity**

From the moment I gained consciousness after being hit by that steel fire door, I continue to be hyper-sensitive to noise, florescent lights, and overcast days. I have listed different tools, strategies, and resources that have helped improve my quality of life in a world filled with loud noise and bright lights. Any loud or high-pitched sound can be disorienting, causing me to lose my balance and disrupt my cognitive process.

Noise Sensitivity:

- Foam earplugs from your local pharmacy can be helpful in blocking out noise. It is not completely foolproof. While muffling sound, these earplugs also make it difficult for me to hear and participate in conversations in public places.

- Molded Ear Filters: These amazing ear filters allow me to enjoy the give and take of conversation, even in noisy environments. They do not muffle all of the sound like foam ear plugs. They help reduce those highs and lows and background noises when out in public making it possible to concentrate and once again enjoy conversation.

The social barrier that was and continues to prevent me from enjoying the world around me no longer exists, thanks to these incredible ear filters. There are a variety of companies that offer ear filtering devices. My audiologist recommended the Sensaphonics Company. Their website address is www.sensaphonics.com. You can search for audiologist referrals in your area on this site that can do an assessment and fit you with a pair of Sensaphonics ear filters. The filters are available in three different decibel filtering ranges, and your audiologist will be able to help you determine which filter is best for your needs. Sensaphonics can be reached by calling toll free 877-848-1717.

Light Sensitivity:

- Many brain injury survivors are hypersensitive to light. Whether it is an overcast day or an office filled with florescent lighting, head and eye pain often times occur when exposed to these elements. Sunglasses are not only helpful when you are outside. If you find that head and eye pain increases when inside your house or in office buildings it may be due to the lighting. Wearing sunglasses or sun clips may be your best defense.

- If you enjoy reading and experience head or eye pain, you can find reasonably priced sunglasses that have a reading glass insert.

Please remember to contact a neuro-optometrist or neuro-opthalmologist if you have any issues or concerns with your vision.

4. <u>Pain Relief Strategies</u>

Even today, when I am under stress, my brain is overtaxed, or I am overwhelmed by outside stimuli I endure intense head pain. Medication can certainly be very helpful for managing pain. You may also want to speak with your doctor about some natural strategies that can help with pain management. I often make use of some of the techniques I utilized as a substance abuse counselor to help reduce stress. These techniques have helped me keep the pain at bay.

As caregivers dealing with your own stressors, these techniques can also help you relax and renew your energy and spirit.

BREATHE …
- Seek out a quiet, calm environment where you can sit or lay down comfortably with no distractions.
- Close your eyes and concentrate on your breathing.
- Breathe in through your nose and exhale out through your mouth with slow, deep breaths.
- Calmly say to yourself, "RELAX" each time you exhale.

VISUALIZE…
(Begin the visualization portion of this exercise when you feel calm and relaxed).

- As you continue your breathing, visualize a place where you feel calm, safe, and at peace. Your "Calm Place" may be a rain forest, a mountain range, a waterfall, or a canyon. I usually visualize lying on a deserted beach in the Caribbean.
- Immerse yourself in your "Calm Place".
- What do you See... Hear... Smell... Taste... Feel...
- As you transport yourself to your "Calm Place" remember to continue breathing slowly and deeply.

(Playing music quietly in the background, such as new-age music, can be an added benefit to your relaxation experience. Purchasing a sound machine that offers a variety of digital nature sounds can also be very effective. Falling asleep while doing either of these exercises is fine. After all, the purpose is to RELAX).

PROGRESSIVE MUSCLE RELAXATION-PMR is a guided muscle relaxation technique that can be used on its own or with the deep breathing and visualization exercises. This step-by-step technique helps you become aware of muscle tension and reduces that tension through a systematic approach that reduces pain. Although PMR can be self-guided, you may need the assistance of a caregiver, professional therapist, counselor, or pain management specialist to get you started. You can also find step-by-step instructions on the internet by searching "PMR Exercise."

If you have never done anything like this before it may seem foreign and maybe even a little strange. But trust me, if you really work hard enough, with practice it may become a very valuable pain management tool.

5. **Short Term Memory Aids**

With an unreliable short-term memory, there is a variety of memory aids that we utilize to help me. Although using these strategies was essential to help me with my memory at the beginning of my recovery, as my memory improved, some of the following strategies were modified and others were no longer needed:

- Compartmentalized pillbox labeled with times of day for dosage.
- Reminder phone calls from a loved one to take your medication and/or for any other daily necessities you need to do each day.
- Setting a countdown timer on a digital watch as a reminder for taking necessary cognitive breaks throughout the day.
- Using a reminder clock on the microwave oven to sound when it is time to eat lunch/dinner.
- Using a specific calendar for all appointments. In the beginning this was my compass and daily navigation tool.
- "Don't Forget" checklists taped to your door to remember necessary items such as house keys, wallet, disability bus pass, ear filters, watch, sun glasses, and cellphone.
- "Reminder" sticky notes:
  - Flush the toilet
  - Wash hands
  - Turn off Water

Note: With all the technology available today, Smartphones provide reminders, alarms, memo notes, shared calendars, and many other tools. Between these functions and an endless selection of "Apps," managing your daily life when you have executive functioning challenges can be a little easier.

6. <u>Cooking in the Kitchen</u>

One of the skills Chris worked on while in occupational therapy was cooking. Excited about this adventure, Chris decided that he would prepare dinner and have it on the table when I returned home from work. However, I would come home to a frustrated husband who was upset that he not only forgot an important piece of the recipe, but who had burned himself or a pot on top of the stove. His brother gave me an idea on how I could create memory aids that provided safety strategies when working in the kitchen:

- Make a magnet that can go on the stove top or oven door to indicate when it is on. (I used a picture of an oven with the heading "oven on").
- Create a clip-on tag or lanyard with the same message as above for your loved one to wear when the stove top or oven is turned on. (The lanyard/clip-on tag acts as an additional memory trigger, should your loved one leave the kitchen).
- When the stove top or oven is turned off return the magnet and clip-on tag or lanyard to a designated spot near the oven.
- New routines take time to learn. Role-play these safety strategies with your loved one until you feel confident that he/she has this new routine down.
- As an added reinforcement, you may want to call your loved one if you are away from the house to remind him/her to use these safety strategies when you know that they may be starting to cook.

Preparing Dinner:

If your loved one has a desire to cook, following a recipe may be a challenge. To reduce the possible frustrations these hints may be helpful:

- Remove or minimize distractions that may impede your loved ones ability to concentrate on the cooking task.
- Pre-plan weekly dinner menus with your loved one.
- Each night put out bowls, pans, spices, and utensils needed to prepare the dinner. If your loved one has difficulty with measuring out ingredients, consider pre-measuring the ingredients the night before.
- Review the recipe with your loved one the night before. If he/she has difficulty following the recipe steps, you may want have them use a colored piece of paper as a guide by placing it over the recipe steps and move the colored paper down exposing the next step as each one is completed. Anticipating potential pitfalls can help mitigate errors, reduce confusion and foster and confidence. This strategy may help your "chef" follow the recipe directions successfully.
- If you own a Nintendo DS, there is a software program called "Personal Trainer: Cooking," which provides hands free step by step voice lead cooking instructions that includes text, images, and video. Each success our loved one experiences is one more victory towards his/her recovery.

7. <u>Keeping up With Conversation</u>

It can be an effort for me to process what people are saying, especially if they are speaking quickly. It was through my participation in a Pragmatic Speech Group where I learned many practical techniques and simple questioning skills to bypass the pitfalls of the communication process. In the beginning I had to really concentrate when using these strategies, but now they are second nature to me.

- Slow it down: Politely request that the person or persons you are talking with to speak slower.
- Repeat, restate, and verify what is being said.
- Delay your response… force a pause to collect your thoughts.
- If asking for directions or instructions, write them down and repeat written instructions to be sure they are accurate.
- Ask people to get to the point by requesting that they summarize their words in a simple sentence since "long winded" sentences can be difficult to break down and comprehend. This will help you get a clear and simple idea on what they are trying to say.
- Tell the person you are talking to that you may repeat yourself, and ask him/her to gently let you know when this happens so you can make your point.

There are many strategies to help the brain injury survivor formulate and organize thoughts before speaking; here are a few:

- When having important conversations, find a quiet room with limited distractions.
- Be prepared: Ask yourself, "What do I really want to say," and say "just that" to the listener.
- Don't worry about finding every word you want to say. Create an image in your mind to help you describe the word.
- Share your conversation objectives with the person you are talking to so that he or she can help you stay focused on the topic.

- Summarize what you heard the person say and elaborate on the topic to stay focused and keep the communication going. (So what you are saying is…) (My experience has been…)

In situations where the person continues to talk fast despite trying to employ these strategies, consider taking the "bull by the horns" and say: "I am a brain injury survivor, and I would really like to understand what you are saying. In order to do that I really need you to slow down so I can follow you." It took a while for me to be comfortable enough to just come right out and say this, but I can tell you that nine times out of ten it works like a charm.

8. Travel Tips

Everyone needs a vacation. A change of scenery, the refreshing sense of new people and new places is revivifying. However, traveling inherently has several obstacles that we have learned how to navigate around.

If you are traveling by plane:
- Call ahead and notify the airline of your health condition and status as a brain injury survivor and request that this information be included on the airline manifest so that the flight staff is aware of your injury.
- If you have challenges with mobility or vestibular issues, ask to be assigned bulkhead seats (the first row of coach following first class), and let the reservationist know if you need wheelchair and/or arm assistance. The bulkhead seating affords easy access to first class or coach restrooms.
- Save your energy for your vacation destination. If you become easily overwhelmed, over stimulated, or are sensitive to noise, or lose your balance easily, you may

want to consider requesting wheel chair assistance. Navigating through an airport these days can really drain your brain quickly, especially with the TSA scanning procedures and baggage screening protocol that every traveler has to go through. Once arriving at the gate, you or your caregiver may want to approach the counter to confirm that the airline representatives are aware of your needs in boarding and disembarking the plane.

WHEN BOOKING HOTEL RESERVATIONS:

Make every effort to ensure your room is in as quiet a location as possible: Free of street noise, the sound of amplified music, away from the elevator or restaurant clatter. Minimizing the stimulation and distraction of noise and activity when relaxing or sleeping will enable you to have the energy you need to successfully make it through the day.

DURING YOUR VACATION:

- Plan "Rest days". Alternating a day of fun with a day of rest will help you restore the energy you need to enjoy your vacation.
- Plan half-day excursions. You can always extend your day depending upon your energy and fatigue level.
- When enjoying an excursion or activity be sure to self-monitor your fatigue. Set a watch or cell phone alarm to remind you to check your fatigue level. You may need to enlist your caregiver to periodically check with you about your fatigue level. Find an escape room or quiet place to recharge, or be prepared to leave the activity early if your fatigue level becomes an issue.
- Go to restaurants at off-peak hours if possible, to avoid the hustle and bustle of a full house. Monitoring your

exposure to over stimulating activities can help you manage your fatigue and stress level more effectively.

- If you have balance, fatigue, or mobility challenges using a wheelchair at tourist attractions or amusement parks can save your energy and help you, your family, and friends enjoy the day more easily. These attractions often times allow you and your party special access by moving to the front of long lines.
- When navigating in public, move around the crowd not through it. Save your energy for more worthwhile adventures.
- Be sure to always have bottled water with you. Drinking water helps you stay hydrated, which is essential for brain function.

9. **Preparing For The Unexpected**

It is impossible to plan for every contingency. Unforeseen things are bound to happen to disrupt the life of someone with a brain injury. The more prepared you are the more likely you will be able to handle those curve balls that will come your way:

- Consider wearing a Medical Alert Bracelet with your type of brain injury and any other major conditions engraved on the back of it; medical personnel can be alerted of your health issues in the event of an emergency.
- Get the "Survivor Identification Card." It was developed by a non-profit organization called The Perspectives Network. Their address is: P.O. Box 121012, W. Melbourne, Florida 32912-1012. Their e-mail address is: TPN@tbi.org. The website: www.tbi.org

o This card identifies the carrier as a brain injured person and provides pertinent information about the general condition, including some of the most common symptoms. If you find yourself in an emergency situation or being pulled over by a police officer and you are unable to communicate effectively, this card may help prevent any problematic incidents or misunderstandings.

10. Suggestions For The Care And Maintenance Of Caregivers

It was about a year after being thrust into the world of care giving that my own health started to decline. My "Auto-Pilot Mode" that had been successful in keeping pace with doctor and therapy visits, maintaining a household, and managing my department at work, suddenly began breaking down. Super humans we are not, and the stress, worry, frustration, and physical demands involved in caregiving, can take its toll on even the best of us.

When speaking at caregiver conferences and workshops I am often asked to share some survival tips that I have found helpful as a caregiver.

- Accept help if it is offered. Ask for help when needed.
    - o Keep a notebook by the phone where you can write down a list of tasks you have to do. When a friend or family member calls and asks how they can help, offer them some suggestions from your list. This can truly be helpful to you.
- Take Five…a little "breather" during the day goes a long way. This short break from caregiving can help you recharge and refocus.

- Sit down for a cup of tea or coffee and read a few pages of a favorite book or magazine.
- Write in a journal about your thoughts, feelings, and concerns.
- Do some of the deep breathing and visualization exercises previously shared.

- Schedule some guilt free "Me" time. You need to renew your strength and energy to effectively take care of your loved one. If all you are doing is giving, you eventually will have nothing left to give. Tell yourself, "I need this time for me." "I'll be much stronger and understanding if I take care of me." Ask a friend or family member to stay with your loved one while you:
  - Run errands
  - Get your hair and nails done
  - Get a massage
  - Enjoy time with a friend at a coffee shop or at the movies
  - Take a yoga class or do some other type of physical activity
  - Go window shopping at a mall

If family or friends are not available contact a respite care service in your area. You may want to contact your statewide Brain Injury Association for assistance as this organization may have a listing of respite care services and other resources available in your local area.

- Set realistic goals and expectations for the day.
- Recognize and respect your own humanity. Give yourself permission to be angry, sad, etc... It's very common and understandable to have these feelings. After all, how prepared are any of us to take on this new life as a caregiver.

- At all costs, resist the temptation to blame yourself for what has happened. Avoid saying "If only I... or What if I..."
- Seek support from counselors, social workers, therapists, clergy, support groups, close friends, and family members. Their support can benefit both you and your loved one during this recovery journey.

Find that "One thing" that brings a little piece of normalcy and balance back into your life. That "One thing" that helps you stay grounded so you can address whatever is thrown at you during the day. Whatever it is, this "One thing" can make all the difference in caring for you and your brain injury survivor.

Knowledge is a mainspring of recovery and rehabilitation. There is a national Brain Injury Association where you can find information about brain injury. This site also provides you with the contact information and websites of other Brain Injury Associations throughout the United States. Their website is www.biausa.org. We strongly suggest that you contact your Statewide Brain Injury Association to inquire about information and resources available within your own community.

For example, in Arizona, the State we have called home since 2006, our Brain Injury Association, now known as Brain Injury Alliance of Arizona, has a variety of resources and referral information on their website. www.biaaz.org. One of the helpful tools on this website is a comprehensive resource for people with brain injury and their families called "Navigating the System." This navigation guide enables the user to view video clips in the following subject areas: "What is Traumatic Brain Injury"; "In the Hospital"; "In Rehabilitation"; "At Home and in the Community"; "Children and TBI"; "I Hurt My Head but Didn't Get Help." There are also links within the guide that provide additional information and resources about brain injury.

While each injury and family circumstance is unique, we hope that our strategies become a foundation for you to build on and develop your own approaches that support you throughout your recovery journey. Keep in mind that as improvement in recovery is made, you may need to change how you use a strategy, aid or tool. What works for you today may need to be modified tomorrow. Through trial and error you will figure out what works best for you. Much like life itself, recovery is about the journey not the destination.

Chris Hotaling, M.A.

Chris holds a Master of Arts Degree in Counseling and a Bachelor of Science degree in Psychology. He has worked in the counseling field for over 20 years, and is a New York State Credentialed Alcoholism and Substance Abuse Counselor Emeritus, retired Credentialed Prevention Specialist and Guidance Counselor. His international consulting experience includes working with the University of LaVerne (Athens campus) and with Akita University (Akita City, Japan).

Over the course of Chris's career he has designed and delivered peer leadership training programs for young adults and in-service training programs for teachers in the secondary education system. Currently he presents at conferences, training programs and workshops for professionals; including licensed counselors, social workers, and other health care providers, as well as for caregivers, family members and survivors impacted by brain injury and other life changing events. It is through his presentations, discussion and support group facilitation, and motivational speaking engagements that Chris enables others to restore hope, reclaim purpose, and ASPIRE TO MOVE FORWARD in their lives.

Chris is currently a Personal Life Adjustment Coach and Consultant for ASPIRE PLACE, the company he and his wife Amy founded.

Amy Hotaling, MBA

Amy holds a Master's degree in Business Administration, a Bachelor of Science degree in Criminal Justice. Amy also is a Certified Paralegal and has worked in the human services field as well as in the banking and finance industry.

Amy presents at workshops, conferences and training programs for professionals who provide brain injury services, as well as for families impacted by brain injury throughout the state of Arizona. She has also trained work groups and business executives in policy and procedure regulations in the business banking sector in New York City. She has worked as an adjunct professor and facilitates support and discussion groups.

As a result of her personal experience supporting Chris every step of the way throughout his recovery journey, and the commitment they made to re-define their relationship, Amy and Chris were inspired to provide support for others who find themselves at a crossroad in their own lives. ASPIRE PLACE, a Personal Life Adjustment Coaching and Consultation company was founded where Amy combines her professional experience with her passion to help others.

Chris and Amy can be reached by contacting ASPIRE PLACE at info@aspireplace.com or by visiting www.aspireplace.com.

(Scan our contact information into your Smartphone)

Mark Leeds, M.A

Mark wrote *"The Passport Guide to Ethnic New York,"* which appeared in two additions and multiple printings and received a positive mention in *New York Magazine's Best of New York* issue *(1995)*. Working out of Greece and Turkey between 1985 and 1990 and in England, Mark free-lanced for a variety of publications from *Catholic Near East* to *Off Duty*. He was also the foreign editor and correspondent for *Lottery Players Magazine*. In 1990, he returned to New York and went to work for the New York City Board Of Education Special Programs, developing and directing a student writing program, while producing a monthly in-house publication. Mark holds a Master of Arts degree in Counseling.

IF YOU WOULD LIKE TO ORDER COPIES OF "LEARNING TO LIVE AGAIN… A DAY AT A TIME"

Go to www.aspireplace.com and place an order through our secure PayPal service by clicking the "Shopping Cart."

Scan this qrcode with your Smartphone and place an order through our secure PayPal service:

You may also find our book at: **www.amazon.com**

For Bulk Orders:

Please contact Aspire Place to determine shipping charges and how to submit purchase orders.

IF YOU WOULD LIKE TO BOOK A SPEAKING ENGAGEMENT:

Contact us at info@aspireplace.com, or by visiting www.aspireplace.com. You can also scan this qrcode with your Smartphone.

TO PURCHASE AMY'S
"A MIRACLE OF LOVE" CD:

Go to www.aspireplace.com and place an order through our secure PayPal service by clicking the "Shopping Cart." You can also purchase Amy's CD at either: CDBABY's online store at
http://www.cdbaby.com/amyhotaling
> or
on iTunes by searching for "Amy Hotaling"

Aspire Place LLC
Web address: www.aspireplace.com
Email us at: info@aspireplace.com
Facebook: www.facebook.com/aspireplace
Follow us on twitter @aspireplace

For your convenience, use your Smartphone and scan the following qrcode to input Aspire Place Contact information into your contact list.